οἱ μοναχοὶ τοῦ ῥαΐθ, ὑπὸ ἀιωπ τοῖς ϛ ταυρο ...

The Life of Michael the Synkellos

BELFAST BYZANTINE TEXTS AND TRANSLATIONS

General editor: Dr M.E. Mullett

Business editor: Mrs Betty Robinson

Editorial board: Mr R.H. Jordan
　　　　　　　　Professor M.J. McGann
　　　　　　　　Dr A.M. Wilson

Advisory board: Dr M.J. Angold
　　　　　　　　Professor A.A.M. Bryer
　　　　　　　　Professor J. Herrin

TITLES IN PREPARATION

BBTT 2: The XL Martyrs of Sebasteia

BBTT 3: The Lives of Meletios of Myoupolis

BBTT 4: Alexios I Komnenos

BBTT 5: Ubertino Pusculo, Constantinopolis

BBTT 6: The Evergetis Monastery

The Life of Michael the Synkellos

Text, Translation and Commentary
by Mary B. Cunningham

BELFAST BYZANTINE TEXTS AND TRANSLATIONS, 1

First published in 1991
by Belfast Byzantine Enterprises
Department of Greek & Latin
The Queen's University of
Belfast, BT7 1NN

© 1991 Belfast Byzantine Enterprises

All rights reserved. No part of this publication may be reproduced, stored in a retrieval system, or transmitted, in any form or by any means, electronic, mechanical, photocopying, recording or otherwise, without the prior permission of the publisher.

ISBN: 0 85389 369 1
ISSN: 0960-9997

British Library Cataloguing-in-Publication Data

A catalogue record for this book is available from the British Library

Printed and bound in Northern Ireland by
The Universities Press

Contents

Editor's Preface	page vii
Foreword	ix
Abbreviations	xi
Chronology	xiv
Introduction	1
The historical accuracy of the *Life*	
The iconophile arguments contained in the *Life*	
The literary form of the *Life*	
Michael the *Synkellos* as a monastic saint	
The writings of Michael the *Synkellos* and his disciples	
The manuscripts	
The text	
Life of Michael the *Synkellos*: text and translation	43
Commentary	131
Bibliography	174
Indexes	
General index	185
Index of Greek words	193
Index to biblical and other quotations	203

Editor's Preface

This is the first volume in a series of texts and translations which aims to publish the work of Belfast scholars and Belfast research projects and to provide a wide range of Byzantine texts for students, scholars and the wider public. It was the experience of our benefactress, Mrs Betty Robinson, while a student of Byzantine Studies at Queen's, which led her to propose that we provide new editions and translations with thorough introductions and commentaries at a reasonable cost. She has been no passive patroness but as Business Editor with an informed interest in Byzantium is actively involved in the project; we owe her a great deal.

I also wish to thank the many who have advised and helped in the planning of the series. The editorial committee, Robert Jordan, Michael McGann and Anna Wilson, has shared all the labour; our advisory committee, Michael Angold, Anthony Bryer and Judith Herrin, has been extremely helpful. Francis and Sandra Cairns, Roy Wallis, Mairead McGlew and Carina Bourke gave me the benefit of their experience. Christine Robertson, Richard Corran and Charlotte Roueché (who brought King's to the rescue of Queen's) have been instrumental in its production. Anna Wilson has always been ready to help with questions of design, and Margaret Jordan has helped in innumerable ways. The board of Belfast Byzantine Enterprises has spent long hours in deliberation and the Arts Faculty Information Technology Users' Committee at Queen's has lent support throughout.

The main burden of the work has fallen on Mary Cunningham, who has done far more to assist the series than could be envisaged of an author. She has patiently allowed us to use her text as a guinea-pig and has worked steadily for its production. It is her book in more than one sense.

Margaret Mullett
General Editor,
BBTT

To my parents

Foreword

My work on the *Life* of St Michael the *Synkellos* began when I was an undergraduate at Harvard University. I presented a translation and commentary of the *Life* as a senior honours essay for the degree of B.A. in the Comparative Study of Religion in March 1977. In preparing the text at that time, I benefited greatly from the help of my supervisor, Professor I. Ševčenko. After it had been examined, he read through the entire text with me and checked my translation. Professor Ševčenko's part in the preparation of this publication lies further in his examination of the Greek text and suggested emendations, and in his contributions to the commentary, some of which emerged from a seminar devoted to the text in 1977-78 at Harvard University.

I also owe many thanks to Dr Jeffrey-Michael Featherstone who helped me with the translation of the text when we were both still undergraduates, and to Professor C. Mango, Dr A.M. Wilson, Professor J. Herrin and Professor M. McGann who all read through the manuscript at different stages and offered many helpful suggestions. I should like to express my gratitude to all of these scholars, while at the same time assuming responsibility for any errors which remain. I am grateful to the Patriarchal Institute for Patristic Studies in Thessalonike for providing me with a microfilm of Cod. Athon. Pantokrator 13 (1047) and to Mrs A. Palau who kindly lent me a microfilm of Cod. 33 of the Congregazione della Missione Urbana in Genoa, along with her notes on the manuscript. The Patriarchal Institute in Thessalonike and the National Library in Madrid generously gave permission to reproduce the photographs of miniatures in the Madrid Skylitzes and in the Lavra codices. I should also like to thank Dr Margaret Mullett and her committee at Queen's University, Belfast, for offering to publish the text as the first volume of a new series of translations of Byzantine texts. Mrs Betty Robinson is generously funding this project and in addition has offered many useful suggestions concerning the text. It is a great honour to be included in this series and to have experienced at first hand the warmth and enthusiasm of the 'Byzantium in Belfast' community as a whole. Finally, I should like to thank Charlotte Roueché and King's

College of the University of London for helping to produce a camera-ready copy of the whole manuscript. My husband, Dr. Richard Corran, provided invaluable advice concerning the Macintosh computer and its software throughout the project. Without his help and support this publication would never have appeared in its present form.

Mary B. Cunningham   Derby, England, 1990

Abbreviations

AASS: *Acta Sanctorum Bollandiana* (Brussels, 1643-)

AmHR: *American Historical Review* (New York, 1895-)

AnalBoll: *Analecta Bollandiana* (Brussels, 1882-)

B: *Byzantion, revue internationale des études byzantines* (Paris & Brussels, 1924-)

BHG: *Bibliotheca Hagiographica Graeca*, 3rd ed., ed. F.Halkin (Brussels, 1957); with *Novum Auctarium* (Brussels, 1984)

BHL: *Bibliotheca Hagiogiographica Latina*, (Brussels, 1898-1901); *Supplément* (Brussels, 1957)

BS: *Byzantinoslavica* (Prague, 1929-)

BZ: *Byzantinische Zeitschrift* (Leipzig & Munich, 1892-)

CH: *Church History* (New York, 1932-)

CSCO: *Corpus Scriptorum Christianorum Orientalium* (Beirut, Paris & Leipzig, 1903-)

CSHB: *Corpus Scriptorum Historiae Byzantinae*, ed. B.G. Niebuhr et al. (Bonn, 1828-)

DOP: *Dumbarton Oaks Papers* (Washington, D.C., 1941-)

DOS: *Dumbarton Oaks Studies* (Washington, D.C. 1951-)

DS: *Dictionnaire de Spiritualité* (Paris, 1932-)

EHR: *English Historical Review* (London, 1886-)

Ehrhard,*Überlieferung*: A. Ehrhard,*Überlieferung und Bestand der hagiographischen und homiletischen Literatur der griechischen Kirche von den Anfängen bis zum Ende des 16 Jahrhundert*, 1-3, *TU*, 50-2 (Leipzig, 1937-52)

EO: *Échos d'Orient, revue bimestrielle d'histoire, de géographie et de liturgie orientales* (Paris, Constantinople & Bucharest, 1898-1943)

GCS: *Die griechischen christlichen Schriftsteller der ersten drei Jahrhünderte* (Leipzig & Berlin, 1897-)

IJSL: *International Journal of the Sociology of Language* (The Hague, 1975)

IRAIK: *Izvestija Russkogo Archeologiceskogo Instituta v Konstantinopole* (Odessa & Sofia, 1896-1912)

JÖB: *Jahrbuch der Österreichischen Byzantinistik* (Vienna, 1951)

JTS: *Journal of Theological Studies* (London, 1899-)

Lampe: G.W.H. Lampe, *A Patristic Greek Lexicon* (Oxford, 1961)

Mansi: J.D. Mansi, *Sacrorum Conciliorum nova et amplissima collectio* (Florence & Venice, 1759-98)

MGH: *Monumenta Germaniae Historica* (Hanover, Berlin, etc., 1826-)

OCA: *Orientalia Christiana Analecta* (Rome, 1923-)

OCP: *Orientalia Christiana Periodica* (Rome, 1935-)

PG: *Patrologiae cursus completa, series graeca,* ed. J.-P. Migne (Paris, 1857-66)

PL: *Patrologiae cursus completus, series latina,* ed. J.-P. Migne (Paris, 1844-64)

RESEE: *Revue des Études Sud-est Européennes* (Bucharest, 1963-)

ROChr: *Revue de l'Orient Chrétien* (Paris, 1896-1936)

SbBayerAW: *Sitzungsberichte* der bayerischen Akademie der Wissenschaften; philosophisch-philologische und historische Klasse (Munich, 1871-)

SC: *Sources Chrétiennes* (Paris, 1955-)

SubsHag: *Subsidia Hagiographica*, ed. Société des Bollandistes (Brussels, 1886-)

Synax.Eccl.CP: *Synaxarium Ecclesiae Constantinopolitanae,* ed. H. Delehaye, *Acta Sanctorum, Propylaeum Novembris* (Brussels, 1902)

TU: *Texte and Untersuchungen zur Geschichte der altchristlichen Literatur* (Leipzig-Berlin, 1882-)

VizVrem: *Vizantijskij Vremmenik* (St Petersburg, 1894-)

Chronology

Michael the *Synkellos*:

AD 761: born in Jerusalem (chap. 1).

764: dedicated by his mother to the church of the Resurrection. Appointed to the rank of reader (chap. 2).

786: aged 25. Michael's father dies and his mother and sisters enter a convent in Jerusalem. Michael enters the *laura* of St Sabas (chaps. 2-3).

798: ordained priest by the patriarch of Jerusalem (chap. 4).

800: Michael receives Theodore and Theophanes, aged twenty-five and twenty-two respectively, as disciples (chap. 5).

809: dispute over the *filioque* between the Greek and Latin monks in Jerusalem. Arab attacks on monasteries in Palestine (chap. 6).

811: appointed *synkellos* to the patriarch of Jerusalem. Moved to the monastery of the Spoudaei (chap. 5).

812: renewed Arab attacks.

812 or 813: Michael sets out for Constantinople and Rome, accompanied by his disciples Theodore, Theophanes and Job (chap. 8).

813: the four monks arrive in Constantinople during the reign of Michael I. They stay in the Chora monastery, delaying their journey to Rome for unknown reasons (chap. 9).

815: Leo V re-introduces iconoclasm. The four monks are interrogated, beaten and confined in the Phiale prison. They are bribed with offers of high ecclesiastical positions if they will accept iconoclasm, but they refuse. Theodore and Theophanes are sent to a fortress at the mouth of the Bosphoros and the Black Sea while Michael and Job remain in the Phiale prison (chaps. 7-14).

820: at the accession of Michael II, Michael the *Synkellos* and Job are sent to a monastery in Prousias or Prousa near Mt Olympos. Here Michael writes the *encomium* of St Dionysios the Areopagite and corresponds with other iconophiles (chap. 15).

834: five years after the accession of Theophilos (829-42), Michael and Job are brought back to Constantinople and confined in the Praetorium

prison. Here they are subjected to solitary confinement and suffer greatly from the difficult conditions (chap. 16).

836: Theophilos transfers Michael from this prison and confines him elsewhere within the Praetorium where he is attended by the nun Euphrosyne. After Theodore and Theophanes are brought back to Constantinople, interrogated and finally tattooed, Michael writes them a consoling letter. During his years of confinement, he has also been able to communicate with other orthodox sympathisers, such as Stephen the *asecretis* and Kallonas the *spatharios* (chaps. 17-24).

843: the triumph of orthodoxy. Michael is appointed abbot of what remains of the monastery of Chora and *synkellos* to the new patriarch Methodios. Michael sets about restoring the monastery with Methodios' and the emperors' help (chaps. 27-32).

4 January 846: Michael dies peacefully, aged eighty-six (chap. 38).

Theodore and Theophanes *Graptoi*:

775: Theodore is born in 'the land of the Moabites', on the eastern side of the Dead Sea (chap. 19).

778: his brother Theophanes is born.

800: the two brothers enter the *laura* of St Sabas and become disciples of Michael (chap. 5).

811: Theodore and Theophanes accompany Michael to the Spoudaei monastery in Jerusalem and are ordained priests (chap. 5).

812 or 813: they journey with Michael and another of his disciples, Job, to Constantinople where they stay at the monastery of Chora (chaps. 8-9).

815: the monks are interrogated, beaten and imprisoned by Leo V (chaps. 10-2).

816: Theodore and Theophanes are sent to a fortress at the mouth of the Bosphoros and the Black Sea.

820: the brothers are allowed to return to Constantinople on the accession of Michael II, but are soon sent to the monastery of Sosthenios on the European side of the Bosphoros.

829: accession of Theophilos. Theodore and Theophanes are interrogated once more and sent to the island of Aphousia, one of the Proconnesian islands west of the Kyzikos peninsula.

8 July 836: the brothers are summoned back to Constantinople and confined in the Praetorium prison (chap. 18).

14 July: Theodore and Theophanes are brought just after daybreak to the Golden Triclinium for an audience with the emperor. The saints are questioned and beaten. After they are dismissed and are being led back to the Praetorium, someone is sent to recall them to the presence of the emperor. They are beaten again and dismissed only when they are scarcely able to walk. And yet for the third time they are summoned back. Since the brothers are unable to return, the logothete of the course follows and questions them again. They arrive back at the prison after dark (chaps. 19-21).

18 July: Theodore and Theophanes are taken to the prefect of the city. He offers them freedom if they will accept communion from the iconoclasts. When they refuse he commands that their faces be tattooed with iambic verses composed by a man named Christodoulos. Theodore and Theophanes are banished again, probably to Apameia (Mudanya) in Bithynia (chaps. 22-4).

27 December 841: Theodore dies in prison, aged sixty-six.

843: the triumph of orthodoxy. Theophanes is appointed metropolitan of Nicaea (chap. 29). Theodore's relics are conveyed to Chalcedon where a monastery in memory of the saint is founded.

11 October 845: Theophanes dies, aged sixty-seven (chap. 31).

Introduction

The Life of St Michael the *Synkellos*,[1] which concerns the second period of iconoclasm (AD 815-843), describes this saint's defence of religious images and consequent persecution at the hands of the iconoclast emperors. The saint was born in Jerusalem in about 761 and spent the first half of his life engaged in spiritual training at the monastery of St Sabas. Several years after he was appointed *synkellos*, or assistant, to the patriarch of Jerusalem in 811, Michael was sent to Constantinople in company with his disciples Theodore, Theophanes and Job. There were two reasons for this journey, which probably occurred in 812 or 813 during the reign of Michael I. A dispute had arisen between the Greek and Frankish monks in Jerusalem over the clause 'filioque' which the Latins were inserting in the Creed. Also, many of the Greek monasteries in Palestine had been devastated because of raids by the Arabs in 809 and 812. Michael the *Synkellos* and his disciples were chosen by the patriarch to carry messages to the pope in Rome, seeking both his arbitration and material aid. The four monks broke their journey in Constantinople and for some reason delayed their journey to Rome for several years. Thus they were in Constantinople when the emperor Leo V re-introduced iconoclasm in 815 and were thrown into prison for refusing to accept this policy.

During the second period of iconoclasm the monks underwent various punishments and exiles under Leo V, Michael II and Theophilos. Because of the bizarre punishment which Theophilos chose to administer to the brothers, Theodore and Theophanes *Graptoi* are well known to all who are familiar with the history of second iconoclasm. Probably in 836 the emperor commanded that the faces of the two monks be tattooed with iambic verses intended to ridicule them. After the death of

---

[1] The *editio princeps* of the Life can be found in Th. Schmitt, 'Kahrie Džame', *IRAIK*, 11 (1906), 227-59. A Russian translation has been made by S.V. Poljakova, *Vizantijskie Legendy* (Moscow, 1972), 114-39.

INTRODUCTION

Theophilos in 842 the holy icons were restored by his widow Theodora. The saints were released from prison and like many other iconophile heroes were now honoured for their steadfast opposition to iconoclasm. Michael the *Synkellos* was appointed abbot of the monastery of Chora in Constantinople and *synkellos* to the newly appointed patriarch Methodios. While his brother Theodore died too early to see the restoration of icons, Theophanes *Graptos* became bishop of Nicaea. In 846 Michael the *Synkellos* died peacefully, having restored the devastated monastery of Chora to its former glory and gained the devotion and reverence of his many disciples.

The Life of Michael is an important document not only for students of Byzantine history, but for all those interested in the history of the Christian Church and its relations with the state. The veneration of religious images or icons, although not originally a feature of Christian worship, gradually increased after the christianisation of the Roman empire, reaching its height in the sixth and seventh centuries.[2] While some prominent churchmen opposed the growing cult of icons on the grounds that it represented idolatry, they received no official backing until 726, when the emperor Leo III introduced an iconoclastic policy. The reasons for his decision are not fully known, but it is likely that he was motivated by political as well as religious considerations. Against the background of the Arab threat, natural disasters and other upheavals within the empire, Leo III believed that he would win God's favour by suppressing what he regarded as idolatrous practices within the Church.[3] While Byzantine emperors had always played an important religious

---

[2] See E. Kitzinger, 'The Cult of Images in the Age before Iconoclasm', *DOP*, 8 (1954), 83-150; N. H. Baynes, 'Idolatry and the Early Church', *Byzantine Studies and Other Essays* (London, 1960), 116-43; *idem.*, 'The Icons before Iconoclasm', *Harvard Theological Review*, 44(1951), 93-106.

[3] A large amount of secondary literature provides a number of theories concerning the causes of iconoclasm in the Byzantine empire. See P.R.L. Brown, 'A Dark-Age Crisis: Aspects of the Iconoclastic Controversy', *EHR*, 346 (1973), 1-34; J.F. Haldon, 'Some Remarks on the Background to the Iconoclast controversy', *BS*, 38 (1977), 161-84; A. Grabar, *L'iconoclasme byzantin. Dossier archéologique* (Paris, 1957); S. Gero, *Byzantine Iconoclasm during the Reign of Leo III* (*CSCO*, 346, Subs 41, Louvain, 1973) and most recently, R. Cormack, *Writing in Gold* (London, 1985), 95-140 and J. Herrin, *The Formation of Christendom* (Oxford, 1987), 307-43.

role, in theory leading the Church as representatives of Christ on earth, it was actually unusual for them to direct ecclesiastical policy. In the first period of iconoclasm, the opposition to Leo III's and Constantine V's iconoclastic policy was centred in the monasteries.[4] The opponents of iconoclasm saw no reason why emperors should suppress what had become a common devotional practice in the Church. From the safety of the monastery of St Sabas in Palestine, which was by that time under Arab rule, St John of Damascus wrote, 'What right have emperors to style themselves law-givers in the Church?'[5]

In fact active persecution of iconophiles, and in particular of monks, does not seem to have started until the 760s, during the reign of Constantine V. The earliest recorded martyrdom is that of St Andreas Kalybites who was whipped to death in the hippodrome of St Mamas. The chronicler Theophanes tells us that Andreas, who was a monk at the monastery of Blachernai, had accused Constantine of impiety and compared him to the pagan emperor Julian.[6] The next martyrdom was that of St Stephen the Younger, who was the victim of an infuriated mob of iconoclasts on the streets of Constantinople. The Life of St Stephen the Younger, written by Stephen the Deacon in the early ninth century, served as a model for many other lives of saints of the same period.[7] After a brief interval following the restoration of icons by the empress Eirene and the council of Nicaea in 787, iconoclastic policies were reintroduced by Leo V in 815. The second period of iconoclasm, which lasted only until 843, differed in some ways from the first. Although the opposition to iconoclasm was more organised under the leadership of Theodore the Stoudite, the parties which supported and opposed the veneration of icons were not divided into specific camps. There is

---

[4] See S. Gero, *Byzantine Iconoclasm during the Reign of Constantine V* (*CSCO*, 384, Subs. 52, Louvain, 1977), 122-42; J.P. Thomas, *Private Religious Foundations in the Byzantine Empire* (*DOS*, 24, Washington, D.C., 1987), 118-30.

[5] John of Damascus, *Orationes de sacris imaginibus*, *PG*, 94, cols. 1296-7.

[6] Theophanes, *Chronographia*, ed. C. de Boor (Leipzig, 1883), I, 432.

[7] I. Ševčenko, 'Hagiography of the Iconoclast Period', eds. A.A.M. Bryer and J. Herrin, *Iconoclasm* (Birmingham, 1977), 115-6. The text of the *Vita s. Stephani iunioris* can be found in *PG*, 100, cols. 1067-186.

INTRODUCTION

evidence that a number of monasteries in Constantinople, including the Chora, agreed to endorse iconoclasm and on the other hand, that some members of the secular clergy remained orthodox.[8] Although the persecution of iconophiles continued, it seems to have been less violent than it had been under Constantine V and it remained confined to Constantinople and its immediate environs.[9]

We gain the impression from the Life of Michael as well as from other sources that the emperors sought obedience from their iconophile opponents more than they cared about their actual acceptance of iconoclasm.[10] Those who did not agree to communicate with the iconoclasts were viewed as traitors as much as religious dissenters. This is especially clear in the section of the Life of Michael which deals with the interrogation of his two disciples Theodore and Theophanes by the emperor Theophilos (829-842). This incident is recorded in a number of sources besides the Life of Michael, all of which depend on a letter possibly written by Theodore himself, which is transcribed in the metaphrastic Life of the saint.[11] According to Theodore's account, the emperor questioned his brother and himself in a series of audiences in the imperial palace. In the first of these interrogations the emperor did not even bring up the issue of iconoclasm. Instead he asked them about their place of origin and their reasons for coming to Constantinople.[12] It is clear that like Leo V, Theophilos felt threatened less by the

---

[8] See P.J. Alexander, *The Patriarch Nicephorus of Constantinople* (Oxford, 1958), 144. According to Theodore of Stoudios, most of the monasteries in Constantinople, including the Chora, accepted iconoclasm after 815. See Ep. 41, ed. A. Mai, *Nova Patrum Bibliotheca*, VIII (Rome, 1871), 34.

[9] For background on the persecution of iconophiles during the first and second periods of iconoclasm, see P.J. Alexander, 'Religious Persecution and Resistance in the Eighth and Ninth Centuries; Methods and Justification', *Speculum*, 52 (1977), 238-64.

[10] In this I agree entirely with David Turner, who discussed the political background of the second period of iconoclasm at more length in his unpublished paper, 'The Second Iconoclasm: Context of a Theology', delivered at the XXIst Spring Symposium of Byzantine Studies, Birmingham, 21-4 March, 1987.

[11] See *PG*, 116, cols. 672-80.

[12] *Ibid.*, col. 676; below, chap. 19.

INTRODUCTION

theological stance of his opponents than by their possible subversive motives towards himself and his government.

While the issue of iconoclasm receives the most emphasis in the Life of Michael, the hagiographer includes several anecdotes which add further interest to the text. At the beginning of the Life as he recounts the events which led up to the saints' journey to Constantinople, the author describes a dispute over the inclusion of the *filioque* in the Creed, which arose between the Greek and the Frankish Benedictine monks in Palestine. As one of the earliest literary sources which deals with this dispute, the Life provides us with valuable evidence about how it first developed.[13] A second feature of the Life is a fairly lengthy passage describing the monastery of Chora in Constantinople and its condition in the ninth century after it had been allowed to decay under the iconoclasts. The author of our Life describes how Michael restored the monastery to its former glory with the help of the emperor Michael III and his mother Theodora.[14]

The Life of Michael the *Synkellos* is anonymous and it is tempting to believe although impossible to prove that it was written not much more than a generation after the saint's death. It is likely that the author was a monk of the monastery of Chora since he devotes so much attention to the monastery in the final section of the Life. The passages which describe Michael's short period as abbot and his death at the monastery suggest the author's acquaintance with a still living tradition surrounding the saint. He claims that he obtained his information from the saint's 'kinsmen, acquaintances, eating and living companions, and disciples, and in addition to these from associates of the tyrant, those who are still alive.'[15] Since the hagiographer is best informed about Michael's

---

[13] On the importance of the Life as a source for these events, see V. Peri, 'Leone III e "il filioque". Echi del caso nell'agiografia', *Rivista di storia della chiesa in Italia*, 25 (1971), 3-58; 'Il simbolo epigrafico di s. Leone III nelle basiliche romane dei ss. Pietro e Paolo', *Miscellanea in onore di E. Josi IV, Rivista di archeologia cristiana*, 45 (1969), 191-222; 'Leone e il "Filioque". Ancora un falso e l'autentico simbolo romano', *Rivista di storia e letteratura*, 6 (1970), 268-97.

[14] See below, chaps. 28 and 32, and commentary, note 4. Similar passages describing a monastery appear in the Life of St Nicholas of Stoudios, written in the first half of the tenth century by a Stoudite monk. *PG*, 105, cols. 869, 901-4.

[15] See below, p. 128, lines 10-3. On this rhetorical *topos* see commentary, note 228.

5

monastic role in Constantinople, it is not surprising that the Life contains some historical inaccuracies regarding his early life, reasons for coming to Constantinople before 815 and his disciples' whereabouts during the reigns of Leo V, Michael II and Theophilos. Such inaccuracies do not necessarily suggest a late date of composition for the Life. The fact that the author refers to Michael III as 'the great and orthodox ruler Michael' suggests that the emperor was still alive at the time he was writing. The deliberate avoidance of the name of 'a certain learned man who was clever at both speaking and listening' (most probably John the Grammarian, the iconoclast who advised Leo V and later became patriarch under the emperor Theophilos) may suggest that he was still living, but could also mean that our author had once been one of his supporters or was on close terms with others who had been.[16]

In addition to its historical interest, the Life of Michael the *Synkellos* represents a fine example of a hagiography written in a 'middle' style.[17] The author displays no real literary pretensions but the Life is carefully constructed in accordance with the rhetorical rules for an encomium.[18] Thus we are told the story of Michael's life according to the conventional rubrics of ancestry, birth, education, achievements and finally death, all of which furnish proof of his sanctity. The greatest stress is placed on the saint's and his disciples' persecution by the

---

[16] E. von Dobschütz questions the early date of the Life of Michael in his study, 'Methodius und die Studiten', *BZ*, 18 (1909), 88, owing to its many chronological inaccuracies. I. Ševčenko on the other hand suggests the two arguments which I have cited for the earlier date of the Life in his 'Hagiography', note 19. Although intriguing, especially in the light of the iconoclasm embraced by the monastery of Chora between 815 and 843, the avoidance of John the Grammarian's name is in fact the less convincing of the two. Since the date of John's death is in any case unknown, it does not furnish a clear *terminus ante quem* for the composition of the Life. Furthermore, the author *does* mention John specifically by name later in the Life; see p. 102, lines 7-9. Michael III died on 23 September 867.

[17] On the different levels of style in Byzantine literature see R. Browning, 'Greek Diglossia Yesterday and Today', *IJSL*, 35 (1982), 49-68; I. Ševčenko, 'Hagiography', 113-31, 127-9; 'Levels of Style in Byzantine Prose', *JÖB*, 31/1 = *XVI IntCong*, I/I (Vienna, 1981), 289-312.

[18] See D.A. Russell and N.G. Wilson, *Menander Rhetor* (Oxford, 1981); L. Spengel, *Rhetores Graeci*, II (Leipzig, 1854), 35-40; 109-12; III (Leipzig, 1856), 368-77; 477-82.

iconoclasts; it is in this context that the hagiographer embarks on his most rhetorical apostrophes, praising the fortitude of the saints and vilifying their persecutors.[19] As the author states in the first paragraph, his purpose in writing the Life of Michael is to inspire other 'lovers of God' to emulate the saint's way of life.[20] This statement is important because it reminds us of the devotional nature of the genre of the saint's life. Great emphasis is placed throughout on Michael's asceticism, both in the context of the monastery of St Sabas and during his period of imprisonment under the iconoclast emperors. It is this spiritual ideal for which he is chiefly honoured although he also excelled as administrator and abbot. In the discussion which follows, we shall examine first the historical content and accuracy of the text, then its theological and literary qualities, and finally its particular vision of monastic spirituality in the early ninth century.

The Historical Accuracy of the Life

The Life of Michael the *Synkellos* contains some chronological errors which suggest either that the hagiographer was not completely informed or that he adapted the story somewhat to fit his own polemical purposes. In the discussion which follows, we shall examine the chronology of the Life and thereby attempt to assess its value as an historical document.[21] Various later texts written in honour of Michael the *Synkellos*, Theodore or Theophanes *Graptos* also provide us with accounts of these saints' struggles during the period of iconoclasm. These sources include the late ninth- or early tenth-century encomium of Theodore by Theophanes

---

[19] See below, pp. 80-1 and 86-9.

[20] See below, p.44, lines 6-8. This preface corresponds almost word for word with that found in Symeon the Metaphrast's Life of St John the Merciful, *PG*, 114, col. 896. On the likelihood that both our hagiographer and Symeon were inspired by the now lost Life of St John composed by Sophronios and John Moschos, see commentary, note 3.

[21] In this discussion I am relying in part on the valuable study of the chronology of the Life by S. Vailhé in his 'Saint Michel le Syncelle et les deux frères Grapti', *ROChr*, 6 (1901), 313-32, 610-42. Vailhé did not have access to the full text of the Life, but used the partial edition by M.M. Gedeon in his Βυζαντινὸν Ἑορτολόγιον (Constantinople, 1899), 231-42.

of Caesarea,[22] the Life of Theodore by Symeon the Metaphrast,[23] the Life of Theophanes composed by Theodora Raoulaina Kantekouzena Palaiologina in the thirteenth century,[24] a fourteenth-century Life of Michael attributed to Nikephoros Gregoras[25] and finally, the notices in the *Menaia* and *Synaxaria*.[26] All of these texts depend to some extent on one another. Theophanes of Caesarea draws most of his information from the anonymous Life of Michael, which probably represents the earliest work composed in the saint's honour. The metaphrastic Life of Theodore is in turn based largely on the encomium, condensing much of the rhetorical eloquence of that work into a more concise narrative.[27] In addition to the encomium however, the Metaphrast employs another important source, excerpts of which he quotes verbatim in his Life, namely the letter written by Theodore *Graptos* to John of Kyzikos, which is accepted by most scholars as authentic.[28] Michael's hagiographer uses this letter as well, scarcely altering the wording of Theodore's own account of the persecution which he and his brother experienced at the hands of the emperor Theophilos.[29] The two later sources, the Life of Theophanes by Theodora Raoulaina and the Life of Michael attributed to Nikephoros Gregoras, both depend primarily on the anonymous Life of Michael. Neither of these Lives contributes any further information to the story, instead omitting such details as place-

---

[22] The encomium survives in one manuscript, the Oec.Patr.Chalcensis Mon. 88, fols. 255-279ᵛ. It has recently been edited by J.-M. Featherstone in 'The Praise of Theodore Graptos by Theophanes of Caesarea', *AnalBoll*, 98 (1980), 93-150.

[23] *PG*, 116, cols. 653-84.

[24] Ed. A. Papadopoulos-Kerameus, Ἀνάλεκτα Ἱεροσολυμιτικῆς Σταχυολογίας, IV (St. Petersburg, 1897), 185-223.

[25] Ed. Schmitt, 'Kahrie-Džame', 260-79. See also R. Guilland, *Essai sur Nicéphore Grégoras. L'homme et l'oeuvre* (Paris, 1926), 175-7; *BHG*, 1297.

[26] *Synax.Eccl.CP*, cols. 324-6; 329-32; *Menaea*, Dec. 18.

[27] Featherstone, 'The Praise', 97-103.

[28] Ševčenko, 'Hagiography', 119, note 44; Vailhé, 'Saint Michel le Syncelle', 623.

[29] See below, pp. 80-95 and commentary, notes 128-61.

names and dates in accordance with the conventions of high-style rhetoric.

Concerning the first half of Michael's life before his departure for Constantinople, his anonymous hagiographer presents a fairly accurate picture. The saint was born in Jerusalem in about 761 and at the age of three was dedicated by his mother to the clergy of the church of the Resurrection under the care of the patriarch of Jerusalem. After the death of his father in 786, Michael, having assisted his mother and two sisters to retire into a convent, entered the *laura* of St Sabas. He remained there, living a solitary, contemplative life, until 811, when he was appointed *synkellos* to the patriarch Thomas and moved back to Jerusalem where he lived in the monastery of the Spoudaei. During the years which he spent at St Sabas, Michael was ordained to the priesthood and two years later received as disciples the brothers, Theodore and Theophanes. Michael was thus present during some of the disruptions which beset the *laura* of St Sabas at the turn of the century, including several attacks by Arabs, when twenty monks were massacred.[30]

The first problem in chronology encountered in the Life concerns the reasons for the departure of Michael, Theodore, Theophanes and another monk Job for Constantinople early in the ninth century. The hagiographer cites three reasons for this journey, which was originally planned as a delegation to Rome, stopping at Constantinople en route. The first of these concerns the addition of the *filioque* clause into the Creed, about which the Greek and the Benedictine monks in Jerusalem had recently been disputing. According to the Life, Michael the *Synkellos* was chosen as a representative to be sent to Rome so that he might help the pope to suppress the misguided Franks in this affair.[31] The second reason for the journey had to do with the Arabs' imposition of a new tax on the churches of Jerusalem. As part of his mission to Rome, Michael was to inform the pope about this tax so that he would assist the churches financially.[32] Finally, the author cites the cause for

---

[30] See commentary, note 23.

[31] See below, chap. 6.

[32] See below, *ibid*.

the visit to Constantinople on the way to Rome. He states that Theodore of Stoudios had sent a letter to the patriarch of Jerusalem, seeking his aid in the struggle against the iconoclast emperor Leo V and his patriarch Theodotos. Michael the *Synkellos*, in company with his disciples, the brothers Theodore and Theophanes, and a monk from the Spoudaei monastery named Job, was thus to set off for Rome, stopping on his way in Constantinople to present a letter from the patriarch of Jerusalem to the emperor condemning his heretical views.[33]

The first of the stated reasons for Michael's departure, that concerning the *filioque*, may indeed be a legitimate one. In 809 pope Leo III received letters from the patriarch of Jerusalem and from Benedictine monks on the Mount of Olives asserting that a monk named John from St Sabas had publicly accused the Benedictines of heresy for their inclusion of the *filioque* in the Creed. The Benedictine monks asked the pope to communicate this incident to the emperor Charlemagne and to examine the writings of the fathers in order to determine the correct wording of the Creed. After the council at Aix-la-Chapelle in December 809, at which Charlemagne approved the inclusion of the *filioque* in the Creed, the pope convoked a synod in which he maintained a more conservative view. The pope condemned the addition of the *filioque*, while nevertheless accepting the procession of the Holy Spirit from both the Father and the Son as a doctrine.[34] Our hagiographer is thus correct in his statement that on considering these matters, the pope refused to support the addition of the *filioque* in the Creed and discouraged the

---

[33] See below, chap. 7.

[34] See Dom B. Capelle, 'Le Pape Léon et le "Filioque"', ed. L. Beauduin, *L'église et les églises*, I (Chevetogne, 1954), 309-22; E. Amann, *L'époque carolingienne*, eds. A. Fliche and V. Martin, *Histoire de l'église* , VI (Paris, 1947), 173-84; J.N.D. Kelly, *Early Christian Creeds* (London, 1960), 358-67; Herrin, *The Formation of Christendom*, 462-4. For the letter sent to Leo III by the Benedictine monks on the Mount of Olives, see *MGH, Epistolae*, V, *Epistolae karolini aevi*, III (Berlin, 1898), 64-6; the letter from Leo III to Charlemagne, *ibid.*, 66-7; the proceedings of Charlemagne's envoys and Leo III in 810, see *MGH, Legum sectio*, III, *Concilia*, II, pt. I (Hanover and Leipzig, 1906), 239-44. On the pope's erection of silver shields in St. Peter's bearing inscriptions of the Creed in Greek and Latin, neither of which contained the *filioque*, see L. Duchesne, ed., *Liber pontificalis*, II (Paris, 1955), 26 and Peter Damian, *Opusculum XXXVIII contra errorem Graecorum de processione Spiritus Sancti*, II, *PL*, 145, col. 635D. See commentary, note 48.

practice, which had already become widespread in the Frankish church. It is unlikely however that the pope would have sent to the patriarch of Jerusalem for assistance in enforcing this decision as the author would have us believe. It seems more likely in view of the pope's conciliatory attitude towards both parties that the patriarch of Jerusalem and the Benedictines sent embassies to Rome of their own accord in an attempt to gain his support for their views. The hagiographer's error in this instance reflects his bias in favour of the Greek monks; it is natural that he should assign them a more active role in this controversy than they in fact played.

The second reason which the hagiographer cites for the journey of Michael and his disciples to Rome concerns a tax which had been imposed on the churches of Jerusalem by the Muslims. I have found no other mention of this tax in either the Greek or the Arabic chronicles dealing with this period, but the chronicler Theophanes does mention the disruption caused by the civil war which followed the death of the Caliph Harun al-Rashid. In both 809 and 812 monasteries in Palestine, including that of St Sabas, were occupied and in some cases destroyed. In 812 the conflict caused many monks to flee to Cyprus and from there to Constantinople where they were received hospitably by the emperor Michael I.[35] Although our hagiographer does not mention this Arab invasion specifically, it is possible that the tax which he describes was in some way connected with it. It would be unusual for an appeal to the pope to be made on a matter such as this, but perhaps since the delegation was already on its way to settle the *filioque* dispute, the patriarch decided to seek his aid in connection with the tax as well.

Whereas the issues of the *filioque* and the Arab attacks could thus represent genuine reasons for Michael's journey, the third reason suggested in the Life presents chronological difficulties. The author states that the patriarch of Jerusalem received a letter from the exiled Theodore of Stoudios, calling for his assistance in contending with the iconoclast doctrines of the emperor Leo V and the patriarch Theodotos.[36] In his study of the Life of Michael, S. Vailhé proves the

---

[35] Theophanes, *Chronographia*, ed. de Boor, I , 484, 499.

[36] See below, chap. 7.

hagiographer's inaccuracy in this instance, pointing out that in May 814, the date which is assigned in the Life for Michael's arrival in Constantinople, Leo V had not yet revived iconoclasm, the patriarch Nikephoros had not yet been replaced by Theodotos, nor was Theodore of Stoudios yet in exile.[37] In fact there is positive proof that the saints arrived in Constantinople even earlier than Michael's hagiographer implies. In the sections of Theodore *Graptos*' letter to John of Kyzikos which Symeon the Metaphrast quotes in his Life of Theodore and which is paraphrased in our Life, the saint describes a conversation which took place shortly after one of the audiences with the emperor Theophilos. As the saints are being taken back to prison, a messenger from the emperor runs after them and asks, 'Why did you rejoice at the death of Leo and why, having taken refuge with him, did you refuse to embrace his faith?' The two brothers answer, 'We did not rejoice at the death of Leo, nor did we seek refuge with him...' The messenger then says, 'What? Did you not come to Constantinople during the reign of Leo?' and the brothers reply, 'By no means. We arrived during the reign of his predecessor.'[38] If we accept the authenticity of this document, we must conclude with Vailhé that the saints arrived in Constantinople in 812 or 813, during the reign of Michael I. The first two reasons given for their departure from Palestine, that of the *filioque* and the Arab threat, make perfect sense in this context, since both occurred several years before the revival of iconoclasm in 815. Once they had arrived in Constantinople, the saints did not continue immediately on their voyage to Rome and thus were still there when Leo V re-introduced iconoclasm.

If two legitimate reasons for Michael and his disciples' departure for Constantinople exist, why does his hagiographer state as a third cause the saints' intention to oppose the iconoclast policy of Leo V? The answer perhaps lies in the author's polemical stance in writing the Life. Since he is about to describe the saints' defence of the faith under the iconoclast emperors, it is natural to suggest that the saints undertook

---

[37] Vailhé, 'Saint Michel le Syncelle', 327-31. On Theodore of Stoudios' exile after the outbreak of iconoclasm, see commentary, note 59.

[38] *PG*, 116, col. 676.

their fateful journey to Constantinople for this reason. The Encomium of Theodore *Graptos* and the metaphrastic Life reproduce this error, both placing the saints' departure within the reign of Leo V.[39] In each of these texts, the authors stress the saints' desire to defend the icons as the reason for their journey to Constantinople.

Thus the true sequence of events surrounding this journey must be as follows: The four monks departed from Palestine during the reign of Michael I for the two reasons mentioned first in the Life of Michael, the dispute over the *filioque* and the threat of the Arabs to the monasteries and churches of Jerusalem. Their final destination was Rome but they stopped in Constantinople, probably in order first to gain the assistance of the emperor. For some reason, perhaps the unexpected welcome which they received there, the saints remained in the imperial city,[40] staying in the monastery of Chora which as our hagiographer suggests, was probably already a haven for Palestinian monks.[41] When in 815 Leo V decided to re-introduce iconoclasm, the saints opposed him and were thrown into the Phiale prison. The journey to Rome was never completed since Michael and his companions remained either in prison or in exile throughout the reigns of Leo V, Michael II and Theophilos.

As Vailhé points out, it is unlikely that the letter from the patriarch of Jerusalem was read out in the first audience of the saints with the emperor.[42] More probably this letter, if it indeed represents a genuine document, was sent several years after the re-introduction of iconoclasm in response to an appeal for help from the exiled Theodore of

---

[39] Featherstone, 'The Praise', 123-5; *PG*, 116, cols. 660-4.

[40] In a letter to Michael the *Synkellos* after his imprisonment, Theodore the Studite writes, Ἀλλ' ὦ πῶς, ἀλλαχῇ ὡρμημένους ὑμᾶς πορεύεσθαι, ἠνάγκασεν ἡ φορὰ τοῦ καιροῦ ἐν ἄρκυσιν ἐμπεσεῖν τῶν τῇδε κρατούντων; (How, when you were planning to go elsewhere, did the train of events force you to fall into the nets of those who were ruling there?) Ep. 218, Lib. II, *PG*, 99, col. 1641.

[41] See commentary, notes 4 and 81.

[42] Vailhé, 'Saint Michel le Syncelle', 613-4.

Stoudios.[43] Michael's hagiographer is probably correct however in stating that during this initial period of imprisonment the emperor attempted to bribe the saints with offers of high ecclesiastical positions. We know from other sources that in the spring of 816 Leo V used such methods of persuasion on those who opposed his doctrines.[44] When Michael and his disciples refused to accept these bribes, they were separated and sentenced to long-term imprisonment.

Our hagiographer is even less well informed about the movements of the *Graptoi* brothers during the reigns of Leo V and his successors. According to Symeon the Metaphrast, Theodore and Theophanes were first exiled not to the island of Aphousia, but to a fortress at the mouth of the Bosphoros and the Black Sea.[45] After the accession of Michael II, they were allowed to return to Constantinople, but soon after were sent to the monastery of Sosthenios.[46] When Michael died and Theophilos came to the throne, the brothers were interrogated once again and then exiled to the island of Aphousia.[47] The author of the Life of Michael has simplified this train of events by stating that Theodore and Theophanes remained on Aphousia from the time of Leo V onwards.

The statement that Michael and Job remained in the Phiale prison until Michael II's accession, on the other hand, appears to be correct. When many iconophile monks were released from prison by the new emperor, Michael and Job went to Bithynia to stay in a monastery in Prousias or

---

[43] Theodore wrote to the patriarch of Jerusalem from his place of exile, Boneta, in the Anatolic theme, in 817 or 818. The letter is published in *PG*, 99, cols. 1160-4. See also commentary, note 59.

[44] See commentary, note 104.

[45] *PG*, 116, col. 665C. Both Vailhé and Featherstone accept the Metaphrast's detailed account of the brothers' movements between 815 and 836 as correct. The latter suggests that these details may have been recorded in the sections of Theodore's letter which the Metaphrast does not quote. See Featherstone, 'The Praise', 101, note 27. If this is the case, one may ask why Michael's hagiographer, who also used the letter, was not aware of Theodore's and Theophanes' precise movements during this period. In any case, it does seem likely that the Metaphrast's more detailed account is the true one, while our hagiographer, either deliberately or through ignorance, simplified the story.

[46] *PG*, 116, col. 668C.

[47] *Ibid.*, col. 669C.

INTRODUCTION

Prousa near Mt Olympos. It is interesting to note that the hagiographer does not acknowledge the more lenient policy of Michael II towards the opponents of iconoclasm. He states that Michael and Job were exiled to the Bithynian monastery 'bound in chains', implying that they merely exchanged one prison for another.[48] The author also reveals however that Michael was free to correspond with other members of the iconophile community from this monastery. Perhaps his freedom of speech and movement was not quite so restricted as his hagiographer would have us believe.

When Theophilos became emperor in 829 he did not immediately reintroduce the persecution of iconophile monks.[49] Five years later however Michael and Job were recalled from their monastery and confined within the Praetorium prison. As for Theodore and Theophanes, Michael's hagiographer forgets to mention one more detail in their story. As we stated above, Symeon the Metaphrast relates that after summoning the brothers to Constantinople from the monastery of Sosthenios and interrogating them, Theophilos banished them to the island of Aphousia.[50] In 836 the brothers were again brought to Constantinople and for the story of their subsequent audiences with the emperor and finally their tattooing with iambic verses, we have the remarkable account by Theodore himself, which is transmitted verbatim in the metaphrastic Life.[51] The author of the Life of Michael relies on

---

[48] See below, chap.15 and commentary, note 112.

[49] See J.B. Bury, *A History of the Eastern Roman Empire* (London, 1912), 135-6.

[50] *PG*, 116, col. 668C.

[51] There is some dispute in the sources about the year when the tattooing actually took place. The letter, which appears in *PG*, 116, cols 672-80, says that it happened on 18 July, but does not state in which year. According to the Chronicle of Symeon the Logothete, the *Encomium* and the metaphrastic Life of the Theodore, the brothers were tattooed after John the Grammarian became patriarch. Against these sources is our Life, which makes no mention of John and places the incident in the fourteenth indiction, in other words, 836. I see no reason to prefer the later accounts on this point and have thus adhered to 836 in this summary. For a different point of view, see W. Treadgold, 'The Chronological Accuracy of the Chronicle of Symeon the Logothete for the years 813-845', *DOP*, 33 (1979), 187-9. V. Grumel and most other scholars believe that John became patriarch on 21 January 837, while Treadgold prefers 21 April 838. See V. Grumel, 'Chronologie des patriarches iconoclastes du IXe siècle', *EO*, 34 (1935), 162-6.

INTRODUCTION

this letter so closely it is likely that he actually had the document in front of him.[52] Unlike Theodore *Graptos*' encomiast, who describes a lengthy theological dispute between the brothers *Graptoi* and the emperor,[53] Michael's hagiographer follows Theodore's letter in suggesting that almost no words were exchanged except for the emperor's questions about the brothers' place of birth and reasons for coming to Constantinople. This account, unlike that found in the later *Encomium*, rings true in its unembroidered simplicity. It is striking that Theophilos' antipathy towards Theodore and Theophanes seems to spring as much from his distrust of them as foreigners as from their steadfast opposition to iconoclasm.[54]

After the tattooing of the brothers' faces, the hagiographer states that they were confined in the Praetorium prison, where they received consoling letters from Michael and from the future patriarch Methodios, both of whom were also imprisoned there.[55] On the movements of Theodore and Theophanes from 836 until the restoration of icons in 843, the hagiographers once again differ in their accounts. According to Theodore's encomiast and Symeon the Metaphrast, the saints were sent to Apameia (Mudanya) in Bithynia where Theodore *Graptos* died in December, 841.[56] Michael's hagiographer on the other hand implies that they remained in the Praetorium prison and that Theodore lived to see the end of iconoclasm. Once again I am inclined to accept the information provided by the two later authors rather than that of

---

[52] See commentary, notes 128-61.

[53] Featherstone, 'The Praise', 133-44.

[54] See Bury, *A History*, 138; note 2, 139. Bury suggests that Theophilos' resentment towards easterners may have been further aroused by the synodical letter which he received from the three eastern patriarchs. See the *Epistola synodica orientalium ad Theophilum imperatorem de cultu ss. imaginum*, edited with an Italian translation by L. Duchesne, *Roma e l'oriente*, V (1912-3), 222 ff. A seminar at the Warburg Institute in London, led by Miss J. Chrysostomides, Dr A. Angelou and Fr J. Munitiz, is currently working on a new edition, translation and commentary of the text.

[55] On the conflicting accounts concerning where Methodios was during the reign of Theophilos, see commentary, notes 167 and 168.

[56] Featherstone,'The Praise', 145-6; *PG*, 116, col. 680.

Michael's hagiographer; the places of exile which they mention seem too specific to have been invented.[57]

After the triumph of orthodoxy in 843, Michael the *Synkellos*, along with other defenders of the faith, was released from prison and restored to favour. Michael's hagiographer states that at this time the saint was acclaimed as a suitable candidate for the patriarchal throne.[58] It is possible that the hagiographer exaggerates the importance of his hero in this instance, but that Michael was indeed held in high esteem is evident in his appointment as abbot of the monastery of Chora and *synkellos* to the patriarch Methodios. Theophanes *Graptos* became metropolitan of Nicaea, which suggests that he also had gained prominence by his experiences during the iconoclast period.[59]

In evaluating the historical accuracy of the Life of Michael the *Synkellos*, it is possible to draw two conclusions. First it is evident that the hagiographer possesses accurate information about the main events in Michael's life except for the actual date of his arrival in Constantinople. He knows less about the activities of the brothers, Theodore and Theophanes *Graptoi*, especially in comparison with the Encomium and the metaphrastic Life of Theodore. Secondly, some of the hagiographer's main errors, such as his account of the reasons for the saints' departure from Palestine for Constantinople, stem from his own bias as an orthodox monk writing after iconoclasm had ended. It suited his polemical purpose to suggest that the monks came to Constantinople in order to combat the iconoclasts; here the hagiographer overlooked the fact that they actually arrived several years before these policies had been re-introduced.

---

[57] Symeon Magister mentions another incident dating from this period which could well be legendary. On their way to Apameia, the brothers sent iambic verses to Methodios who, according to the chronicler, was then imprisoned in a tomb on the island of Antigoni. See commentary, note 167.

[58] See below, chap. 25.

[59] See commentary, note 197.

INTRODUCTION

The Iconophile Arguments Contained in the Life

The theological arguments in defence of icons which appear in the Life of Michael the *Synkellos* are at first glance no more sophisticated than those which are found in the majority of other hagiographies concerning the iconoclastic period. The lives of iconophile saints generally refute iconoclasm with the help of a few standard patristic arguments, scriptural examples of God's approval of certain types of images, or the existence of miraculous icons such as those 'made without hands' (*acheiropoietai*).[60] On closer inspection however, the Life of Michael the *Synkellos* contains a more sophisticated style of polemic than at first appears. While the doctrinal arguments which our author explicitly sets out are not complex, the Life in its very structure, language and use of scriptural quotations conveys in a subtle way aspects of the orthodox theology of images. In addition, by identifying his iconophile heroes with Christ and with the early Christian martyrs, the hagiographer underlines the importance of the iconoclast controversy in the history of the struggle between the Church and the heretical movements which have repeatedly threatened it.

The arguments in defence of icons are set out in two passages, once in the context of a letter purported to have been written by the patriarch of Jerusalem to the emperor Leo V and once in an apostrophe addressed by the hagiographer himself to the iconoclasts. In the letter, after a short excursus on the Incarnation of our Lord and His place in the holy Trinity, the nature of man as the image and likeness of God and Christ's role as Saviour, the arguments used are mostly drawn from the testimony of tradition.[61] The writer lists examples of legitimate icons, including the prophets (this argument is drawn from St John of Damascus' oration on the holy icons),[62] the miraculous image which Christ sent to Abgar, king of Edessa, and the icon of Christ and the

---

[60] See Ševčenko, 'Hagiography', 127.

[61] See below, chap. 11.

[62] See commentary, note 88.

INTRODUCTION

Theotokos which was believed to have been painted by St Luke.[63] In the second passage the hagiographer denounces the iconoclasts for comparing the icons of Christ, the Mother of God and the saints to idols of Apollo, Artemis and other false gods.[64]

In these passages the author succeeds in conveying the basic arguments against iconoclasm in a concise, almost formulaic manner. This is the political answer to iconoclasm: a doctrine which can be summed up in a few words and repeated even by the average person in the street. If we look beyond this, however, there emerges a deeper, more symbolic level in the Life of Michael which both reinforces these arguments and endows the text with a broader religious significance. The first and most striking feature on this level is the theme of the saints' (that is, both Michael's and his disciples') resemblance to Christ, which pervades the Life from the very beginning. This device is of course common to all saints' lives, but it seems possible that in the context of iconophile polemic it acquires special meaning. At the interrogation of the *Graptoi* brothers by the emperor Theophilos, for example, the hagiographer writes, 'What is more fitting and marvellous than this, that they were made equal to their Creator in contest? For just as my Christ was smitten in the face as He stood in the presence of Pilate, so His true servants rejoiced as their countenances were struck for His sake and for the sake of His icon.'[65] After the two saints are tattooed with the iambic verses, they defiantly quote Matthew 25:40: 'You will recognise all of these letters in the countenance of Christ, for He said,"Inasmuch as ye have done it unto one of the least of these My brethren, ye have done it unto Me."'[66]

While the gospels remain the fundamental source of inspiration for the Life of Michael, it is fascinating to perceive also the influence of

---

[63] See commentary, notes 93 and 95.

[64] See below, p. 80.

[65] See below, p. 84, lines 12-5.

[66] See below, p. 94, lines 21-3.

apocalyptic texts and in particular, of the Book of Revelation.⁶⁷ The iconoclast emperors are described in colourful language as beasts who resemble the father of all evil, the devil himself. Leo V is 'the serpent of the sea and beast who bore the name of lion' and 'gnashes his teeth at the saints,'⁶⁸ while Theophilos is 'savage in ways and harsh in mind, breathing forth Christ-hating anger and fury' and 'gnashes his teeth like a lion.'⁶⁹ Whereas such imagery can be found in other lives concerning the iconoclast period and in the passions of earlier martyrs,⁷⁰ our hagiographer succeeds in tying it into his narrative in an original and striking way. The symbolism of Revelation can be used to describe not only the heretical persecutors but also the heroes of the story. Michael is indirectly identified with the archangel Michael, who defeats the bestial kings in the apocalyptic books from Daniel to Revelation.⁷¹ The

---

⁶⁷ I am very grateful to Dr.A.M. Wilson for pointing out to me the dependence of the Life on apocalyptic texts and in particular on the Book of Revelation.

⁶⁸ See below, p. 62, line 3 and p. 68, lines 1-2.

⁶⁹ See below, p. 72, lines 20-1; p. 78, line 24. For other examples of the final phrase, which appears as λεοντιαῖον βρύξας in the Life of Michael, cf. *Passio Paphnutii*, *BHG*, 1419, *AASS*, Sept, VI, 68, n. 2; *Passio s. Margaretae*, *BHL*, 5308, *AASS*, Jul, V, 36, n.16; *Passio ss. XL martyrum*, *BHG*, 1201, in O. von Gebhardt, *Acta martyrum selecta* (Berlin, 1902), 173. All of these examples are cited in Delehaye, *op.cit.*, 246, note 4. The original source of the expression is scriptural. See Psalm 34:16 (35:16); Acts 7:54 etc.

⁷⁰ On the genre of epic passions, see H. Delehaye, *Les passions des martyrs et les genres littéraires* (Brussels, 1921), 226-315.

⁷¹ 'Michael, which means "general of God"...' below, p. 46, lines 5-6. The epithet 'general of God' refers to the archangel Michael with his military attributes, see commentary, note 10. Apocalyptic writing developed during the period of the Jews' exile (587-538 B.C.). It can be found first in the Book of Ezekiel and in Isaiah 40-55. Apocalyptic writing appears in a fully developed form in the Book of Daniel 7-12, which was written during the great persecution of 167-164 B.C. by Antiochus IV Epiphanes, the Seleucid king of Antioch. Many of the apocryphal books of the Old Testament are also much influenced by this tradition. In the New Testament, the apocalyptic style is used by Jesus (Mark 13) and in one of the finest examples of the genre, the Book of Revelation. For further background, see R.H. Charles, *The Apocrypha and Pseudepigraphica of the Old Testament in English*, I-II (Oxford, 1913); S.B. Frost, *Old Testament Apocalyptic: Its Origin and Growth* (London, 1952). Apocalyptic writing continued to flourish in the late Roman and Byzantine periods. See H. Weinel, 'Die spätere christliche Apocalyptic', in Εὐχαριστήριον, *Studien zur Religion und Literatur des alten und neuen Testaments*, II (Göttingen, 1923), 141-73; P.J. Alexander, *The Oracle of Baalbek: The Tiburtine Sibyl in Greek Dress*, (*DOS*, 10,

Graptoi brothers, on the other hand, represent the saints and martyrs in Revelation. The tattooing of iambic verses on their faces marks them out as the chosen ones, like the hundred and forty-four thousand who have the Father's name written on their foreheads (Rev. 14:1).[72] After they are tattooed, Theodore and Theophanes cry, 'Understand that when they have seen these letters, the cherubim will withdraw and the fiery sword, retreating before us, will yield entrance to paradise, revering these countenances which were so ignominiously engraved for the sake of their Lord...'[73] The hagiographer draws further on the imagery of Revelation in a rhetorical apostrophe in the midst of his account of the saints' punishment: 'But because you were eager to persecute them, God Who judges righteously through His righteous wrath will hinder you from such an aim in order that the holy and exceedingly glorious city of God, the New Jerusalem, may not be deprived of such luminaries, but may place them around herself as an adornment, fixing them as all-precious stones in the diadem of the empire.'[74]

The use of the gospels and of the Book of Revelation performs two functions in the Life of Michael the *Synkellos*. First, it places the story of Michael and his disciples within the history of the Church and identifies their struggles with the early persecutions. The eschatological dimensions of their experience are thus revealed: like Christ and the early martyrs, these saints through their sufferings transcend this world and will be resurrected in glory on the final day. Secondly, however, and purely in the context of the iconoclastic controversy, the Life conveys much about the saints' role as living icons of Christ. While historians have recently placed much emphasis on the iconoclasts' 'ethical' theory of images, that is, the doctrine that holy men are true icons of Christ, they have sometimes neglected to point out that this

---

Washington, 1967); 'Medieval Apocalypses as Historical Sources', *AmHR*, 73 (1968), 997-1018; *The Byzantine Apocalyptic Tradition* (Berkeley-Los Angeles-London, 1985).

[72] see below, p. 88, lines 12-5 and 94, lines 15-8.

[73] See below, p. 94, lines 15-8.

[74] See below, p. 88, lines 15-20.

concept was no less important to the iconophiles.⁷⁵ If we look at the Life of Michael the *Synkellos* as a whole, it is this point which the hagiographer strives above all to convey. He first demonstrates Michael's and his disciples' likeness to Christ in their conduct and then shows how they were persecuted on behalf of Christ and His icon. Michael the *Synkellos* writes to Theodore and Theophanes after their ordeal in the following words:

> I praise above measure and embrace the breasts and backs which were sprinkled with blood on account of the divine and saving blood which flowed on our behalf from the life-giving side which was pierced with a lance. I salute those honourable and most beloved countenances which are marked with letters on behalf of the sacred image of Christ. I caress the living icons and forms which were pricked with iron and blackened on behalf of the erected and painted icon and form of my Redeemer and Saviour.⁷⁶

In the conduct and suffering of an iconophile saint, various strands of the orthodox theology of images overlap and intertwine. Not only the material, but also the living icons of Christ, His true saints, are desecrated. Just as honour passes from an image to its prototype, so does dishonour, and the hagiographer emphasises again and again that the outrages committed by the iconoclasts were outrages against the Saviour Himself. In this way the orthodox resistance to iconoclasm is placed not only within a wider historical, but also a theological context. As the great theologian John of Damascus stated in the previous century:

> For the saints are the Lord's army... if [they] are heirs of God and co-heirs with Christ, they will also share in the divine glory and dominion. If they have partaken of Christ's sufferings, and are His friends, shall they not receive a share of glory from the Church on earth?... I

---

⁷⁵ See M.V. Anastos, 'The Ethical Theory of Images Formulated by the Iconoclasts', *DOP*, 8 (1954), 151-60; P.J. Alexander, 'The Iconoclastic Council of St Sophia (815) and its Definition (*Horos*)', *DOP*, 7 (1953), 37-66.

⁷⁶ See below, p. 96, lines 19-26.

INTRODUCTION

> bow before the images of Christ, the incarnate God; of our Lady, the Theotokos and Mother of the Son of God; and of the saints, who are God's friends. In struggling against evil they have shed their blood; they have imitated Christ Who shed his blood for them by shedding their blood for Him. I make a written record of the prowess and sufferings of those who have walked in His footsteps, that I may be sanctified and be set on fire to imitate them zealously...[77]

While Theodore of Stoudios has less to say on the iconic qualities of saints,[78] the Life of Michael the *Synkellos* along with other representatives of its genre suggests the centrality of this idea to iconophile thought. It is possible that because these lives were written after the triumph of orthodoxy when the finer points of iconoclast theology had already faded from peoples' minds, the significance of the saints who defended the icons and their role as images of Christ could again be fully appreciated. In fact it is unlikely that the iconoclasts ever possessed sole claim to the 'ethical' theory of images. Indeed this concept seems more consistent with the iconophile attitude to images, the body and the material world than it is with what we know of iconoclast theology.

The Literary Form of the Life

As a literary work, the Life of Michael the Synkellos follows a traditional form which is based on the rules for the pagan encomium or the βασιλικὸς λόγος.[79] The first Christian saints' lives and encomia to

---

[77] *PG*, 94, col. 1252. Translated by D. Anderson, *St John of Damascus, On the Divine Images* (New York, 1980), 28-9 (I, 21). I would like to thank the St Vladimir Seminary Press for allowing me to reprint this translation here.

[78] Theodore of Stoudios, *Antirrhetici adversus iconomachos*, *PG*, 99, cols. 327-436. The writings of the patriarch Nikephoros, which still require a detailed study, contain more on the veneration of saints. See K. Parry, 'Theodore Studites and the Patriarch Nicephorus on Image-making as a Christian Imperative', *B*, 59 (1989), 164-83; Alexander, *The Patriarch Nicephorus of Constantinople* and P. O'Connell, *The Ecclesiology of St. Nicephorus I (758-828)* (Rome, 1972).

[79] See above, note 10; H. Delehaye, *Les passions des martyrs*, 183-235.

INTRODUCTION

adopt this form, including Athanasius' Life of St. Anthony,[80] and Gregory of Nazianzus' funeral orations,[81] served as models for the later works. For this reason, we find many examples of borrowings between hagiographies. *Topoi*, or rhetorical commonplaces, often reappear in different works. In fact the very elements which modern scholars sometimes discard as lacking originality are those which conveyed the most meaning to the Byzantines.[82] Like an icon, a saint's life must contain recognizable features which reveal the sanctity of its subject.[83]

Most hagiographical *topoi*, in order to illustrate the holiness of the saint, underline his or her resemblance to Christ. In the Life of Michael this is immediately evident as we read the account of the saint's birth and upbringing. The hagiographer compares Michael's conception to that of Samuel. Samuel's mother Anna was sterile until she prayed unceasingly to God for a male child (I Kings 1: 1-20 LXX).[84] This *topos*, which appears in a number of other saints' lives and encomia, would have evoked for the Byzantines the story of Anna's namesake, the mother of the Virgin Mary and by implication the miraculous conception of Christ Himself.[85] The canticle of Anna (I Kings 2: 1-10)

---

[80] *PG*, 26, cols. 835-976; J. List, 'Das Antoniosleben des hl. Athanasius d. Gr. Eine literarhistorische Studie zu den Anfängen der byzantinischen Hagiographie', *Texte und Forschungen zur byzantinisch-neugriechischen Philologie*, II (Athens, 1930).

[81] Gregory of Nazianzus wrote funeral orations on his father, his brother Caesarius and Basil the Great, among others. These are published in *PG*, 35 and 36. Translations of some of these texts can be found in H. Wace and P. Schaff, *A Select Library of Nicene and Post-Nicene Fathers of the Christian Church*, VII (Oxford-New York, 1894).

[82] The traditional approach towards hagiography has been to disregard commonplaces and to concentrate on the elements which may be historically true. See for example, F. Halkin, 'L'hagiographie byzantine au service de l'histoire', *XIII International Congress* (Oxford, 1966), Main Papers XI, 1-10; H. Delehaye, *Les légendes hagiographiques* (Brussels, 1905). A more constructive approach is suggested by E. Patlagean in her 'Ancienne hagiographie byzantine et histoire sociale', *Annales ESC*, 23 (Paris, 1968), 106-26, whose chief merit is that it recognises the importance of the overall form and structure of saints' lives.

[83] The similarity between the lives of saints and icons was recognised by St John of Damascus. See his *Orationes de sacris imaginibus*, *PG*, 94, col 1248.

[84] See below, chap. 1.

[85] See commentary, note 8.

was sung at Christmas in the orthodox church by the ninth or tenth centuries, which suggests its early association with the Nativity of Christ.[86]

The language used to describe Michael's education and monastic training is likewise derived from the gospel accounts of Christ's childhood. Like Christ, 'the boy increased in stature and in knowledge before God' (Luke 2:52). The subjects which Michael studies, grammar, rhetoric, philosophy, poetry and astronomy, represent five of the seven liberal arts (if poetry corresponds to music).[87] Whereas this listing of the subjects studied is a common *topos* in Byzantine hagiography, it varies enough in individual lives to suggest that hagiographers were approaching as near as possible to the truth.[88] The underlying point of the *topos* however is again to compare the saint with Christ. Although Luke does not suggest that Christ was educated in pagan letters and philosophy, he does describe His learned discussions with the doctors in the temple, which amazed His parents (Luke 2: 46-8). Michael again imitates Christ when after the death of his father he sells all his moveable possessions and landed property and enters the *laura* of St Sabas.[89] This taking up of the ascetic way, inspired by Jesus' commands to His disciples in Matthew 10: 5-42 and 16: 24, appears in countless other lives of saints, beginning with Athanasius' Life of St Anthony.[90]

In the next section of the Life, the hagiographer emphasizes the monastic role of the saint. Emulating his illustrious predecessors in

---

[86] J. Mateos, ed. and tr., *Le typicon de la grande église*, I (*OCA*, 165, Rome, 1962), 154-5.

[87] See below, chap. 2.

[88] For a summary of the subjects studied by other saints in this period, see P. Lemerle, *Le premier humanisme byzantin* (Paris, 1971), 100-4. Also see A. Moffatt, 'Schooling in the Iconoclast Centuries', *Iconoclasm*, eds. Bryer and Herrin, 91-2. The *topos* appears first however in much earlier works. Gregory of Nazianzus in his *In laudem Basilii*, for example, lists rhetoric, grammar (and poetry), philosophy, astronomy, arithmetic and medicine, *PG*, 36, col. 528.

[89] See below, chap. 3.

[90] Athanasius, *Vita s. Antonii*, *PG*, 26, col. 841: ...ἐλογίζετο περιπατῶν, πῶς οἱ μὲν ἀπόστολοι πάντα καταλιπόντες ἠκολούθησαν τῷ σωτῆρι...

INTRODUCTION

Palestine, St Euthymios and St Sabas, he is ultimately allowed to withdraw into a solitary cell in order to hold private conversation with God. Some time later, Michael achieves the status of a spiritual father in the tradition of the earlier desert fathers. Theophanes and Theodore come to be trained by him in the monastic way of life; it is interesting that Michael teaches them grammar, philosophy and the composition of poetry in addition to the art of prayer.[91] This part of the Life, dealing with the monastic training of Michael and his disciples, is clearly based on the accounts found in earlier lives of ascetic saints. The biographer stresses the spiritual training of the monks who have as their goal solitary contemplation and tranquillity (*hesychia*).[92] It is somewhat surprising to find in this context the emphasis on both Michael's and his disciples' education in the liberal arts, as well as their continued contact with the patriarch of Jerusalem. It is possible that in view of the saints' changed roles somewhat later, the hagiographer wishes to point out their fitness not only for the monastic, but also for the pastoral way of life.

Whereas the first section of the Life thus stresses the monastic and ascetic roles of the saints, the character of the text changes once they have arrived in Constantinople. The Life no longer follows the conventional form of the monastic *bios*, but is rather inspired by the 'epic' passions of the early Christian martyrs.[93] On examining this section of the Life in detail, however, it becomes clear that while it shares many conventional *topoi* with these mainly fictional passions, it

---

[91] See below, chap. 5.

[92] Examples of saints' lives which describe the ascetic training of their subjects include Cyril of Skythopolis, *Vitae ss. Euthymii et Sabae*, ed. E. Schwartz (*TU*, 49, 2, Leipzig, 1939), 5-200 as well as many others. It is important to remember that physical asceticism, called *praktike* by Evagrios, leads to *physike*, or natural contemplation, and finally *theologia*, knowledge of God Himself. It was never practised by monks as an end in itself. See as an introduction to the subject of mysticism in the eastern monastic tradition, A. Louth, *The Origins of the Christian Mystical Tradition* (Oxford, 1981), esp. 98-131.

[93] The genre which Delehaye calls 'epic' passions differ from the monastic *bioi* in that they rarely include an account of their heroes' birth and upbringing. Instead these texts concentrate on the scenes of interrogation and martyrdom, which they often elaborate considerably. It is likely that one of the apocryphal books of the Old Testament, the fourth book of Maccabees, had an important influence on the genre. See Delehaye, *Les passions des martyrs*, 314-5; Charles, *The Apocrypha*, 653-85.

also remains faithful to the probably truthful account of these events contained in Theodore *Graptos*' letter to the bishop of Kyzikos.

It is striking that in the passages describing Leo V's and Theophilos' interrogations of Michael and his disciples, the hagiographer does not record lengthy dialogues on the subject of icons. This contrasts with the accounts of other saints' encounters with emperors during the iconoclast period. According to Stephen the Deacon, St Stephen the Younger, when eventually summoned to the presence of Constantine V, debated with him at length about the sanctity of icons.[94] Such dialogues, which would normally be on the subject of Christianity versus paganism, feature prominently in the passions written from the fourth century onwards to commemorate the struggles of the early Christian martyrs. To take one example, the pre-metaphrastic Passion of St Eustratios and his companions contains a long discussion between Eustratios and his interrogator, the governor Agrikolaos. In this audience, the saint displays his knowledge not only of Christian teachings, but also of the pagan philosophers.[95] In contrast, the dialogues between the *Graptoi* brothers and the emperor Theophilos described in Theodore's letter and in our Life are short and to the point.[96] One aspect of the latter text which might seem to have been influenced by the epic passions, but which also appears in Theodore's letter, is the series of interrogations to which the two brothers are subjected. This is a classic *topos* in passions of martyrs which serves to build up the suspense and to provide further

---

[94] See *Vita s. Stephani iunioris*, *PG*, 100, cols. 1156-60. Although we have no biography of the martyr Andreas Kalybites, Theophanes suggests that he also debated with Constantine V and accused him of impiety and of resembling the emperors Valens and Julian. Theophanes, *Chronographia* , I, 432.

[95] *PG*, 116, cols. 468-505. The audience with the emperor is described in cols. 489-500. Although the *passio* was included in the metaphrastic *Menologion* compiled in the late tenth to early eleventh centuries, it has also been discovered in a number of pre-metaphrastic *menologia* and in a fragment of a ninth-century manuscript. See F. Halkin, 'L'épilogue d'Eusèbe de Sebastée à la passion de s. Eustrate et ses compagnons', *AnalBoll*, 88 (1970), 279; Ehrhard, *Überlieferung* I, 509-32, 112, note 2.

[96] See below, chaps. 19 and 21; *PG*, 116, cols. 672-80. I am grateful to Dr J. Herrin for suggesting another close parallel to these short interviews, namely the trials of St Maximos Confessor in the mid-seventh century. Verbatim accounts of the interrogation are discussed in J.M. Garrigues, 'Le martyre de s. Maxime le Confesseur', *Revue thomiste*, 76 (1976), 410-52.

opportunities for theological discussion.⁹⁷ In the Life of Michael and in Theodore's letter, the second summons of the saints underlines the cruelty of Theophilos. The brothers are beaten again until 'their blood like the stream of a river... stained the whole floor.'⁹⁸ It is not altogether clear why after leaving the Chrysotriklinos Theodore and Theophanes are again pursued and questioned, this time by the logothete of the course. If this account is true, it may indicate the emperor's puzzlement at the obstinacy of the saints and his desire to break their resolve before administering his bizarre punishment.

In the last part of the Life, when Theophilos has died and orthodoxy is restored, the hagiographer renews his emphasis on the monastic and pastoral roles of Michael and his disciples. Here the sanctity of the heroes is revealed in a number of ways, but most of all in their care for the spiritual flocks entrusted to them, whether monastic or lay. Michael plays an active part in restoring the monastery of Chora to its former prosperity. He seeks the aid not only of the patriarch Methodios, but also the patronage of the emperor Michael III and his mother Theodora. Theophanes likewise, as bishop of Nicaea, having 'guided his spiritual flock in an orthodox manner for four years and borne ripe fruits for God... stored up within the haven of the heavenly kingdom the blessed souls of those who had been saved by him and by his all-wise teachings.'⁹⁹

In this section of the Life, Michael's biographer is able to draw not only on the *vitae* of monastic saints for inspiration, but also on those of bishops and patriarchs.¹⁰⁰ The treatment of holy men is in fact similar in the two genres, since ascetics like Theodore of Sykeon and even the

---

⁹⁷ See Delehaye, *Les passions des martyrs*, 256.

⁹⁸ See below, p. 90, lines 22-3.

⁹⁹ See below, p. 112, lines 4-8.

¹⁰⁰ See, for example,*Vita s. Eutychii, PG*, 86, cols. 2273-6 (a translation and commentary by A.M. Wilson and A. Cameron will soon appear in this series); *Vita s. Nicephori,* ed. C. De Boor, *Nicephori archiepiscopi CP opuscula historica* (Leipzig, 1880), and many others. To my knowledge no study has yet been done on the differences between the lives of episcopal and ascetic saints.

stylite saints generally play an active pastoral role in their later years.[101] Nevertheless, the stress on both Michael's and Theophanes' responsibility towards their monastic or lay communities is striking here. We gain the impression that it is this aspect of the saints' mission which is most vividly remembered in their separate communities and which perhaps inspired the hagiographer to undertake the composition of the Life.

The biographer provides an extended description of the events leading up to Michael's death, beginning with a vision and continuing with his visit to the patriarch and emperors, his return to the monastery and his prayers and sermon to the monks.[102] All of these elements serve not only to emphasize Michael's sanctity and the extent to which he will be missed, but also lend dignity and grandeur to his death. The description of Michael's disciples coming to meet him with candles and incense and of the saint's prayers at the tombs of holy people buried in the monastery is a vivid one. Finally when Michael dies, a miracle occurs, offering absolute proof of his holiness.[103]

The structure of the Life of Michael the *Synkellos* is thus a composite one. Beginning as a monastic *bios*, laying stress on the spiritual development of the saint, the work moves on to adopt the form of an epic passion as it relates the story of his and his disciples' persecution, finally reverting to the conventional treatment of a monastic or episcopal saint's final years and death. While most of the Life is written in a straightforward narrative style, the hagiographer breaks out occasionally into more high-flown rhetorical apostrophes. Two such passages occur in the context of the saint's persecution by the emperor Theophilos. Directing a series of rhetorical questions concerning the nature of the persecution and the theology of icons at Theophilos, the hagiographer employs language and imagery drawn from the scriptures.[104] The

---

[101] See H. Delehaye, *Les saints stylites* (*SubsHag*, 14, Brussels, 1923); A.-J. Festugière,*Vie de Théodore de Sykéon*, I-II (*SubsHag*, 48, Brussels, 1970). Theodore was in fact ordained bishop, but later resigned the office. *Ibid.*, chaps. 58 and 74.

[102] See below, chaps. 33-7.

[103] See below, chap. 39. See commentary, note 227.

[104] See below, chaps. 18 and 20.

polemical tone of the text is apparent throughout, but it is also clearly intended to instruct its audience both morally and spiritually.

Michael the *Synkellos* as a Monastic Saint

The Life of Michael the *Synkellos* provides much information not only about iconoclasm, but also about monasticism in the late eighth to the early ninth centuries. The ascetic life which Michael undertakes at the *laura* of St Sabas belongs to the tradition of the early desert fathers. The saint's chief aim at this stage is to embark on the way of life of a solitary ascetic, living in a cell for the purpose of contemplation and private conversation with God.[105] Much later, when he becomes abbot of the monastery of Chora, the hagiographer implies that Michael is no longer leading the life of a contemplative, but is actively administering to his community's spiritual and physical needs. This change in Michael's monastic role parallels that of many other Byzantine saints who moved, often reluctantly, from a life of solitude to one of responsibility and leadership. The founders of monasticism in Palestine, St Euthymios and St Sabas for example, experienced a similar transition when they had acquired circles of disciples and were forced to found monasteries to house them.[106] Michael the *Synkellos'* monastic life however differs in some ways from those of the early desert fathers, reflecting developments in institutional monasticism which had taken place in the intervening centuries.

At the beginning of the Life, we are given a clear and detailed account of the ascetic exercises which Michael practised at the *laura* of St Sabas. The saint observed a continuous fast of unsalted vegetables, eating bread only on Saturdays, Sundays and feast-days; in addition, he undertook all-night vigils and other difficult feats.[107] His goal in performing these acts was to prove to his abbot that he was worthy of entering into an even

---

[105] See below, chap. 3.

[106] See D.J. Chitty, *The Desert a City* (Oxford, 1966), 82-122; *Vitae s Euthymii et s Sabae*, ed. Schwartz, 5-200.

[107] See below, chap. 3.

INTRODUCTION

more demanding, solitary style of spiritual life. In spite of its origins as a foundation for hermits to live in close proximity while maintaining lives of solitary prayer, the *laura* of St Sabas appears to have evolved into a coenobitic monastic community by the ninth century.[108] This transformation is certainly implied in this section of our Life, since Michael's request to withdraw into a cell is granted only after eighteen years of communal life. Nevertheless it appears that the ideal of the solitary life remained at the monastery in theory, if not always in practice. The abbot complied with Michael's request, evidently recognizing with him the value of complete withdrawal.

This section of the Life of Michael raises interesting questions about the nature of coenobitic monastic life in this period. To judge by contemporary lives of saints, it was not uncommon for solitary ascetics to live within *coenobia*, not only in Palestine but also in Asia Minor.[109] However it is unclear to what extent the solitary contemplative life was combined with the life of communal worship. Did monks like Michael cut themselves off entirely from their communities and if so, what was their spiritual effect on those communities? As we have seen, even when living in his cell Michael remained under the authority of his abbot. When Theodore and Theophanes presented themselves to him as disciples, Michael went to the abbot to request permission to train them.[110] The biographer does not state how often Michael and his two disciples joined in the liturgical worship of the monastery as a whole, but one assumes that they followed the traditional procedure of the *laura*, rejoining the rest of the community on Saturdays and Sundays.[111] On week-days, the hagiographer states that Michael and his disciples

---

[108] See D. Papachryssanthou, 'La vie monastique dans les campagnes byzantines du VIIIe au XIe siècles', *B*, 43 (1973), 166-73, 179.

[109] *Ibid.*, 165-6; see also V. Corbo, 'L'ambiente materiale della vita dei monaci di Palestina nel periodo bizantino', *Il monachesmo orientale* (*OCA*, 153, Rome, 1958), 245, 249.

[110] See below, chap. 5.

[111] On the history of the *laura* as an institution in Palestine, see Chitty, *The Desert a City*, 13-6, 82-6, 105-18. Also see commentary, note 22.

were engaged in singing the daily offices and in lessons in rhetoric and philosophy.

When Michael was fifty years old, he was appointed *synkellos*, or advisory assistant, to the patriarch of Jerusalem. The reasons for this appointment are not entirely clear, but Michael's hagiographer suggests that it was due to his distinction not only in asceticism, but also in learning and lineage.[112] The patriarch's choice of Michael and his disciples as envoys to the pope offered them a further opportunity for widening their horizons. Caught in Constantinople at the beginning of second iconoclasm, the saints then assumed the role of confessors and martyrs. This in fact led them back to a life much closer to that which they had left at the *laura* of St Sabas. Twenty-eight years of solitary imprisonment or exile under the iconoclasts followed; the hardships which they endured resulted in an even greater prestige as holy figures than before.

In the final section of the Life, Michael assumes once again a more active, administrative role. Like many other iconophile monks who suffered during the period of iconoclasm, Michael played a part in the restoration of the church after the triumph of orthodoxy in 843. He was made abbot of the monastery of Chora and *synkellos* to the newly appointed patriarch Methodios, who was also of monastic background and a former victim of the iconoclasts. The hagiographer describes how Michael went about obtaining imperial aid for the monastery and restoring it to its former prosperity. Furthermore, he taught and inspired not only his own flock but also laymen and clerics in Constantinople: '... his virtuous way of life shone like a star, so that almost all of those belonging to the palace and to the catholic church came to him for the sake of his prayer and for the benefit of his all-wise teaching.'[113]

These passages, besides telling us much about the part which iconophile monks like Michael played after the restoraton of icons, also

---

[112] See below chap. 5; it was in fact not uncommon for Palestinian monks to become patriarch or to assume active roles within the patriarchate. The patriarch Elias (494-516) was one example. See commentary below, note 43.

[113] See below, p. 116, line 26-9.

contain some information about monasticism as an institution in this period. It is interesting to note for example Michael's initiative in seeking the aid of the emperor after he became abbot of the monastery of Chora. The exchange of prayers for material aid represented a return to the traditional relationship between emperors and holy men or monasteries before the introduction of iconoclasm. It is likely that holy figures like Michael the *Synkellos* who had acquired distinction through their sufferings under the iconoclasts not only offered spiritual support, but also gave practical advice to the orthodox emperors, Michael III and his mother Theodora.

While Michael was thus actively administering to his community's needs at the end of his life, we are left in some doubt about the nature of his own spiritual life. The biographer states that after the vision which informed Michael of his approaching death, the saint commanded that the sounding-board (*semantron*) be struck and the monks summoned for Mattins. This caused surprise within the community, as if Michael had not been in the habit of performing the daily offices in the company of the monks.[114] It is possible that in spite of his active role as abbot, Michael was nevertheless accustomed to pray privately in his cell. This could have been due either to his level of training as a solitary ascetic or simply to the fact that as an infirm octogenarian he had been forced to reduce the hours which he spent in communal worship. Unfortunately, since the biographer does not state in what way the sounding of the gong was contrary to custom, it is impossible to draw any definite conclusions.

What emerges most clearly in the final section of the Life is the extent to which Michael was venerated by his disciples and the importance of his role as spiritual father. As abbot, Michael was entrusted with the care of the entire community and it was he who would ultimately be

---

[114] See below, chap.34. The phenomenon of an abbot living the life of a recluse within his own monastery is attested in other saints' lives of the period. See for example the Life of St Stephen the Younger, *PG*, 100, col. 1100b and Theodore of Stoudios' *Laudatio s.Platonis Hegumeni*, *PG*, 99, cols. 813 and 817. For further examples, see Papachryssanthou, 'La vie monastique', 164, note 3.

responsible for their souls.[115] In his final prayer to the monks, Michael begged them to remain obedient to the abbots who would succeed him, stating, 'I shall render account to God on your behalf on the fearful day of judgment, on which He will come to reward every man according to his works.'[116] In spite of the saint's quest for *hesychia* at the beginning of his life, it was as a spiritual leader entrusted with the care of many souls that he died.

From this and other texts, we know that many different forms of monastic life existed in the early ninth century, from the solitary asceticism practised by hermits like St Ioannikios on Mt Olympos[117] to the fully-fledged coenobitic monasticism of the type best exemplified in the monastery of Stoudios in Constantinople.[118] Many intermediate forms existed as well, of which Michael's retreat into a cell within the *laura* of St Sabas at the beginning of his life and the possibility that he led a separate prayer life at the monastery of Chora are both examples. Whatever the personal spiritual aims of Michael may have been, it is clear that by the end of his life he was living in a world in which coenobitic monasticism had an important role to play. All of Michael's prayers for the monastery of Chora indicate that he envisaged it as a coenobitic community in the strictest sense. Above all he demanded obedience and humility from his monks. In this context one does not imagine Michael encouraging such ascetic feats or seclusion as he himself practised at the *laura* of St Sabas.

---

[115] The role of the spiritual father assumed great importance in eastern monasticism from an early period. The idea that the spiritual father or mother (most often an abbot or abbess) will answer to God for his or her disciples' souls appears in the *Pratum spirituale*, *PG*, 87, col. 2992C (this story concerns an abbess), John Klimakos' *Scala Paradisi*, *PG*, 88, cols. 680A, 705C and other texts. See R.J. Barringer, 'Penance and Byzantine Hagiography, le Répondant du Peché', *Studia Patristica*, 17, ed. E.A. Livingstone (Oxford, 1982), II, 552-7.

[116] See below, p.126, lines 22-4.

[117] See below, chap. 26 and commentary, note 179.

[118] For a detailed account of the coenobitic way of life at the monastery of Stoudios, see J. Leroy, 'La vie quotidienne du moine Studite', *Irénikon*, 27 (1954), 21-50; also 'La réforme studite', *OCA*, 153 (1958-9), 181-214.

INTRODUCTION

The Life of Michael the *Synkellos* represents an example of the hagiographical genre which has its roots in the monastic way of life. The hagiographer commemorates the saint's demonstration of Christian virtue to the extent that he renounced all worldly ties and retreated into a life of contemplation. It is in this context that the description of Michael's spiritual training at the beginning of the Life acquires importance. That the saint perceived his own role primarily as a spiritual one is also evident at the end of the Life, when the hagiographer describes his guidance of the monastery during the difficult period following the restoration of orthodoxy. It is thus first for his role as a monastic saint and as abbot of Chora that Michael the *Synkellos* is commemorated. The part which Michael played in the dispute over images represents an extension of his spiritual and ascetic ideals. The saint is depicted as upholding the way of Christian virtue, having renounced all personal freedom in his dedication to the true faith. Like Christ before Pilate and like the early Christian martyrs, he remains steadfast in his beliefs. In opposing the iconoclasts, the saint does not question the ideal authority of the emperor in the spiritual as well as the temporal realms; rather he combats rulers who have embraced heretical doctrines. When orthodoxy is restored, Michael regains his traditional relationship with the emperors, that of counsellor and spiritual guide, who depends on their munificence to carry out his way of life. Once again the spiritual and temporal realms proceed in mutual harmony and dependence.

The Writings of Michael the *Synkellos* and his Disciples

1. Michael the *Synkellos*
A large number of works attributed to Michael, monk or *synkellos* of Constantinople, survive. Unfortunately, it is still not known which of these should be ascribed to our Michael and which to another Michael, also monk and *synkellos* of Constantinople, who flourished later in the

ninth century.[119] Until a stylistic analysis has been made of all of these works, their authorship will remain an open question. In the following list, we have included all of the works which could possibly have been written by Michael, *synkellos* of Jerusalem and Constantinople and abbot of Chora, *or* by his successor, also *synkellos* of Constantinople. Those texts whose authorship is still in doubt are indicated below with an asterisk:

    a) Encomium of St Dionysios the Areopagite[120]
    b) Encomium of Zacharias, father of St John the Baptist*[121]
    c) Encomium of the holy angels (incip. Τὸν μὲν λόγον)*[122]
    d) Encomium of the holy angels (incip.Σχεδὸν γὰρ ἀγαπητοὶ)*[123]
    e) Encomium of the archangels Gabriel and Michael*[124]

---

[119] See H.-G. Beck, *Kirche und theologische Literatur im byzantinischen Reich* (Munich, 1959), 503-5. R. Loenertz would like to attribute the *encomia* on Zacharias, Ignatios, the archangels Gabriel and Michael, the holy angels, St Mokios, St Isaakios and St Dalmatos and the oration on the translation of the girdle of the Mother of God to the later Michael. See R.Loenertz, 'Le panégyrique de l'Aréopagite par Saint Michel le Syncelle', *AnalBoll*, 68 (1950), 103-4. A. Ehrhard attributes the *encomium* on St Isaakios and St Dalmatos, as well as several others on Eustratios and his companions, the prophet Daniel and the three children in Babylon, and the apostle Philip to a third Michael, who was possibly a Stoudite monk. This Michael might also be the author of the Life of St Theodore of Stoudios (*PG*, 99, cols. 233-328) as well as the encomia of St Ignatios and St Mokios. Beck, *Kirche und theologische Literatur*, 504; Ehrhard, *Überlieferung,* I, 1, 486, 489, 491, 510, 680, 622.

[120] (*BHG*, 556). *PG*, 4, cols. 617-68; Loenertz, 'Le panégyrique', 94-107. This work was pronounced on 3 October during the period when Michael was exiled to Prousa or Prousias (821-33). This is the only *encomium* which Loenertz attributes to our Michael.

[121] (*BHG*, 1881n). Still unedited. In the earliest manuscripts this work is ascribed to 'the humble monk Michael'. Loenertz, 'Le panégyrique', 103.

[122] (*BHG*, 127). Ed. F. Combefis, *Novum auctarium*, I (Paris, 1648), 1525-80. For the manuscripts containing this text, which mostly attribute it to a Michael the *Synkellos* or the monk, cf. Loenertz, 'Le panégyrique', 103-4 and Ehrhard, *Überlieferung*, I, 3, 462, 24 and 494, 30.

[123] (*BHG*,129a). Cod. Athon. Kausokalyb. 6, 15th c., ff. 254v-258. Ehrhard, *Überlieferung*, III, 241, note 1.

[124] (*BHG*, 1294a). Still unedited. The text survives in six manuscripts, in the earliest of which it is attributed to 'the humble monk Michael', Loenertz, 'Le panegyrique', 104.

INTRODUCTION

f) Encomium of St Mokios*[125]
g) Encomium of St Ignatios*[126]
h) Encomium of St Isaakios and St Dalmatos* [127]
i) Martyrium of the forty-two martyrs of Amorion*[128]
j) Life and Miracles of St John of Damascus and St Kosmas the Melodist*[129]
k) Life of St John of Damascus* [130]
l) Oration on the girdle of the blessed Theotokos* [131]
m) Oration on the dead*[132]
n) Translation into Greek of the Arabic text of a profession of the Chalcedonian faith written circa 813 by the Christian writer and former monk of St Sabas, Theodore Abu Qurrah, in the form of a letter to the Armenians[133]

---

[125] (*BHG*, 1298h). Ed. H. Delehaye, *AnalBoll*, 31 (1912), 176-87.

[126] (*BHG*, 818). Fragmentary. It is impossible for the earlier Michael to be the author of this work since Ignatios died in 877. See J.D. Mansi, *Sacrorum Conciliorum Nova et Amplissima Collectio*, XVI (Venice, 1771) 292-4; *AnalBoll*, 28 (1909), 383.

[127] (*BHG*, 956d). Cod. Paris. gr. 548, ff. 279v-296v (10th-11th c.)

[128] (*BHG*, 1213). Ed.V.Vasilievskij-P.Nikitin, *De XLII martyribus Amoriensibus narrationes et carmina sacra, Mémoires de l'Académie Imp. de S Petersbourg*,VIIIe série, VII, 2 (1905), 22-36, from a manuscript copied in 1023 which attributes the work to Michael, monk and *synkellos*. The difficulty of assigning this work to our Michael is the fact that it was read out on 7 March 843, 844 or 845, when the saint would have been a very old man.

[129] (*BHG*, 394) A. Papadopoulos-Kerameus, Ἀνάλεκτα, IV, 271-302. The text is attributed to Michael by J.H. Hoeck, 'Stand und Aufgaben der Damaskenos-Forschung', *OCP*, 17 (1951), 10-11.

[130] (*BHG*, 884a). Still unedited. Ehrhard, *Überlieferung*, III, 1024-5.

[131] (*BHG*, 1147) Ed. Combefis, *Novum auctarium*, II, 790-802.

[132] *PG*, 95, cols. 248-77. On this attribution, see Hoeck, 'Stand und Aufgaben', 39, 44.

[133] *PG*, 97, cols. 1504-21; I. Dick, 'Un continuateur arabe de saint Jean Damascène: Théodore Abuqurra, évêque melkite de Harran', *Proche-orient chrétien*, 12 (1963), 1209-23, 319-32; 13 (1963), 114-29; S.H. Griffith, 'Theodore Abu Qurrah's Arabic Tract on the Christian Practice of Venerating Images', *Journal of the American Oriental Society*, 105 (1985), 53-73..

o) *Libellus* on the orthodox faith [134]
p) Anacreontic verses written to commemorate the triumph of orthodoxy[135]
q) Four canons[136]
r) Letters addressed to the Sicilian monks on the subject of the *filioque* (now lost)[137]
s) Greek Syntax[138]

2. Theodore *Graptos*

The writings which are attributed to Theodore *Graptos* are as follows:

a) Letter sent to the bishop John of Kyzikos describing his and his brother Theophanes' ordeals at the hands of the emperor Theophilos. An excerpt is preserved in Symeon the Metaphrast's Life of Theodore.[139]

b) A lost work against the iconoclasts, entitled Κυνόλυκος. According to the Life of Michael the *Synkellos*, this consisted of passages quoted from the scriptures and the Church fathers in defence of the icons.[140]

---

[134] Ed. B. Montfaucon, *Bibliotheca coisliniana* (Paris, 1715), 90-3.

[135] L. Allatius, *De ecclesia occidentalis et orientalis perpetua consensione* (Cologne, 1648), 1433-55. Cf. also Th. Nissen, 'Die byzantinischen Anakreonteen', *SbBayerAW*, 3 (Munich, 1940), 48-52.

[136] See D. Stiernon, 'Michel le Syncelle', *DS*, 68-9, col. 1197.

[137] See below, p.56, lines 15-16.

[138] The text is published in D. Donnet, *Le traité de la construction de la phrase de Michel le Syncelle* (Brussels-Rome, 1982). Also see his 'Le traité de grammaire de Michel le Syncelle. Inventaire à l'histoire du texte', *Bull. Inst. Hist. Belge Rome*, 40 (1969), 33-67; 'La tradition imprimée du traité de grammaire de Michel le Syncelle de Jérusalem', *B*, 42 (1972), 441-508; 'Un travail inédit de l'humaniste Nicaise van Ellebode: Notes sur le traité de grammaire de Michel le Syncelle', *Bull.Inst.Hist.Belge Rome*, 43 (1973), 401-57; 'Transmission et revision: à propos du traité de grammaire de Michel le Syncelle', *Revue de l'histoire des textes*, 5 (1975), 73-86. According to some manuscripts, the work was written in Edessa. See H. Hunger, *Die hochsprachliche profane Literatur der Byzantiner*, II (Munich, 1978), 15.

[139] *PG*, 116, cols. 672B-680A.

[140] See below, chap. 30.

c) Oration on the dead.[141]
d) Paracletic canon in honour of the Theotokos[142]

3. Theophanes *Graptos*
Theophanes *Graptos* is remembered in the orthodox church for his composition of a large number of hymns, including *canons*, *stichira* and *idiomela*.[143]

The Manuscripts

For this new edition of the text of the Life of Michael the *Synkellos* I have used the two known manuscripts in which it survives,[144] which are as follows:

1) Cod. 33 of the Congregazione della Missione Urbana of Genoa (this manuscript is now kept in the Biblioteca Franzioni in Genoa) (G)[145] 11th c.; 207 ff.; 32.3 x 22.5cm.; parchment[146]

---

[141] See L. Allatius, *De purgatorio* (Rome, 1655), 211.

[142] Unedited, this survives in a Mt Sinai manuscript. V. Gardthausen, *Catalogus codicum graecorum sinaiticorum* (Oxford, 1886), cod. 1004, p. 218.

[143] W. Christ and M. Paranikas, *Anthologia graeca carminum christianorum* (Leipzig, 1871), 264; J.-B. Pitra, *Analecta sacra spicilegio solesmeni parata* I (Paris, 1876), 236-42, 408; C. Emereau, 'Hymnographi byzantini', *EO*, 25 (1926), 179-82; S. Eustratiades, 'Θεοφάνης ὁ Γραπτός', *Nea Sion,* 31 (1936), 339-44.

[144] These are the same two manuscripts which Th. Schmitt used for his edition of the text in 1906. See Schmitt, 'Kahrie-Džame'. 227.

[145] L. Perria, *I manoscritti citati da Albert Ehrhard, Testi e studi bizantino-neoellenici*, IV (Rome, 1979), 70; Ch. Samberger, *Catalogi codicum graecorum qui in minoribus bibliothecis Italicis asservantur,* I (Leipzig, 1965), 292. I am most grateful to Mrs A. Palau for lending me a microfilm of this manuscript along with her notes describing it. Mrs Palau is presently preparing a new catalogue of all the manuscripts in this collection.

[146] Descriptions of this manuscript can be found in Ehrhard, *Überlieferung*, I, 544 and 'Zur catalogisierung der kleineren Bestände griechischer Handschriften in Italien', *Centralblatt für Bibliothekswesen*, 10 (1893), 208-10. In the latter description, which is the earlier one, Ehrhard gives the measurements as 31 x 72 cm.(!) and dates the manuscript to the tenth century. Having been unable to visit Genoa myself to examine the manuscript, I have depended here on Mrs Palau's description, which is the latest and

INTRODUCTION

The first part of a two volume *Menologion* for January, this manuscript contains texts for the days between 3 and 13 January, including homilies for the Theophany by Basil of Caesarea and Gregory of Nazianzus. Most of the texts, however, are premetaphrastic lives or passions of saints. A. Ehrhard believes that 74 folios (9 1/4 quires) are missing at the beginning of the manuscript, which would have contained texts for the first two days of January. It is not certain, however, whether it would originally have ended on the thirteenth, or seventeenth or eighteenth day of the month like other examples of this type of collection.[147] The Life of Michael the *Synkellos* is contained in ff. 7-44.

2) Cod. Athon. Pantokrator 13 (1047) (A)
12th c.; 319 ff.; parchment.[148]

The first part of a mixed metaphrastic *Menologion* for January, containing texts for the first through the eighteenth day of that month. Like G, the collection includes sermons for the Theophany, including one by St John Chrysostom. Most of the remaining texts are lives, passions or encomia of saints, some of which are identical with those in G. Ehrhard believes that this collection is nearly complete in its present form. It contains four metaphrastic lives, all of which occur near the end of the collection.[149] The Life of Michael the *Synkellos*, which is missing its conclusion, appears in ff. 85-114 v.

The Text

Although the text of the Life of Michael which appears below represents a new critical edition, it does not differ greatly from that prepared by

---

most comprehensive one. She tells me that Dr Nigel Wilson concurs with her in dating the manuscript to the eleventh century.

[147] Ehrhard, *Überlieferung*, I, 544-5.

[148] Again, I have been able to examine this manuscript only on microfilm, for which I am most grateful to the Patriarchal Institute of Patristic Studies in Thessalonike. S. Lambros provides only a very summary description of the manuscript in his *Catalogue of the Greek Manuscripts on Mt. Athos*, I (Cambridge, 1895), 95.

[149] Ehrhard, *Überlieferung*, III, 196-7.

INTRODUCTION

Th. Schmitt, except in a few readings and in the organisation of the apparatus. The original purpose of republishing the text here was to make it once more easily available to scholars. On checking Schmitt's edition with the manuscripts, it became apparent that he occasionally misread them, especially in the case of A.[150] Also since his critical apparatus is somewhat cumbersome and in Russian, it was decided that a new edition of the text would be appropriate here. The page numbers of the Schmitt edition are indicated for ease of reference and in several cases his emendations have been retained. I should like to acknowledge here my indebtedness to his fine work and to express the hope that this new edition will not supersede his, but that it will complement it and make the text available to a wider audience. Like Schmitt, I have adopted in most cases the readings of A, which represents a more reliable witness than G. Besides containing a number of *lacunae*, of one or two words to whole phrases, G contains more orthographical and grammatical mistakes than A. In a few instances, the text itself is non-standard in its syntax, as at p. 124, line 16 (εἰσέρχεται ἐν τῷ ναῷ). These idiosyncracies, usually involving misplaced datives or incorrect sequences of tenses, may be attributed to the hand of the writer rather than to that of the scribe. For this reason I have allowed these readings to remain in the text rather than emending them, adding a note in the commentary to signal their presence.

The English translation is intended to be as faithful to the Greek as possible, while nevertheless remaining understandable to the reader. Elegance may sometimes be sacrificed to accuracy, for example in retaining such expressions as 'the aforementioned', which appear repeatedly in the text. One of the aims of this translation is to suggest as much as possible the slightly stilted and yet colloquial style of the Greek. The frequent quotations from the scriptures and use of biblical language are rendered in the style of the authorized (King James) version. Quotations are identified beside the translation and are sometimes

---

[150] In his collation of A, Schmitt makes very few mistakes which affect the text itself. Strangely however, errors which he records in the *apparatus* do not in fact always appear in the manuscript. It is just possible that the manuscript itself was corrected since his edition was published, but this is not detectable on the microfilm.

INTRODUCTION

discussed further in the commentary. The transliteration of names from the Greek follows the current convention among Byzantinists: κ remains k, endings are -os, rather than the Latinized -us, and so on.

The primary aim of this publication is to make this text, which is an important one for the history of the second iconoclastic period, once again easily available to scholars. The English translation and notes are intended for students of all levels in Byzantine studies and related fields. It is hoped therefore that they will provide enough general and specific information to meet everyone's various needs.

The Life of Michael the Synkellos:

Text and Translation

ΒΙΟΣ ΤΟΥ ΜΙΧΑΗΛ ΤΟΥ ΣΥΝΚΕΛΛΟΥ

Μηνὶ τῷ αὐτῷ δ'

Βίος καὶ πολιτεία καὶ ἀγῶνες τοῦ ὁσίου πατρὸς ἡμῶν καὶ ὁμολογητοῦ Μιχαὴλ πρεσβυτέρου καὶ συγκέλλου γεγονότος πόλεως Ἱεροσολύμων.

Τὰς τῶν ἀγαθῶν ἀνδρῶν ἀναγράπτους τίθεσθαι πράξεις καὶ τὴν
5 τούτων μνήμην τῷ μετὰ ταῦτα χρόνῳ παραδιδόναι πρᾶγμα πολλῆς ὠφελείας τῷ βίῳ καθέστηκε πρόξενον. Ζήλου γάρ τι κέντρον ἐνίησι ταῖς τῶν φιλοθέων ψυχαῖς ἡ τῶν αὐτοῖς κατορθωθέντων διήγησις καὶ πρὸς τὴν τῶν ὁμοίων ἐργασίαν παρακαλεῖ. Ὧν εἷς ἐστι καὶ ὁ νῦν ἡμῖν εἰς διήγησιν προκείμενος βίος, Μιχαήλ φημι τοῦ ὁμολογητοῦ καὶ συγκέλλου,
10 ὃν ἤνεγκε μὲν ἡ ἁγία Χριστοῦ τοῦ Θεοῦ ἡμῶν πόλις Ἱερουσαλήμ, καὶ ὥς τι φυτὸν εὐθαλὲς καὶ ἀρεταῖς κατάκομον ἀνεθρέψατο, ἡ περιφανὴς δὲ Κωνσταντινούπολις ὁμολογητὴν Χριστοῦ καὶ ἀρχιμανδρίτην μονῆς τῆς Χώρας εὐμοίρησεν.

(1) Οὗτος τοίνυν ὁ περιφανέστατος ἄνθρωπος τοῦ θεοῦ καὶ τῶν
15 Ἱεροσολύμων πολίτης ἐκ τίνων μὲν ἔφυ γονέων οὐκ ἴσμεν· οὐδὲ γὰρ ἦν ὁ τὰς κλήσεις αὐτῶν ἡμῖν ἀπαγγέλλων. Περσογενὴς δὲ ὑπῆρχεν ἐκ προγόνων, καθὼς αὐτὸς ἐν ταῖς αὐτοῦ ἐπιστολαῖς διαγορεύων γράφει. Οἱ δὲ γεννήτορες αὐτοῦ πολύπαιδες μὲν ὑπῆρχον, οὐκ ἐτίκτετο δὲ αὐτοῖς παιδίον ἄρρεν, καὶ οὐ μικρῶς ἠθύμουν περὶ τούτυυ. Ἡ δὲ μήτηρ αὐτοῦ,
20 θεοφιλὴς καὶ πιστὴ ὑπάρχουσα, συχνοτέρως παρέβαλλε τοῖς τοῦ Θεοῦ εὐκτηρίοις οἴκοις σχολάζουσα καὶ δεομένη τοῦ Θεοῦ νυκτὸς καὶ ἡμέρας, ὅπως δῴη αὐτῇ Κύριος καρπὸν κοιλίας ἀρρενικόν, καθάπερ ποτὲ τῇ τοῦ Ἐλκανᾶ Ἄννῃ, μητρὶ δὲ τοῦ τὰ ἔμπροσθεν βλέποντος προφήτου Σαμουήλ, μονονουχὶ λέγουσα πρὸς αὐτόν· ' Ἀδωναὶ Κύριε Ἐλωὶ Σαβαώθ·
25 ἐὰν ἐπιβλέπων ἐπιβλέψῃς ἐπὶ τὴν ἐμὴν ταπείνωσιν καὶ παράσχῃς μοι καρπὸν κοιλίας ἀρρενικόν, σοὶ δώσω αὐτόν, ὅπως γένηται λειτουργὸς ἐναντίον σοῦ ἀεὶ προσεδρεύων τῷ ἁγίῳ θυσιαστηρίῳ.' Ὁ δὲ τῶν ὅλων Θεός, ὁ βραδὺς μὲν εἰς ὀργήν, ταχὺς δὲ εἰς ἀντίληψιν τοῖς αὐτὸν ἀνενδοιάστως ἐπικαλουμένοις, εἰσήκουσεν αὐτῆς τῶν ὀδυρμῶν καὶ τῆς
30 εὐχῆς αὐτῆς ἀκήκοε, καὶ παρέσχεν αὐτῇ κατὰ τὴν αὐτῆς αἴτησιν παῖδα

AG
10. ἁγία : τῆς ἁγίας codd. | ὥς A: ὅς G 13. εὐμοίρησεν G: εὐμοίρησε A 22. δῴη αὐτῇ A: δώῃ αὐτὴ G 25. ἐπιβλέψῃς A: ἐπιβλέψις G | παράσχῃς A: παράσχις G

LIFE OF MICHAEL THE SYNKELLOS

[227] On the fourth day of the same month[1]

The life, conduct and struggles of our holy father and confessor Michael, priest and *synkellos*[2] of the city of Jerusalem

To set the deeds of good men down in writing and to pass their memory on to the times that follow after them is something which furnishes much profit for our lives. For the narrative of the things they accomplished inspires a goad of emulation in the souls of lovers of God and exhorts them to the working of similar exploits. One <such account> is the *Life* which is now set before us for narration, namely the *Life* of Michael, the confessor and *synkellos*, whom the holy city of Christ our God, Jerusalem, bore and reared as a flourishing plant, luxuriant in virtues, while the famed Constantinople was blessed in possessing him[3] as a confessor of Christ and archimandrite of the monastery of Chora.[4]

1. The birth of Michael

I do not know who were the parents of this most notable man of God and citizen of Jerusalem, for no one reported their names to me. He was of Persian ancestry,[5] as he writes plainly in his letters.[6] His parents had many children, but a male child had not been born to them and they were greatly disheartened by this. His mother, who was a lover of God and a pious woman, often visited God's houses of prayer, spending time there and beseeching God by night and by day that the Lord might grant male fruit to her body as He once did to [228] Anna, wife of Elkanah, mother of Samuel, the prophet who perceived things in advance. She addressed him in almost those words: ' O Lord of Sabaoth, if Thou wilt indeed look on my affliction, and wilt grant male fruit to my body, then I will give him unto Thee that he may be a servant in Thy presence and always stay near the holy altar.' And the Lord of all creation, who is slow in turning to wrath yet swift in succouring those who call on Him without doubting, hearkened to her lamentations, heard her prayer and granted to her

---

22. 'fruit to her body': cf. Ps. 131: 11 (132:11)   24-7. cf. I Kings 1:11 (I Sam. 1:11)

ἄρρενα, ὃν καὶ ἀπογαλακτισθέντα προσέφερεν αὐτῷ δῶρον εὐπρόσδεκτον. Κατὰ γὰρ τὰς ἡμέρας ἐκείνας καθευδήσασα μετὰ τοῦ ἀνδρὸς αὐτῆς συνέλαβε κατὰ γαστρὸς καὶ ἔτεκεν ἄρρεν, καὶ ἐκάλεσε τὸ ὄνομα αὐτοῦ ἐν τῷ τῆς παλιγγενεσίας λουτρῷ Μιχαήλ, ὃ ἑρμηνεύεται ΄στρατηγὸς Θεοῦ΄, μονονουχὶ διαρρήδην βοῶσα καὶ προφητεύουσα διὰ τῆς τοῦ ὀνόματος κλήσεως, καθότι ἔμελλεν ἀριστεύειν κατὰ τῶν ἀθέων αἱρετικῶν.

(2) Ἀπογαλακτισθέντος δὲ τοῦ παιδὸς καὶ τριετοῦς ἤδη γεγονότος, προσήγαγεν αὐτὸν τῷ Θεῷ κατὰ τὴν αὐτῆς ὑπόσχεσιν. Μετὰ γὰρ τοῦ ἀνδρὸς αὐτῆς καταλαβοῦσα τὴν ἁγίαν Χριστοῦ τοῦ Θεοῦ ἡμῶν Ἀνάστασιν, προσήγαγε τὸν υἱὸν αὐτῆς τῷ τότε τελεταρχοῦντι τῇ ἁγίᾳ Χριστοῦ τοῦ Θεοῦ ἡμῶν πόλει καὶ ὀρθοδόξως ἰθύνοντι τὸν ἐν αὐτῇ ἀποστολικὸν θρόνον, λέγουσα οὕτως· ΄Δέξαι, δέσποτα ἅγιε, καὶ προσάγαγε τῷ ἀρχιποίμενι Χριστῷ τὸν ἐξ ἐμῶν τεχθέντα σπλάγχνων, κατατάξας αὐτὸν ἐν τῷ τῆς ἁγίας Χριστοῦ τοῦ Θεοῦ ἡμῶν Ἀναστάσεως κλήρῳ.΄ Καὶ ἐξεῖπεν αὐτῷ πᾶσαν τὴν ἀλήθειαν, καὶ πῶς ὁ Κύριος εἰσήκουσεν αὐτῆς τῶν εὐχῶν, καὶ ὅπως αὐτὴ ὑπέσχετο προσάξαι τοῦτον δοτὸν τῷ Θεῷ. Ὁ δὲ δεξάμενος τὴν αὐτῶν ἱκετείαν καὶ ἐπευξάμενος τῷ παιδὶ ἀπέκειρεν αὐτοῦ τὴν κόμην καὶ τέως ἐν τῷ τῶν ἀναγνωστῶν βαθμῷ κατέταξεν τῆς ἁγίας Χριστοῦ τοῦ Θεοῦ ἡμῶν Ἀναστάσεως.

Λαβόντες δὲ οἱ τούτου γονεῖς τὸν αὐτῶν θεόσδοτον υἱὸν κεκαρπωμένον καὶ κεκληρωμένον ἐν τῇ ἁγίᾳ Χριστοῦ τοῦ Θεοῦ ἡμῶν Ἀναστάσει, ὑπέστρεψαν ἐν τῷ αὐτῶν οἴκῳ μετὰ πολλῆς θυμηδίας. Καὶ δὴ παραδίδουσιν αὐτὸν διδασκάλῳ, ὅπως προπαιδεύσῃ αὐτὸν τὰ τῆς προπαιδείας γράμματα. Ὁ δὲ παῖς *προέκοπτε τῇ τε ἡλικίᾳ καὶ τοῖς μαθήμασι παρὰ Θεῷ καὶ ἀνθρώποις*. Μετὰ δὲ τὸ ἐκπαιδευθῆναι αὐτὸν τὰ τῆς προπαιδείας γράμματα, καθὼς ἔφημεν, κατὰ πρόσταξιν τοῦ αὐτὸν ἀποκείραντος πατριάρχου παραδίδοται εἰς τὰ τῆς γραμματικῆς καὶ ῥητορικῆς καὶ φιλοσοφίας διδάγματα. Καὶ δὴ ὡς γῆ λιπαρὰ καὶ πίων, οὕτως ἐν ὀλίγῳ χρόνῳ ἀνεμάξατο τά τε τῆς γραμματικῆς καὶ ῥητορικῆς

AG
15. ἐξ G: om. A   20. κόμην A: κώμην G   21. κατέταξεν A: κατέταξε G   24. θυμηδίας G: θυμηδείας A   25. παραδίδουσιν : παραδιδοῦσιν codd. | προπαιδεύσῃ A: προπαιδεύση G   26. προέκοπτε G: -ν A   27. δὲ A: om. G   30. πίων A: πίον G

according to her request a male child;⁷ and when he was weaned, she offered him up to Him as an acceptable gift.⁸

For during those days, when she had lain with her husband, she conceived in her womb and bore a son. In the bath of regeneration⁹ she called his name Michael, which means 'general of God',¹⁰ all but explicitly proclaiming and prophesying on account of the endowment of his name that he would gain the highest distinction against the ungodly heretics.

2. Michael is dedicated to the clergy of the church of the Resurrection

When the boy had been weaned and had reached the age of three, she offered him to God in accordance with her promise. She went to the holy church of the Resurrection of Christ our God¹¹ with her husband and offered her son to the chief priest in the holy city of Christ our God¹² who ruled on the apostolic throne in an orthodox manner, saying the following words: 'Receive, saintly lord, and dedicate the offspring of my womb to the chief shepherd Christ. Appoint him to the clergy of the holy church of the Resurrection of Christ our God.' And she revealed to him the whole truth: how the Lord had hearkened to her prayers and how she had promised to offer him as a gift to God. After yielding to their supplication and praying for the boy, he cut off his hair and appointed him at that time to the grade of the readers¹³ of the holy church of the Resurrection of Christ our God.

When they had taken their God-given son to be offered¹⁴ and assigned to the holy church of the Resurrection of Christ our God, his parents joyfully returned to their house. And they handed him over to a teacher in order that he might give him instruction in the letters of preliminary training.¹⁵ The boy increased in stature and in knowledge before God and men. After he was completely educated in the letters of preliminary training, as I have said, he was sent by the order of the patriarch who had tonsured him for lessons in grammar, rhetoric and philosophy. Indeed, he was like unto rich and fertile ground¹⁶ and assimilated his lessons in grammar, rhetoric and philosophy in

---

1-2. 'acceptable gift': cf. I Pe. 2:5; Ro. 15:16   5. 'the bath of regeneration': cf. Tit. 3:5   15. cf. I Pe. 5:4   26-7. cf. Lu.2:52

καὶ φιλοσοφίας μαθήματα ὡς ἄλλος τῷ τότε χρόνῳ οὐδείς. Οὐ μόνον δὲ ταῦτα, ἀλλὰ καὶ ποιητικῶν καὶ ἀστρονομίας ὅσον τὸ κάλλιστον.

Τούτων δὲ οὕτως ἐχόντων καὶ τοῦ παιδὸς προκόπτοντος τῇ τε σοφίᾳ καὶ ἡλικίᾳ καὶ χάριτι καὶ ταῖς κατὰ Θεὸν ἀρεταῖς (οὐ γὰρ παρελείπετό 5 ποτε τοῖς τοῦ Θεοῦ εὐκτηρίοις οἴκοις καὶ τῇ αὐτοῦ δοξολογίᾳ, νηστείαις καὶ ἀγρυπνίαις καὶ εὐχαῖς ἑαυτὸν ἐθίζων καὶ τὸ τῆς νεότητος ἀμείλικτον καταμαλάσσων καὶ ναὸν εὔχρηστον τῷ Θεῷ ἀφιερῶν ἑαυτόν, ὅπως ἐξ ἁπαλῶν ὀνύχων κατοικητήριον τῷ Θεῷ, ὅσον ἐστὶ δυνατὸν ἀνθρώπῳ, ἑαυτὸν ποιήσῃ) τούτου δὲ οὕτως ἀσκουμένου καὶ θεαρέστως βιοῦντος, 10 ἦν πᾶσι ποθεινὸς καὶ ἐπέραστος, ἀδόμενος ἐν τοῖς ἁπάντων στόμασι διὰ τὴν ἐνάρετον αὐτοῦ πολιτείαν.

Τοῦ δὲ πατρὸς αὐτοῦ τέλει τοῦ βίου χρησαμένου καὶ τῆς τούτου μητρὸς χηρευσάσης, ἦν αὐτῷ οὐ μικρὰ φροντὶς τὸ πῶς διοικήσῃ τὴν αὐτοῦ μητέρα καὶ τὰς αὐτοῦ ἀδελφάς. Ὡς δὲ κατενύγη οὐ μετὰ πολὺν 15 χρόνον ἡ αὐτοῦ μήτηρ ταῖς αὐτοῦ θείαις παραινέσεσι, βλέπουσα τὸν ἐξ αὐτῆς φύντα οὕτως ἐναρέτως βιοῦντα, ᾑρετίσατο μονάσαι σὺν ταῖς αὐτῆς θυγατράσιν ἔν τινι τῶν μοναστηρίων τῆς ἁγίας Χριστοῦ τοῦ Θεοῦ ἡμῶν πόλεως.

(3) Ὁ δὲ παμμάκαρ Μιχαὴλ μετὰ πάσης προθυμίας τοῦτο πεποίηκεν, 20 ἀποκείρας αὐτὴν μετὰ τῶν αὐτῆς δύο θυγατέρων, καθὼς προείπομεν, ἔν τινι μοναστηρίῳ πλησίον τῆς ἁγίας Σιών, τῆς μητρὸς πασῶν τῶν ἐκκλησιῶν, ἀφιερώσας κτήματα πάμπολλα ἐν τῷ αὐτῷ μοναστηρίῳ. Τὰ δὲ λοιπὰ κινητά τε καὶ ἀκίνητα αὐτοῦ πεπραχὼς πράγματα καὶ διανείμας ταῦτα πτωχοῖς μικρά τινα καὶ πάνυ ὀλίγα χρήματα εἰς 25 ἑαυτὸν καταλιπὼν φυγῇ ἐχρήσατο, ὥστε μὴ κρατηθῆναι αὐτὸν παρά τε ἀγχιστῶν καὶ γνωρίμων καὶ συγγενῶν, καὶ τὸν αὐτοῦ θεάρεστον σκοπὸν εἰς πέρας ἀγαγὼν καταλαμβάνει τὴν μεγίστην Λαύραν τοῦ ἐν ἁγίοις πατρὸς ἡμῶν καὶ καθηγητοῦ τῆς ἐρήμου Σάβα καὶ λιπαρεῖ τὸν αὐτῆς προεστῶτα δεχθῆναι αὐτὸν καὶ καταταγῆναι ἐν τῇ αὐτοῦ ἐναρέτῳ καὶ

AG
1. ὡς -- οὐδείς : om. 7. ἑαυτόν : ἑαυτῷ codd. 9. ποιήσῃ A : ποιήσει G | ἀσκουμένου καὶ A: om. G 10. ἦν post πᾶσι trsp. G | πᾶσι A: -ν G | στόμασι G: -ν A 13. τὸ A: om. G | διοικήσῃ : διοικήσει codd. 14. κατενύγη : κατηνοίγη A κατηνοίγει G 16. ᾑρετίσατο A: ἡρετίσατο G 20. προείπομεν A: προείπωμεν G 25. καταλιπὼν A: καταλειπῶν G 27. καταλαμβάνει A: καταλιμπάνει G 28. λιπαρεῖ A: λιπαρῇ G

such a short time that he outdid all of his contemporaries. Not only these subjects did he learn, but what is best of poetry and astronomy as well.[17]

[229] As these things were taking place and the boy increased in wisdom, stature, favour and the virtues according to God (for he never neglected God's houses of prayer nor to sing His praises, accustoming himself to fasts, watches, and prayers, softening the recalcitrance of youth and consecrating himself as a serviceable temple of God in order that from the earliest infancy[18] he might make himself an habitation of God, as far as this is possible for a man[19]) as he was thus training himself and living in a manner pleasing to God, he was desired and beloved of all, and was praised in the mouths of all on account of his virtuous way of life. When his father came to the end of his days and his mother was widowed, Michael was greatly concerned about how he might provide for his mother and his sisters. As his mother was spurred on after a short time by his godly preaching and by seeing the virtuous life of her son, she chose with her daughters to become a nun in one of the monasteries of the holy city of Christ our God.

3. Michael becomes a monk at the *laura* of St Sabas

The all-blessed Michael accomplished this eagerly; he tonsured her and her two daughters, as I have said before, in a certain monastery near the holy Sion,[20] the mother of all churches, and consecrated many possessions to the same monastery. When he had sold his remaining movable possessions and landed property and distributed them to the poor, he put aside for himself a very small and meagre amount of money and took to flight, that he might not be held back by family, friends, and kinsfolk.[21] Bringing his God-pleasing aim to fulfilment, he went to the great *laura*[22] of our father and teacher of the desert, Sabas of saintly memory,[23] and entreated its abbot[24] to receive and enrol him in his virtuous and God-loving community, giving him as much

---

7-8. 'serviceable temple of God...habitation of God': cf. II Tim. 2:21; Eph. 2:21-2

θεοφιλεῖ συνοδίᾳ, δεδωκὼς αὐτῷ καὶ ἅπερ ἐπεφέρετο μεθ᾽ ἑαυτοῦ χρήματα, ὥστε, καθὼς αὐτὸς βούλεται, ταῦτα διοικήσῃ. Ὁ δὲ πανάριστος ἐκεῖνος ποιμὴν κατανοήσας τό τε εὐσταθὲς καὶ ταπεινὸν καὶ φιλόσοφον τοῦ νέου (ἦν γὰρ ὡς ἐτῶν εἴκοσι καὶ πέντε) εἶξε τῇ αὐτοῦ παρακλήσει.
5 Καὶ μετ᾽ οὐ πολλὰς ἡμέρας προσκαλεσάμενος αὐτὸν καὶ πολλὰ κατηχήσας καὶ προτρεψάμενος πρὸς τὸν τῆς ἀσκήσεως ἐνάρετον βίον, ἀπέκειρεν αὐτοῦ τὴν κόμην καὶ συναρίθμιον πεποίηκε τῇ αὐτοῦ ἐναρέτῳ καὶ θεοφιλεῖ συνοδίᾳ.

Ὁ δὲ πατὴρ ἡμῶν καὶ μέγας Μιχαήλ, τούτου τυχὼν τοῦ πανιέρου καὶ
10 ἀγγελικοῦ σχήματος, οὕτως ἐπέδωκεν ἑαυτὸν πρὸς τὸν τῆς ἀσκήσεως δρόμον καὶ τοιαύτην ἑαυτῷ ἐπέθηκε νηστείαν, ὥστε λαχάνοις μόνοις ἀρκεῖσθαι πᾶσαν τὴν ἑβδομάδα ἄνευ ἁλός, καὶ τοῦτο κατὰ δύο ἢ καὶ τρεῖς ἡμέρας ποιῶν. Οὐκ ἤσθιεν ἐκτὸς σαββάτου καὶ κυριακῆς καὶ ἑορτῆς ἄρτον ἐπὶ δέκα καὶ ὀκτὼ ἔτη. Πάμπολλα δὲ παρὰ τοῦ αὐτοῦ
15 καθηγητοῦ ἤγουν τοῦ τῆς μονῆς προεστῶτος παρακαλούμενος ἐνδοῦναι μικρὸν πρὸς τὸ ἐξαρκεῖν τὸ αὐτοῦ σῶμα ἐν τῇ τοῦ Θεοῦ λειτουργίᾳ καὶ τῇ διακονίᾳ τῆς Λαύρας, οὐκ ἠνείχετο, ἀλλὰ μᾶλλον προέκοπτε τῇ κατὰ Θεὸν πολιτείᾳ καὶ τῇ νηστείᾳ καὶ ἀγρυπνίᾳ καὶ ταῖς παννύχοις στάσεσί τε καὶ εὐχαῖς, ὥστε θαυμάζεσθαι αὐτὸν παρὰ πάσης τῆς ἀδελφότητος.
20 Ἐξερχομένων δὲ πάντων τῶν πατέρων ἐν συλλογῇ τῶν μαννουθίων καὶ πάντων πρὸς ἓν φορτίον βασταζόντων, αὐτὸς δύο φορτία ποιῶν ἐν τῷ ἀρτοκοπείῳ ἐκόμιζεν.

(4) Διαπρέψας δὲ ἐν πάσῃ διακονίᾳ χρόνους δύο καὶ δέκα καὶ σχεδὸν πάντας ὑπερακοντίσας τῇ τε ὑπακοῇ καὶ ταπεινώσει, ἀξιοῦται ψήφῳ
25 Θεοῦ καὶ τῇ τοῦ προεστῶτος προστάξει τῆς τοῦ πρεσβυτέρου ἀξίας. Παραλαβὼν γὰρ αὐτὸν ὁ προλεχθεὶς τῆς Λαύρας προεστὼς καὶ ἀνελθὼν πρὸς τὸν ἐν ἁγίοις πατριάρχην Θωμᾶν τοὔνομα παρακαλεῖ τοῦτον, ὅπως χειροτονίας ἀξιώσῃ τὸν πανσεβάσμιον Μιχαήλ. Ὁ δὲ πατριάρχης μηδὲν μελλήσας τοῦτο πεποίηκεν. Χειροτονηθέντος δὲ τοῦ ἐν ἁγίοις πατρὸς
30 ἡμῶν Μιχαὴλ ἐν τῇ ἁγίᾳ Χριστοῦ τοῦ Θεοῦ ἡμῶν Ἀναστάσει παρὰ τοῦ προλεχθέντος ἀρχιεράρχου, κατῆλθε σὺν τῷ αὐτοῦ ποιμένι ἐν τῇ

AG
1. θεοφιλεῖ A : θεοφιλῆ G 2. διοικήσῃ : διοικήσει codd. 8. θεοφιλεῖ A : θεοφιλῆ G 11. ἐπέθηκε G : -ν A 12. καὶ² G : om. A 17. προέκοπτε G : -ν A 18. καὶ τῇ νηστείᾳ A : om. G 22. ἀρτοκοπείῳ G : ἀρτοκοπίῳ A 24. ὑπερακοντίσας A : ὑπερακοντήσας G 27. τοῦτον A : αὐτὸν G 29. πεποίηκεν A : πεποίηκε G 31. κατῆλθε G : -ν A

money as he had brought with him that he might administer it as he wished. And that most virtuous shepherd perceived the firmness and humility and wisdom of the youth (for he was twenty-five years old) and yielded to his entreaty. After a few days he summoned him and gave him ample instruction, spurring him on to the virtuous life of spiritual training. He then tonsured his hair and numbered him among his virtuous and God-loving community.

Our great father Michael, after becoming part of this all-holy and angelic order, gave himself over so much to the way of spiritual training and undertook such fasting that he was satisfied with vegetables alone without salt throughout the week and even of those he partook only every second or third day. He did not eat bread except on Saturdays, Sundays and feast-days for eighteen years. [230] He was often commanded by his teacher, that is to say the abbot of the monastery, to relax his fast slightly that his body might retain enough strength to perform the liturgy of God and service of the *laura*. He would not acquiesce but rather advanced in the way of life according to God, in fasts and vigils made up of all-night standing and prayers, so that all the brethren marvelled at him. When all the fathers went out gathering faggots[25] and each carried only one burden,[26] he bore two burdens and would bring them to the bakery.

4. Michael's ordination to the priesthood and *askesis*

When he had excelled for twelve years in every service and had outdone almost everyone in obedience and in humility, he was deemed worthy of priestly dignity by the verdict of God and by the command of the abbot. The aforementioned abbot of the *laura* took him and going to the patriarch named Thomas of saintly memory, begged him to ordain the most venerable Michael.[27] The patriarch did so without delay. When our holy father Michael of blessed memory had been ordained by the aforesaid bishop in the holy church of the Resurrection of Christ our God, he went back with his shepherd

προρρηθείση Λαύρα. Καὶ δὴ εἴχετο τῆς προτέρας αὐτοῦ σκληραγωγίας, μᾶλλον δὲ καὶ ἐπέτεινε τῇ τε νηστείᾳ καὶ ἀγρυπνίᾳ καὶ χαμευνίᾳ καὶ ταῖς παννύχοις στάσεσι, σπουδάζων ἄξιον ἑαυτὸν τῆς ἐπιτεθείσης αὐτῷ ἱερωσύνης καὶ ἀνεπαίσχυντον ἐργάτην παραστῆσαι τῷ παμβασιλεῖ καὶ
5 ἀρχιεράρχη Θεῷ ἡμῶν.

Μετὰ δὲ δύο χρόνους παρακαλεῖ τὸν αὐτοῦ προεστῶτα ὥστε δοθῆναι αὐτῷ ἀναχωρητικὸν κελλίον πρὸς τὸ ἡσυχάσαι καὶ καταμόνας τῷ Θεῷ προσομιλεῖν. Ὁ δὲ θέλων αὐτὸν εἰς πάντα πληροφορεῖν (ἐγίνωσκε γὰρ τὴν αὐτοῦ ἐνάρετον πρόθεσιν) δέδωκεν αὐτῷ κελλίον καὶ σπήλαιον
10 μικρὸν ὥστε κατὰ τὴν αὐτοῦ θεάρεστον βούλησιν ἡσυχάζειν καὶ τῷ Θεῷ προσεύχεσθαι. Ἦν δὲ πάνυ ἀκτήμων ὁ πανίερος Μιχαήλ, μηδὲν κεκτημένος τοῦ ματαίου βίου τούτου ἐν τῷ αὐτοῦ κελλίῳ εἰ μὴ ἓν χιτώνιον, ὃ περιεβέβλητο, καὶ ψιάθιον, εἰς ὃ ἐκάθευδεν, καὶ βαυκάλιον, ἐν ᾧ τὸν ἄρτον βρέχων ἤσθιεν, καθὼς προλέλεκται.
15 (5) Τούτων δὲ οὕτως γεγονότων καὶ τοῦ πατρὸς ἡμῶν οὕτως ἀσκουμένου, πέμπονται αὐτῷ παρὰ Θεοῦ ἡ τιμία ξυνωρὶς τῶν αὐταδέλφων, φημὶ Θεοδώρου καὶ Θεοφάνους, τοῦ μὲν ἁγίου Θεοδώρου εἴκοσι καὶ πέντε ἐτῶν ὑπάρχοντος, τοῦ δὲ ὁσίου Θεοφάνους εἴκοσι καὶ δύο. Ἀνελθὼν δὲ ὁ πατὴρ ἡμῶν καὶ μέγας Μιχαὴλ πρὸς τὸν τῆς Λαύρας προεστῶτα καὶ
20 ταῦτα δῆλα τούτῳ πεποιηκὼς προσετάχθη παρ' αὐτοῦ δέξασθαι τούτους καὶ ὁδηγῆσαι ἐν τῇ κατὰ Θεὸν πολιτείᾳ. Ἀποκείρας δὲ τούτους κατὰ τὴν πρόσταξιν τοῦ προεστῶτος καὶ δεδωκὼς αὐτοῖς τὸ ἀγγελικὸν τοῦ μονήρους βίου σχῆμα ἦν σὺν αὐτοῖς ἐκτελῶν τὴν τοῦ Θεοῦ δοξολογίαν, προβιβάζων αὐτοὺς ἐν τῇ τῆς σωτηρίας ὁδῷ, ὡς καλὸς παιδοτρίβης,
25 διδάξας αὐτοὺς τήν τε γραμματικὴν καὶ φιλοσοφίαν καὶ τῶν ποιητικῶν οὐκ ὀλίγα σκέμματα, ὥστε ἐν ὀλίγῳ χρόνῳ πανσόφους ἀναδειχθῆναι τοὺς πανιέρους αὐταδέλφους καὶ διαδραμεῖν τὴν φήμην αὐτῶν μέχρι τῶν περάτων τῆς γῆς ἐκείνης, καὶ ἕως αὐτὸν τὸν τὸν ἀποστολικὸν θρόνον καλῶς καὶ ὀρθοδόξως διέποντα. Ὅστις πατριάρχης συχνοτέρως

AG
2. ἐπέτεινε G: -v A   3. στάσεσι G: -v A | ἑαυτὸν τῆς ἐπιτεθείσης A: εἶναι καὶ ὀνομάζεσθαι τῆς ἐπιτεθείσης αὐτῷ G   5. ἀρχιεράρχη : ἀρχιεράρχει codd.   15. οὕτως²:θεοφιλῶς add. G   19. πατὴρ ἡμῶν καὶ : om. G   20. πεποιηκὼς A: πεποικὼς G
28. τὸν ¹ G: om. A

to the aforementioned *laura*. And he continued in his former austerity or rather even increased it with fasts, vigils, sleeping on the ground and all-night standing, as he was zealous to present himself as worthy of the priesthood that had been bestowed on him and as a worker with no cause for shame before our universal Sovereign and supreme Pontiff, God.[28]

After two years, he begged his abbot that he might be given a solitary cell for contemplation[29] and for holding private conversation with God. The abbot, wishing to satisfy[30] him in everything (for he knew his virtuous disposition), gave him a cell and a small cave so that in accordance with his God-pleasing desire he might live in contemplation and offer prayers to God. The all-holy Michael was entirely without possessions, having nothing of this vain life in his cell except one robe which he wore, a rush mat[31] on which he lay, and a small vessel[32] in which he dipped the bread he ate, which I have already mentioned.

5. The arrival of Theodore and Theophanes at St Sabas

After these events had come to pass and our father was following such spiritual exercises, there were sent to him by God a pair of honourable brothers: I refer to Theodore and Theophanes. The holy Theodore was twenty-five years of age and the saintly Theophanes was twenty-two.[33] When our great father Michael went to the abbot of the *laura* and explained this matter to him, he was commanded by the abbot to accept them and to guide them in the way of life according to God.[34] After he had tonsured them in accordance with the abbot's command and bestowed upon them the angelic habit[35] of the monastic life, he was engaged in carrying out with them the praises of God, [231] guiding them forward in the way of salvation as a good teacher.[36] He taught them grammar, philosophy, and a number of works[37] of poetry[38] so that in a short time the all-holy brothers were proclaimed supremely wise and their fame spread to the ends of that land, even to the one who administered the apostolic throne well and in an orthodox manner. That

---

28. Ps. 45:10 (46:9); Mt. 12:42; Lu. 11:31

προσεκαλεῖτο πρὸς ἑαυτόν, ὁμιλίας χάριν καὶ συζητήσεως τῶν θείων γραφῶν. Καὶ ἀκούων αὐτῶν τῆς πανσόφου διδασκαλίας τὴν χύσιν, ὥσπερ ῥεῦμα ποταμιαῖον χεόμενον, ἔχαιρε καὶ ἠγαλλιᾶτο τῷ πνεύματι, δοξάζων τὸν φιλοικτίρμονα Θεόν, τὸν ἐν ταῖς αὐτοῦ ἡμέραις τοιούτους
5 φωστῆρας ἀναδείξαντα. Ἐθαύμαζε δὲ καὶ τὴν ἄκραν ταπείνωσιν καὶ εἰς πάντα ἐγκράτειαν τοῦ πανσόφου Μιχαήλ, ὅτι μετὰ τοσαύτην περιουσίαν λόγου καὶ ὕψος ἀρετῆς καὶ εὐγένειαν γένους τοσαύτῃ ταπεινώσει κατεκεκόσμητο.

Οὕτως δὲ τῶν ἁγίων ἀσκουμένων καὶ τῷ Θεῷ εὐαρεστούντων διὰ τῆς
10 καθαρᾶς αὐτῶν πολιτείας, ηὔξανέ τε καὶ ἐπληθύνετο ὁ τοῦ Θεοῦ λαὸς ἐν τῇ αὐτῶν διδασκαλίᾳ φωτιζόμενος καὶ τῇ τῶν θείων δογμάτων ὀρθότητι. Τῷ δὲ πεντηκοστῷ τῆς τοῦ μεγάλου Μιχαὴλ ἡλικίας χρόνῳ κατὰ ἀποκάλυψιν Θεοῦ ὁ προλεχθεὶς πατριάρχης Θωμᾶς καθίστησι τὸν μακάριον καὶ μέγαν Μιχαὴλ σύγκελλον ἑαυτοῦ. Ὅθεν καὶ μεταστήσας
15 τοῦτον ἐκ τοῦ προλεχθέντος ἀναχωρητικοῦ κελλίου ἤγαγεν αὐτὸν ἐν τῇ ἁγίᾳ Ἀναστάσει Χριστοῦ τοῦ Θεοῦ ἡμῶν μετὰ καὶ τῶν αὐτοῦ δύο φοιτητῶν, Θεοδώρου φημὶ καὶ Θεοφάνους, δεδωκὼς αὐτοῖς κατοικίαν ἐν τῇ μονῇ τῶν Σπουδαίων, τῇ κτισθείσῃ παρὰ τοῦ ἁγιωτάτου πατριάρχου Ἠλία πλησίον τῆς ἁγίας Χριστοῦ τοῦ Θεοῦ ἡμῶν Ἀναστάσεως. Μετ' οὐ
20 πολλὰς δὲ ἡμέρας λαβὼν τοὺς μαθητὰς αὐτοῦ (τοῦ πανσόφου λέγω Μιχαήλ), Θεόδωρον καὶ Θεοφάνην, πρεσβυτέρους ἐχειροτόνησεν τῆς ἁγίας Χριστοῦ τοῦ Θεοῦ ἡμῶν Ἀναστάσεως. Καὶ ἦσαν τοῦ λοιποῦ ἀχώριστοι ὅ τε μέγας Μιχαὴλ καὶ ὁ προλεχθεὶς ἁγιώτατος πατριάρχης Θωμᾶς.

25 (6) Εἶχεν δὲ ἐκ πολλοῦ τοῦ χρόνου ὁ πανόσιος καὶ μέγας Μιχαὴλ ἔφεσιν καὶ ἦν δεόμενος τοῦ Θεοῦ νυκτὸς καὶ ἡμέρας, ὥστε εἰ ἀρεστὸν αὐτῷ ἐστιν, ἀξιωθῆναι αὐτὸν τῆς προσκυνήσεως τῶν ἁγίων λειψάνων τῶν κορυφαίων ἀποστόλων, Πέτρου καὶ Παύλου, τῶν μαρτυρησάντων ἐν τῇ μεγίστῃ τῶν πόλεων Ῥώμῃ ἐπὶ Νέρωνος τοῦ ἐν αὐτῇ ἀσεβῶς
30 βασιλεύσαντος. Ἐν δὲ ταῖς ἡμέραις ἐκείναις ἀνέστησάν τινες ἐκ τοῦ ἔθνους τῶν Φράγων, ἱερεῖς καὶ μονάζοντες, λέγοντες ἐν τῷ θείῳ συμβόλῳ τὸ ἐκτεθὲν παρὰ τῶν ἑκατὸν πεντήκοντα ἁγίων πατέρων, τῶν ἐν τῇ

AG
6. πάντα A: ἅπαντα G   8. κατεκεκόσμητο : κατακεκόσμητο codd.   10. ηὔξανέ G: -ν A   12. Μιχαὴλ A: om. G   18. κτισθείσῃ G: κτισθήσει A

patriarch often summoned them so that he might benefit from their conversation and discussion about the divine scriptures. Listening to the torrent of their all-wise teaching, which was like unto a river's flowing stream,[39] he was delighted and rejoiced greatly in spirit, praising God the merciful for having revealed such luminaries in his days. And he marvelled at the all-wise Michael's utter humility and self-control in all things, that besides such abundant eloquence, sublime virtue, and noble lineage he was adorned with so much humility.

As the holy men were undergoing such spiritual training and pleasing God well by their pure way of life, the number of people of God enlightened by their teaching and by the orthodoxy of divine doctrines increased and multiplied. In the great Michael's fiftieth year,[40] the aforesaid patriarch Thomas appointed in accordance with divine revelation the holy and great Michael as his *synkellos*.[41] For that reason he moved him from the aforesaid solitary cell and led him with his two disciples, Theodore and Theophanes, to the holy church of the Resurrection of Christ our God and gave them an habitation in the monastery of the Spoudaei[42] which was built by the most holy patriarch Elias[43] near the holy church of the Resurrection of Christ our God. After a few days, taking his (that is, the all-wise Michael's) disciples Theodore and Theophanes, he ordained them priests of the holy church of the Resurrection of Christ our God. And the great Michael and that most holy patriarch Thomas were inseparable thereafter.

6. The *filioque* conflict and Arab threat

For a long time the all-holy, great Michael had longed and was beseeching God by night and by day that should it please Him, he might be deemed worthy of venerating the holy relics of the chief apostles Peter and Paul,[44] who were martyred in the very great city of Rome under Nero who had impiously ruled there.[45] In those days certain priests and monks belonging to the nation of the Franks rose up, reciting in the divine Creed the passage formulated by the hundred and fifty holy fathers gathered in the second synod in Constantinople

---

3. 'rejoiced... in spirit': cf. Lu. 10:21   10. 'increased and multiplied': cf. Ex. 1:7; Acts 7:17   30. Ge. 6:4; I Ma. 2:1; Mt. 3:1; 24:38; Acts 2:18; 9:37; Rev. 9:6

δευτέρᾳ συνόδῳ συναθροισθέντων ἐν Κωνσταντινουπόλει κατὰ τοῦ ἀθεωτάτου Μακεδονίου, τοῦ εἰς τὸ Πνεῦμα τὸ Ἅγιον βλασφημῆσαι τολμήσαντος, ἐπὶ τῆς βασιλείας Θεοδοσίου τοῦ Μεγάλου· Καὶ εἰς τὸ Πνεῦμα τὸ Ἅγιον, τὸ κύριον καὶ ζωοποιοῦν, τὸ ἐκ τοῦ Πατρὸς καὶ τοῦ
5 Υἱοῦ ἐκπορευόμενον. Ὅθεν οὐ μικρῶς ἐτάραξαν τὴν μεγαλόπολιν Ῥώμην, ἀνθισταμένου τοῦ τότε τελεταρχοῦντος πάπα τῆς τῶν Ῥωμαίων μεγαλοπόλεως καὶ μὴ καταδεχομένου προστεθῆναί τι, ὃ οὐκ ἐρρέθη παρὰ τῆς τῶν θείων πατέρων ὁμηγύρεως ἐν τῷ θείῳ συμβόλῳ. Οὗτινος πάπα ἐπιστολαῖς χρησαμένου πρὸς τὸν μέγαν πατριάρχην Θωμᾶν τῆς
10 ἁγίας Χριστοῦ τοῦ Θεοῦ ἡμῶν πόλεως, τοῦ βοηθῆσαι τῇ αὐτοῦ ἐκκλησίᾳ κινδυνευούσῃ ἐξαποστεῖλαι αὐτῷ ἐκ τοῦ αὐτοῦ ἀποστολικοῦ καὶ ἱερατικοῦ θρόνου τινὰς λόγῳ καὶ σοφίᾳ κατακεκοσμημένους, πρὸς τὸ ἀντιπαρατάξασθαι τοὺς κακῶς ἐθελοφρονήσαντας περὶ τῆς προσθήκης τῆς ἐν τῷ θείῳ συμβόλῳ προστεθείσης παρὰ τῶν Φράγγων, καθὼς ὁ μέγας
15 Μιχαὴλ ἐν ταῖς αὐτοῦ θείαις ἐπιστολαῖς ταῖς πεμφθείσαις παρ' αὐτοῦ πρὸς τοὺς ἐν Σικελίᾳ ὄντας ὀρθοδόξους μοναχοὺς διηγούμενος γράφει. Ὅθεν ὁ προλεχθεὶς ἁγιώτατος πατριάρχης Θωμᾶς, συμβούλιον ποιήσας μετὰ τῆς αὐτοῦ ὀρθοδόξου καὶ ἁγίας συνόδου καὶ τῆς τῶν θείων πατέρων ὁμηγύρεως τῶν ἐν τῇ ἐρήμῳ οἰκούντων τῆς ἁγίας Χριστοῦ τοῦ Θεοῦ ἡμῶν
20 πόλεως, ἐψηφίσαντο πάντες ὁμοθυμαδόν, ὥστε ἀποσταλῆναι τὸν μέγαν καὶ ἅγιον Μιχαὴλ πρὸς τὸν προλεχθέντα πάπαν ἐν τῇ μεγάλῃ τῶν πόλεων Ῥώμῃ, ἅτε δυναμένου αὐτοῦ συγκροτῆσαι τὴν τοῦ Θεοῦ ἐκκλησίαν καὶ φιμῶσαι τὰ τῶν ἀθέων Φράγγων ἀπύλωτα στόματα καὶ διδάξαι τούτους ὀρθολεκτεῖν τὴν ἀλήθειαν καὶ μὴ ὑπερφρονεῖν, παρ' ὃ
25 δεῖ φρονεῖν, καὶ ἕπεσθαι τῇ τῶν ἁγίων πατέρων ἀκριβεῖ διδασκαλίᾳ τῇ ἐκφωνηθείσῃ παρὰ τῆς τοῦ Ἁγίου ἐμπνεύσεως Πνεύματος, τὸ ''Ἐκ τοῦ Πατρὸς ἐκπορευόμενον, τὸ σὺν Πατρὶ καὶ Υἱῷ συμπροσκυνούμενον καὶ συνδοξαζόμενον.'

Συνέβη δὲ ἐν ταῖς αὐταῖς ἡμέραις χρηματικήν τινα μεγίστην
30 ζημίαν γενέσθαι παρὰ τῶν ἀθέων Ἀγαρηνῶν τῇ ἁγίᾳ Χριστοῦ τοῦ Θεοῦ ἡμῶν Ἀναστάσει καὶ ταῖς λοιπαῖς τοῦ Θεοῦ ἐκκλησίαις ταῖς οὔσαις ἐν τῇ ἁγίᾳ Ἰερουσαλήμ, ὥστε μὴ ἰσχύειν τὴν τοιαύτην χρηματικὴν ζημίαν

AG
5. ἐτάραξαν: ἐτάραξε codd.   7. ἐρρέθη : ἐρέθη codd.   10. αὐτοῦ post ἐκκλησίᾳ trsp. G   16. γράφει A: γράφη G   17. πατριάρχης A: om. G   25. ἀκριβεῖ A: ἀκρινῆ G
29. χρηματικήν τινα A: χρηματικὴν τινὰ G

during the reign of Theodosius the Elder[46] against the impious Macedonius[47] who dared to blaspheme against the Holy Spirit, reciting it as follows: 'And in the Holy Ghost, the Lord and Giver of Life, Who proceeds from the Father and Son.' On account of this they stirred up in no small way the great city of Rome. [232] The pope who was then in office in the great city of the Romans was opposed to it and did not consent to anything being added to the divine Creed which had not been expressed by the assembly of divine fathers.[48] The same pope sent letters to the great patriarch Thomas of the holy city of Christ our God, beseeching help for his endangered Church and asking him to send from his apostolic and priestly throne certain men adorned with eloquence and wisdom who would stand in array against those with wilful opinions concerning the addition made in the divine creed by the Franks,[49] even as the great Michael writes and describes fully in the divine letters which he sent to the orthodox monks who were in Sicily.[50] For this reason the aforesaid most holy patriarch Thomas called a council with his orthodox and holy synod and the assembly of divine fathers who lived in the desert near the holy city of Christ our God and they all decided with one accord to send the great and holy Michael to the aforementioned pope in the great city of Rome, inasmuch as he would be able to sustain the Church of God, silence the unbridled mouths of the impious Franks, teach them to speak the truth correctly and not to hold overbearing opinions contrary to the correct views and to follow the exact teaching of the holy fathers which was pronounced by the inspiration of the Holy Ghost, Who 'proceeds from the Father, and is worshipped and glorified together with the Father and the Son.'[51]

It came to pass in those days that a certain heavy fine was imposed by the impious Hagarenes[52] on the holy church of the Resurrection of Christ our God and on the other churches which were in holy Jerusalem,[53] to the extent that those who lived in the holy city of Christ our God were unable to pay this

---

23. 'silence': cf. I Pe. 2:15 | 'the unbridled mouths': cf. Aristophanes, *Ranae*, 838

ἀποδοῦναι τοὺς ἐν αὐτῇ τῇ ἁγίᾳ Χριστοῦ τοῦ Θεοῦ ἡμῶν πόλει οἰκοῦντας. Τούτων ἕνεκεν τῶν δύο αἰτιῶν συνεῖδον ὅ τε πατριάρχης καὶ ἡ ἁγία αὐτοῦ σύνοδος ἀποστεῖλαι τὸν πανόσιον αὐτοῦ Μιχαὴλ πρὸς τὸν προλεχθέντα πάπαν, ὅπως καὶ τοὺς κακῶς δογματίσαντας περὶ τοῦ θείου
5 συμβόλου καταπαύσῃ καὶ περὶ τῆς χρηματικῆς ζημίας τῆς ἐπιτεθείσης τῇ ἁγίᾳ Ἀναστάσει ἀπαγγείλῃ τῷ Χριστοῦ ἱεράρχῃ, ἵν᾽ ὅπως χεῖρα βοηθείας ὀρέξῃ κινδυνευούσῃ τῇ τοῦ Θεοῦ πόλει. Ὅθεν ἐπιστολῆς γενομένης πρὸς τὸν προλεχθέντα πάπαν παρὰ τοῦ ἁγιωτάτου πατριάρχου καὶ τῆς ἁγίας συνόδου καὶ τῶν πατέρων περὶ τοῦ θείου συμβόλου καὶ τῆς
10 ἐπιτεθείσης ζημίας, συνεῖδον καὶ πρὸς τὸν ἐν Κωνσταντινουπόλει πατριαρχοῦντα Θεόδοτον τοὔνομα, ὄντα ἔξαρχον τῆς τῶν εἰκονοκαυστῶν αἱρέσεως, καὶ πρὸς τὸν βασιλέα Λέοντα, τῷ γένει Ἀρμένιον, ἐπιστολὴν ἀποσταλῆναι, ἴσως ἰσχύσωσι καὶ τούτους μεταστρέψαι ἐκ τῆς τῶν εἰκονομάχων αἱρέσεως καὶ προσαγαγεῖν τῇ καθολικῇ καὶ ἀποστολικῇ
15 καὶ ὀρθοδόξῳ ἐκκλησίᾳ. Τοῦτο δὲ ἦν ἐν ταῖς ἀρχαῖς τῆς αὐτοῦ βασιλείας τοῦ προλεχθέντος Λέοντος. Ἔμελλεν γὰρ ἐκεῖθεν τὴν πορείαν ποιεῖσθαι ὁ μέγας Μιχαήλ, κατερχόμενος πρὸς τὸν ἐν ἁγίοις πάπαν ἐν τῇ μεγάλῃ τῶν πόλεων Ῥώμῃ, ὅπως ἐν ἀπολαύσει γένηται καὶ τῶν ἐν τῇ θεοστέπτῳ καὶ βασιλίδι τῶν πόλεων τοῦ Θεοῦ εὐκτηρίων οἴκων.
20 (7) Ὁ γὰρ ἐν ἁγίοις καὶ ὁμολογητὴς Θεόδωρος ὁ τῶν Στουδίων, ὢν ὑπερόριος ἐν τῇ ἀνατολῇ ἐπὶ Νικηφόρου τοῦ βασιλέως, ἐπιστολὴν πέπομφε πρὸς τὸν προλεχθέντα ἀρχιτελετάρχην τῆς ἁγίας Χριστοῦ τοῦ Θεοῦ ἡμῶν πόλεως, πρὸς τοῦ βοηθῆσαι καὶ συνεπαμύνασθαι αὐτῷ τῇ κατὰ Κωνσταντινουπόλει τοῦ Θεοῦ ἐκκλησίᾳ κινδυνευούσῃ παρὰ τῶν
25 ἀθέων καὶ εἰκονομάχων αἱρετικῶν. Ταύτης ἕνεκα τῆς αἰτίας τὴν ἐπιστολὴν ἐποιήσαντο πρὸς τὸν προλεχθέντα Θεόδοτον πατριάρχην, μᾶλλον δὲ φατριάρχην, καὶ τὸν ἄνακτα Λέοντα, τοῦτο μὲν ἐπιστομίζοντες, τοῦτο δὲ καὶ νουθετοῦντες ἀποστῆναι τῆς μυσαρᾶς τῶν εἰκονοκαυστῶν αἱρέσεως.

AG
1. τοὺς : τοῖς codd.   2. αἰτιῶν A: ἐτῶν G I συνεῖδον G: συνίδων A 4. κακῶς A: καλῶς ante corr. G I περὶ : τῇ add. G   5. καταπαύσῃ A: καταπαύσει G   10. συνεῖδον A: συνείδων G   13. εἰ ante ἴσως add. Šev. I ἰσχύσωσι G: -ν A   15. καὶ ὀρθοδόξῳ A: om. G   23-4. τοῦ Κωνσταντινουπόλει A: τὸ ἐπαμῦναι καὶ βοηθῆσαι τῇ G   25. ἕνεκα A: ἕνεκεν G   26. ἐποιήσαντο : ἐποιήσατο codd.

monetary fine.⁵⁴ For these two reasons the patriarch and his holy synod resolved to send his all-holy Michael to the aforementioned pope, so that Michael might both check those who held wrong opinions concerning the divine Creed and report to the pontiff of Christ about the fine imposed on the holy church of the Resurrection, and that the latter might extend a hand of assistance to the endangered city of God. Thus the most holy patriarch and the holy synod and fathers composed a letter to the aforementioned pope concerning the divine Creed and the imposed fine, and they also resolved to send a letter to the patriarch in Constantinople, Theodotos by name, who was leader of the heresy of image-burners, and to the emperor Leo of Armenian descent⁵⁵ that they might perhaps be able to turn them away from the heresy of the icon-fighters and lead them to the catholic, [233] apostolic, and orthodox Church. This was in the beginning of the reign of the aforesaid Leo.⁵⁶ For the great Michael was to make the journey from Constantinople, going on from there to the pope of blessed memory in the great city of Rome, so that he might benefit from the churches of God in the God-crowned imperial city as well.

7. The revival of iconoclasm by Leo V

The confessor Theodore of Stoudios of saintly memory, when he was banished to the east during the reign of Nikephoros the emperor,⁵⁷ had sent a letter to the aforesaid chief priest⁵⁸ of the holy city of Christ our God soliciting his help and assistance on behalf of the holy Church of God in Constantinople which was endangered by the impious and icon-fighting heretics.⁵⁹ For this reason, they composed a letter to the aforesaid patriarch or rather 'factionarch'⁶⁰ Theodotos⁶¹ and to the ruler Leo, both refuting⁶² them and admonishing them to turn away from the foul heresy of the burners of icons.

(8) Ὁ δὲ πατὴρ ἡμῶν καὶ μέγας Μιχαήλ, μὴ γινώσκων παρακούειν, μᾶλλον δὲ καὶ ὡς ἐκ Θεοῦ δεξάμενος τὴν τοιαύτην παρὰ τῶν ἁγίων πατέρων κέλευσιν, καὶ ὡς ἐκ πολλοῦ ἦν εὐχόμενος, ὥστε καταξιωθῆναι αὐτὸν τῆς τῶν κορυφαίων ἀποστόλων προσκυνήσεως, εὐχὴν μετ᾽ αὐτῶν
5 ποιησάμενος καὶ λαβὼν παρ᾽ αὐτῶν πρόθεσιν καὶ οἱονεὶ συνταξάμενος αὐτοῖς ἐξῆλθε τῆς ἁγίας Χριστοῦ τοῦ Θεοῦ ἡμῶν πόλεως μετὰ τῶν αὐτοῦ μαθητῶν, Θεοδώρου φημὶ καὶ Θεοφάνους, καὶ ἑτέρου τινὸς τῶν Σπουδαίων Ἰὼβ τοὔνομα, μαρτυρουμένου παρὰ πολλῶν ἐν τῇ κατὰ Θεὸν ἀκριβεῖ πολιτείᾳ, προπεμφθεὶς παρὰ τοῦ ἐν ἁγίοις πατριάρχου, καὶ τῶν
10 αὐτοῦ ἱεραρχῶν, καὶ τῆς τῶν ἁγίων πατέρων συνόδου, μέχρι Διοσπόλεως καὶ Λύδδης. Καὶ τούτους ἀσπασάμενος καὶ τὸ τελευταῖον χαίρειν εἰπὼν ἤρξατο τῆς ὁδοιπορίας.

Καὶ δὴ διερχόμενος ἐν τῇ πόλει Σελευκείας, εὗρεν ἐκεῖσέ τινας μοναχοὺς ἀνθισταμένους καὶ μὴ κοινωνοῦντας μήτε μὴν καταδεχομένους
15 τῇ κατὰ Νίκαιαν ἑβδόμῃ συνόδῳ, τῇ συναθροισθείσῃ ἐπὶ Κωνσταντίνου καὶ Εἰρήνης, τῆς αὐτοῦ μητρός, τῶν θεοστέπτων βασιλέων, καὶ Ταρασίου πατριάρχου, οὔτε μὴν ἀναφέροντας ἐν τοῖς ἱεροῖς διπτύχοις τοὺς ἁγίους καὶ ὁμολογητὰς καὶ μεγάλους πατριάρχας Ταράσιον καὶ Νικηφόρον. Ὅθεν τῇ πανσόφῳ αὐτοῦ διδασκαλίᾳ καὶ τῷ καθ᾽ ἑαυτὸν ὑποδείγματι
20 ἔπεισε τούτους συνθέσθαι καὶ κοινωνῆσαι τῇ ἁγίᾳ συνόδῳ. Οὐ μόνον δὲ τούτους πέπεικε συνθέσθαι τῇ ἁγίᾳ συνόδῳ καὶ τῇ τοῦ Θεοῦ καθολικῇ καὶ ἀποστολικῇ ἐκκλησίᾳ, ἀλλὰ καὶ πᾶσιν, οἷς ἂν ἔλαχε κατὰ τὴν ὁδὸν τούτῳ προσομιλῆσαι, λέγων πᾶσι καὶ διαβεβαιούμενος ὅτι ἡ τοῦ Θεοῦ ἐκκλησία ἡ ἐν Ἱεροσολύμοις καὶ ὁ ταύτης τελετάρχης σὺν τοῖς αὐτοῦ
25 ἀρχιεράρχαις καὶ τῆς ἐρήμου πατράσι καὶ ἀπεδέξατο καὶ συνήνεσε καὶ συντέταχεν ἐν τοῖς ἱεροῖς διπτύχοις τὴν ἁγίαν καὶ οἰκουμενικὴν ἑβδόμην σύνοδον μετὰ τῶν πρὸ αὐτῆς ἓξ ἁγίων καὶ οἰκουμενικῶν συνόδων, καὶ τοὺς ταύτης ἀρχιεράρχας Ταράσιον καὶ Νικηφόρον ὡς ὁμοτρόπους καὶ ὁμογνώμονας ἀπεδέξατο καὶ ὡμολόγησεν. Ὅθεν τούτων ἀκούσαντες
30 καὶ πληροφορηθέντες, συνήνεσαν πάντες καὶ ἐκοινώνησαν τῇ ἁγίᾳ καὶ οἰκουμενικῇ ἑβδόμῃ συνόδῳ.

AG
9. ἀκριβεῖ A: ἀκριβῇ G   11. τῆς ante καὶ ¹ add. Šev. l Λύδδης G: Λίδδης A   20. ἔπεισε G: -ν A 21. πέπεικε G: -ν A 22. ἔλαχε G: -ν A 25. πατράσι G: -ν A l συνήνεσε G: -ν A 29. ὡμολόγησεν A: ὁμολόγησεν G

8. Michael and his disciples depart on their journey to Constantinople

Our great father Michael, who did not know how to disobey but rather received this command from the holy fathers as if from God since he had been wishing for a long time to be deemed worthy of venerating the chief apostles, prayed with the fathers, took their counsel[63] and as it were took leave of them. He then departed from the holy city of Christ our God with his disciples, I mean Theodore and Theophanes, and another from the Spoudaei monastery named Job, for whom there were many witnesses to his strict way of life according to God. Michael was escorted by the patriarch of saintly memory[64] and his hierarchs and the synod of holy fathers as far as Diospolis which is also called Lydda.[65] After embracing them and bidding them the final farewell, he began his journey.

When he arrived in the city of Seleukeia,[66] he found certain monks there who were opposing, not adhering nor even acceding to the seventh council of Nicaea[67] which was convened under the God-crowned emperor Constantine and his mother Eirene[68] and the patriarch Tarasios.[69] Nor did they mention the saints, confessors and great patriarchs Tarasios and Nikephoros in their holy diptychs.[70] By means of his all-wise teaching and his own example Michael persuaded them to be reconciled with and to adhere to the holy synod. Not only did he persuade these men to be reconciled with the holy synod and the catholic, apostolic Church, but he stated and maintained to all those with whom[71] he happened to converse on his way that the Church of God in Jerusalem and her chief priest with his bishops and fathers of the desert accepted, agreed with, and included the holy and universal seventh council in the holy diptychs along with the six holy and [234] universal councils which preceded it, and that this body also accepted and confessed its bishops Tarasios and Nikephoros as being of one manner and mind with it. When they had heard and were wholly satisfied with these matters, they all agreed and adhered to the holy and universal seventh council.

(9) Οὐ μέντοι διέλαθε τοῦτο τῷ ἀσεβεῖ καὶ θεομάχῳ καὶ θηριωνύμῳ ἄνακτι, καὶ τῷ τούτου ἱεράρχῃ, μᾶλλον δὲ αἱρεσιάρχῃ, Θεοδότῳ. Ὅθεν καὶ ἔβρυχον κατ᾽ αὐτοῦ τοὺς ὀδόντας. Ὡς δὲ εἰσῆλθεν ὁ ἐν ἁγίοις πατὴρ ἡμῶν καὶ τῆς εὐσεβείας ἀγωνιστὴς Μιχαὴλ ἐν τῇ πανευδαίμονι
5 Κωνσταντινουπόλει μηνὶ μαΐῳ ἰνδ. ζ΄ σὺν τοῖς αὐτοῦ μαθηταῖς καὶ δῆλα τὰ κατ᾽ αὐτὸν τῷ τε βασιλεῖ καὶ τῷ πατριάρχῃ Θεοδότῳ πεποίηκε, τέως τὸν δόλον ἀπέκρυψαν τὸν κατὰ τῶν ἁγίων. Δεξάμενοι δὲ τὴν ἐπιστολὴν ὅ τε βασιλεὺς καὶ ὁ πατριάρχης καὶ ἀναγνόντες οὐ μόνον οὐδὲν ὠφελήθησαν τοῦ συνθέσθαι τῇ ἀληθείᾳ, ἀλλὰ καὶ μᾶλλον εἰς τὸ
10 χεῖρον ἐξήφθησαν. Καὶ δὴ κελεύουσι τὸν ἐν ἁγίοις πατέρα ἡμῶν καὶ μέγαν Μιχαήλ, ἐν τῇ τῆς Χώρας μονῇ καταλῦσαι σὺν τοῖς αὐτοῦ μαθηταῖς καὶ ἀνάπαυλαν ἐκ τῶν τῆς ὁδοιπορίας πόνων δέξασθαι, ὁρίσαντες τὴν αὐτῶν διατροφὴν ἐκ τῶν βασιλικῶν ταμιείων χορηγεῖσθαι.
(10) Μετὰ δὲ ὀλίγας ἡμέρας τῆς αὐτοῦ παρουσίας ἀποστείλας ὁ βασιλεὺς
15 προσεκαλέσατο τὸν ἅγιον Μιχαὴλ ἐν τῷ παλατίῳ σὺν τοῖς αὐτοῦ μαθηταῖς, ἐν τῷ λεγομένῳ Χρυσοτρικλίνῳ, παρούσης καὶ τῆς συγκλήτου. Εἰσελθόντες δὲ οἱ ἅγιοι καὶ θεοφόροι πατέρες ἔστησαν ἔμπροσθεν τοῦ βασιλέως, καὶ ὁ βασιλεὺς πρὸς αὐτοὺς ἔφη· Τίς ἡ αἰτία, πατέρες ἅγιοι, δι᾽ ἣν ἐσκύλητε πρὸς τὴν τοῦ κράτους ἡμῶν μετριότητα; Ἀποκριθεὶς δὲ
20 ὁ ἐν ἁγίοις πατὴρ ἡμῶν Μιχαὴλ λέγει τῷ βασιλεῖ· Ὁ τὸν ἀρχιερατικὸν θρόνον ἐπέχων τῆς ἁγίας Χριστοῦ τοῦ Θεοῦ ἡμῶν πόλεως, ὁ ἁγιώτατος πατριάρχης, ἀπέστειλεν ἡμᾶς πρὸς τὴν τοῦ κράτους ὑμῶν γαληνότητα, σὺν τῇ κατ᾽ αὐτὸν ἁγίᾳ συνόδῳ καὶ τῶν τῆς ἐρήμου πατέρων, ὑπομνῆσαι τὴν θεοκυβέρνητον ὑμῶν βασιλείαν ἕνεκεν τῆς ἁγίας καθολικῆς καὶ
25 ἀποστολικῆς τοῦ Χριστοῦ ἐκκλησίας καὶ τοῦ ὀρθοδόξου λαοῦ, ὅπως κελεύσῃ ἡ σὴ θειότης τὴν τῶν ἁγίων εἰκόνων ἀνατύπωσιν μετὰ παρρησίας εἰκονίζεσθαί τε καὶ προσκυνεῖσθαι ὑπὸ πάντων ἀκωλύτως, καθὼς καὶ ἡ παρ᾽ αὐτῶν σοι ἀποσταλεῖσα ἔγγραφος ἐπιστολὴ περιέχει.

AG
1. διέλαθε G: -ν A   2. δὲ : τῷ add. G   5. μηνὶ -- ζ΄ A: κατὰ τὸν μάϊον μῆνα τῆς ἑβδομῆς ἰνδικτιῶνος G   6. τε A: τότε G | πεποίηκε G: -ν A   7. Δεξάμενοι A: Δεξάμενος G   12. ὁρίσαντες A: ὡρήσαντες G

9. The arrival of the holy fathers in Constantinople

These events however did not escape the notice of the impious, God-fighting ruler[72] who was named after a beast[73] or that of his hierarch, or rather heresiarch,[74] Theodotos.[75] And so they gnashed their teeth at him. As our father of saintly memory and champion[76] of piety Michael entered[77] all-fortunate[78] Constantinople with his disciples in the month of May of the seventh indiction[79] and explained his affairs to the emperor and the patriarch Theodotos, they concealed their deceit[80] towards the saints for the time being. When the emperor and patriarch had received and read the letter, not only did they in no way derive profit and assent to the truth, but they were even inflamed to worse things. They ordered our great father Michael of saintly memory to take up quarters in the monastery of Chora[81] with his disciples, and to take rest from the hardships of the journey, decreeing that their sustenance should be furnished from the imperial treasuries.

10. The audience with Leo V

Several days after his arrival, the emperor sent for the holy Michael, summoning him with his disciples to the palace, to[82] the so-called 'Golden Triclinium'[83] in the presence also of his senate. The holy and God-inspired[84] fathers entered and stood before the emperor. The emperor said to them, 'For what reason, holy fathers, have you troubled yourselves to come to my humble majesty?' Our father Michael of blessed memory answered and said to the emperor, 'The most holy patriarch who holds the pontifical see of the holy city of Christ our God, with the holy synod that he convened and the fathers of the desert, sent us before your serene majesty to petition your divinely led empire on behalf of the holy, catholic, and apostolic Church of Christ and the orthodox people that your divinity may command that the representation of holy icons may occur openly and that they may be venerated by all without restraint, even as is contained within the written letter which they have sent to you.'[85]

---

3. 'they gnashed their teeth at him': cf. Ps. 34:16 (35:16); 36:12 (37:12); 111:10 (112:10); Acts 7:54

(11) Ὁ δὲ βασιλεὺς ἐκέλευσεν ἐνεχθῆναι τὴν ἐπιστολὴν καὶ ἐπαναγνωσθῆναι εἰς ἐπήκοον πάντων. Ἤχθη δὲ ἡ πεμφθεῖσα ἐπιστολὴ παρὰ τοῦ ἁγιωτάτου πατριάρχου Ἱεροσολύμων ἐν Κωνσταντινουπόλει τῷ πατριάρχῃ Θεοδότῳ καὶ τῷ βασιλεῖ Λέοντι, καὶ εἶχεν ἐπὶ λέξεως οὕτως· Τοῦ Κυρίου καὶ Θεοῦ καὶ Σωτῆρος ἡμῶν Ἰησοῦ Χριστοῦ, τοῦ ἑνὸς τῆς ἁγίας καὶ ὑπερουσίου καὶ ζωαρχικῆς Τριάδος, τοῦ σὺν Πατρὶ καὶ Πνεύματι ἐκ μὴ ὄντων τόνδε τὸν κόσμον εἰς τὸ εἶναι παραγαγόντος, καὶ κατ᾽ ἰδίαν εἰκόνα καὶ ὁμοίωσιν ἐκ γῆς ἰδίᾳ χειρὶ πλαστουργήσαντος τὸν ἄνθρωπον, ἐπ᾽ ἐσχάτων δὲ τῶν ἡμερῶν διὰ τὴν ἡμῶν σωτηρίαν ἐκ παρθένου τεχθέντος καὶ ἐνανθρωπήσαντος καὶ ἐνδυσαμένου τὸν παλαιὸν Ἀδάμ, τὸν φθόνῳ διαβόλου καὶ γυναικὸς ἀπάτῃ ἐξόριστον γενόμενον ἐκ τῆς τοῦ παραδείσου διαίτης καὶ ὑπόδικον τῷ πονηρῷ δαίμονι γεγονότα, ὅπως ἀνασώσῃ καὶ ἀνεγείρῃ τὴν αὐτοῦ εἰκόνα, συγχωσθεῖσαν τοῖς πάθεσιν, καὶ διὰ τοῦτο πάντα ὑπομείνας, σταυρόν τε καὶ θάνατον καὶ τἆλλα πάντα, ὅσα ἡ τῶν θείων εὐαγγελίων περιέχει βίβλος. Τούτου τοίνυν τοῦ μεγάλου Θεοῦ καὶ Σωτῆρος ἡμῶν Ἰησοῦ Χριστοῦ ἐξ ἀρχῆς καὶ ἄνωθεν τῷ Μωσεῖ ἐπὶ τοῦ ὄρους νομοθετοῦντος, ποιῆσαι ἐκέλευσε δύο χερουβεὶμ κατασκιάζειν τὸ ἱλαστήριον τῆς δόξης τοῦ Θεοῦ. Ἀλλὰ καὶ ἡ σκηνὴ τοῦ μαρτυρίου εἰκόνα ἔφερε τῆς ἁγίας Θεοτόκου καὶ ἀειπαρθένου Μαρίας. Ὡσαύτως καὶ οἱ προφῆται ἃ ἐθεάσαντο, Ἡσαΐας, Ἱερεμίας, Δανιήλ, Ἰεζεκιὴλ καὶ πάντες, εἰκόνες καὶ τύποι ἦσαν τῆς ἀληθείας. Αὐτὸς δὲ ὁ τῶν ὅλων Θεός, ὁ Κύριος ἡμῶν Ἰησοῦς Χριστός, οὐχὶ εἰκὼν καὶ ἐκσφράγισμα τοῦ ἀοράτου Θεοῦ καὶ Πατρὸς λέγεταί τε καὶ ἔστι καὶ πιστεύεται; Τί δαὶ καὶ οἱ ἅγιοι καὶ πανσεβάσμιοι ἀπόστολοι, οὐχὶ καὶ αὐτοὶ φαίνονται εἰκόνας ποιήσαντες, ἀλλὰ καὶ σεπτῶς προσκυνήσαντες καὶ τιμήσαντες; Οὐχ ὁ πρῶτος τῆς ἐκκλησίας ποιμὴν καὶ διδάσκαλος, ᾧ τὰς κλεῖς τῆς βασιλείας Χριστὸς ἐνεπίστευσε, καὶ ποιμαίνειν καὶ βόσκειν τὰ αὐτοῦ λογικὰ πρόβατα παρεκελεύσατο, τῷ τρισσῷ τῆς ἐρωτήσεως τὸ τρισσὸν τῆς ἀρνήσεως ἰασάμενος, οὐχὶ καὶ

AG
8. πλαστουργήσαντος : πλαστουργήσας codd. 10. ἐνανθρωπήσαντος : ἐνανθρωπίσαντος ante corr. A | ἐνδυσαμένου A: ἐνδυσάμενον G 11. ἐξόριστον : ἐξώριστον codd. (ante corr. A) 17. ἐκέλευσε G: -ν A 18. κατασκιάζειν A: κατασκευάζειν G 21. εἰκόνες: εἰκόναι codd. 24. ἔστι G: -ν A | δαὶ A : δὲ G 27. ἐνεπίστευσε G: -ν A

11. The letter from the patriarch of Jerusalem to Leo V

The emperor commanded that the letter be brought forth and read aloud in the hearing of all. The letter which the most holy patriarch of Jerusalem had sent to the patriarch Theodotos in Constantinople and to the emperor Leo was brought in and was word for word as follows: 'Our Lord, God and Saviour, Jesus Christ, One of the holy, supra-essential and life-giving Trinity, Who with the Father and the Spirit brought this world from non-being into being and Who fashioned man from earth with His own hand according to His own image and likeness, Who was born from a Virgin [235] for the sake of our salvation in the final days, Who became man and Who put on the person of the first Adam (who was banished from the abode of paradise through the envy of the devil and the deceit of woman and made subject to the wicked demon), in order that He might save and raise up His image, which had been covered up with passions, Who on this account suffered everything, the cross, death, and all the other things which are contained in the book of the divine gospels: when He, our great God and Saviour, Jesus Christ, in the beginning and from on high gave the law to Moses on the mountain, He commanded that two cherubim be made to cover over the mercy seat of the glory of God.[86] Even the tabernacle of testimony bore the image of the holy Mother of God and ever-Virgin Mary.[87] Likewise what the prophets, Isaiah, Jeremiah, Daniel, Ezekiel and all of the others perceived were images and likenesses of the truth.[88] And is not the God of all things, our Lord Jesus Christ, Himself said and believed to be the image and impression of the unseen God and Father, and is He not indeed?[89] Are not the holy and all-venerable apostles seen not only to have fashioned icons, but even reverently to have worshipped and honoured them? Is not the first shepherd and teacher of the Church, to whom Christ entrusted the keys of the kingdom and commanded to feed and tend his spiritual flock,[90] and whose triple denial He

---

13-4. 'covered up with passions': cf. Greg.Naz. Or. 38 (*PG*, 36, 328B)

αὐτὸς φαίνεται Παγκρατίῳ τῷ αὐτοῦ μαθητῇ δεδωκὼς δύο εἰκόνας, τοῦ τε Χριστοῦ καὶ τῆς αὐτοῦ μητρὸς τῆς εὐλογημένης Θεοτόκου καὶ ἀειπαρθένου Μαρίας, παρεγγυήσας αὐτῷ ἐξεικονίζειν πᾶσαν τὴν ἔνσαρκον οἰκονομίαν τοῦ ἀληθινοῦ ἡμῶν Θεοῦ ἐν τῇ ἁγίᾳ ἐκκλησίᾳ ἀπό
5 τε τῆς τοῦ ἀγγέλου πρὸς τὴν Παρθένον λεχθείσης φωνῆς, τὸ 'Χαῖρε, κεχαριτωμένη, ὁ Κύριος μετά σου,' μέχρι τῆς αὐτοῦ ἀναλήψεως καὶ τῆς τοῦ Ἁγίου Πνεύματος παρουσίας, ὥστε δύνασθαι καὶ τὸν ἰδιώτην καὶ ἀγράμματον ἐκ τῆς τῶν ἁγίων εἰκόνων στηλογραφίας κατανοεῖν, ὅσα ἀνθ' ἡμῶν καὶ τῆς ἡμῶν σωτηρίας ᾠκονόμησεν ὁ προαιώνιος Θεός, ὁ
10 Κύριος ἡμῶν Ἰησοῦς Χριστός, ποιῆσαί τε καὶ παθεῖν; Τί δαὶ καὶ ὁ εὐαγγελιστὴς Λουκᾶς, οὐχὶ καὶ αὐτὸς φαίνεται πρῶτος στηλογραφήσας τὴν σαρκομοιόμορφον εἰκόνα Χριστοῦ τοῦ Θεοῦ καὶ τῆς αὐτοῦ μητρός, ἥτις καὶ μέχρι τοῦ νῦν σώζεται ἔν τε τῇ μεγάλῃ Ῥώμῃ καὶ ἐν τῇ ἁγίᾳ τοῦ Θεοῦ ἡμῶν πόλει; Τί δὲ λέγωμεν προφήτας καὶ ἀποστόλους; Αὐτὸς ὁ
15 Κύριος ἡμῶν καὶ Θεός, Ἰησοῦς ὁ Χριστός, ἡ εἰκὼν τοῦ ἀοράτου Πατρός, οὐχὶ καὶ αὐτὸς ῥάκος περιθεὶς τῇ ἑαυτοῦ ὄψει καὶ ἀναμάξας τὴν αὐτοῦ τῆς σαρκὸς εἰκόνα, Ἀβγάρῳ τῷ πιστοτάτῳ τοπάρχῃ πόλεως Ἐδέσης πέπομφε διὰ τοῦ αὐτοῦ οἰκέτου; Ἥτις καὶ μέχρι τοῦ νῦν σώζεται ἐν τῇ αὐτῇ πόλει; Καὶ ταῦτα μὲν διεξήλθομεν, δεῖξαι πειρώμενοι ὡς ὅτι οὐχὶ
20 νεαρὰ καὶ πρόσφατός ἐστιν ἡ τῶν εἰκόνων ἀνατύπωσις, ἀλλά γε μὴν ἐξ ἀρχῆς καὶ ἄνωθεν παραδοθεῖσα καὶ πιστευθεῖσα ἔν τε τῇ παλαιᾷ καὶ νέᾳ διαθήκῃ. Ὅθεν δυσωποῦμεν τὸ ὑμέτερον κράτος, ὅπως ἀποστῇ τῆς νεαρᾶς ταύτης καὶ μυσαρᾶς τῶν εἰκονοκαυστῶν αἱρέσεως, καὶ κοινωνοὶ γένησθε τῆς πατροπαραδότου ἁγίας καὶ ἀποστολικῆς πίστεως, καὶ
25 ἀπολάβῃ ἡ τοῦ Θεοῦ ἐκκλησία τὴν ἰδίαν εὐκοσμίαν τῆς τῶν θείων εἰκόνων ἀνατυπώσεως, καὶ μὴ αἰωνίῳ καὶ ἀτελευτήτῳ ἀναθέματι περιβάλησθε, ἀλλ' εἴξαντες τῇ ἡμῶν παρακλήσει, ἐν ὀρθοδόξῳ καὶ ἀσφαλεῖ πίστει τελειωθήσεσθε, καὶ εἰς τὰς αἰωνίους σκηνὰς μετὰ τῶν προφητῶν καὶ ἀποστόλων, μαρτύρων τε καὶ δικαίων ἀγαλλιαθήσεσθε,
30 αἰωνίαν λύτρωσιν εὐράμενοι.'

AG
14. λέγωμεν G: λέγομεν A   15. ὁ A: om.G   16. ῥάκος : ῥάκκος codd.   19. διεξήλθομεν A: διεξήλθωμεν G   24. γένησθε : γένεσθε codd.   27. περιβάλησθε : περιβάλεσθε codd.

healed with His triple question,⁹¹ seen to have given to his disciple Pankratios⁹² two icons, one of Christ and another of His mother, the blessed Mother of God and ever-Virgin Mary, and to have instructed him to represent the entire incarnate dispensation of our true God in the holy Church from the time of the speech of the angel to the Virgin, who said, 'Hail, thou that art highly favoured, the Lord is with thee,' until His Ascension and the coming of the Holy Spirit, so that even the uncultivated and illiterate might be able to contemplate through the depiction of holy icons all that our Lord God Who is before all ages, Jesus Christ, dispensed to do and suffer on our behalf and on behalf of our salvation? And is not the evangelist Luke seen to have been the first to depict the life-like icon of Christ our God and His Mother which is preserved even now in the great city of Rome and in our holy city of God?⁹³ But why should we speak of prophets and apostles? Did not our Lord and God Jesus Christ Himself, the image of the unseen God, after placing a strip of cloth over His visage and wiping off the image of His flesh, send it through His household servant to Abgar, the most faithful toparch⁹⁴ of the city of Edessa?⁹⁵ And is not this cloth preserved even now in the same city? We have recounted these matters in detail, endeavouring to show [236] that the fabrication of icons is by no means new and recent, but was transmitted from the beginning and from on high, and confirmed in both the old and new covenants. Therefore we entreat your majesty to renounce this abominable new heresy of the icon-burners that you may become a communicant of the ancestral, holy, and apostolic faith,⁹⁶ that the Church of God may recover its proper adornment in the representation of divine icons, and that you may not be subject to eternal and unending anathema but yielding to our exhortation, you may pass away in the orthodox and unswerving faith and that you may rejoice in the everlasting habitations with the prophets and apostles, the martyrs and the righteous, having found eternal redemption.'⁹⁷

5-6. Lu.1:28   28. Lu.16:9

(12) Τούτων δὲ εἰς ἐπήκοον πάντων ἀναγνωσθέντων, θυμομαχήσας ὁ βύθιος δράκων καὶ λεοντώνυμος θήρ, ὁ ἀνάξιος τῆς βασιλικῆς ἁλουργίδος, οὐ μετρίως τούτους τυφθῆναι καὶ ἐναποκλείστους γενέσθαι ἐν τῇ τῆς Φιάλης εἱρκτῇ ἐκέλευσε, πάμπολλα κατηγορήσας καὶ ἀναθέμασι
5 περιβαλὼν τόν τε ἁγιώτατον πατριάρχην καὶ τὴν αὐτοῦ ἁγίαν καὶ ἀποστολικὴν σύνοδον, οὐ μὴν ἀλλὰ καὶ τὴν τῶν ἁγίων πατέρων ὁμήγυριν, ὡς ἅτε αἱρετικοὺς καὶ εἰδωλολάτρας ὄντας καὶ μὴ ὀρθῶς φρονοῦντας, 'Οὐ μόνον δὲ ἀλλὰ καὶ ἡμᾶς ἀναγκάζοντας εἰδωλολατρεῖν,' τοῦτο προσειπών. Ὡς δὲ ἐναπόκλειστοι γεγόνασιν οἱ ἅγιοι καὶ θεοφόροι πατέρες,
10 εὐχαριστηρίους ᾠδὰς ἀνέπεμπον Χριστῷ τῷ Θεῷ, τῷ τούτους ἀξιώσαντι ὑπὲρ αὐτοῦ καὶ τῆς αὐτοῦ εἰκόνος τοιαῦτα παθεῖν, ἱκέτευον δὲ καὶ μέχρι τέλους ὑπομονὴν δοθῆναι καὶ παρρησίαν αὐτοῖς, ὅπως καταισχύνωσι τὸν ἀπηνῆ καὶ μισόχριστον τύραννον.

Ἡμερῶν δὲ διαγενομένων οὐκ ὀλίγων καὶ ἀσίτων διατελούντων τῶν
15 ἁγίων καὶ μὴ θελόντων δέξασθαί τι βρώσιμον παρὰ τῶν τοῦ ἀνηλεοῦς τυράννου ὑπηρετῶν, ὡς ἅτε αἱρετικῶν αὐτῶν καὶ μισοχρίστων ὄντων, καίπερ πολλὰ τοῦ βασιλέως πέμψαντος αὐτοῖς, φοίνικάς τε καὶ ἰσχάδας, καὶ ὅσα πρὸς τροφὴν ἐπιτήδεια ἀσκητῶν ἐγίνωσκεν εἶναι, οὐκ ἐδέξαντο, τὸ τοῦ ἱεροψάλτου Δαυὶδ λόγιον πρὸς αὐτὸν εἰπόντες, τὸ φάσκον, ' Ἔλαιον
20 ἁμαρτωλοῦ μὴ λιπανάτω τὴν κεφαλήν μου,' αἱρούμενοι λιμῷ φθαρῆναι ἤ τι αὐτῶν ἀπογεύσασθαι.

(13) Ὁ δὲ βασιλεὺς διά τινος λογίου δυναμένου λέγειν τε καὶ ἀκούειν, οὗ τὸ ὄνομα ἑκὼν ὑπερβήσομαι, ἐδήλωσεν αὐτοῖς λέγων · 'Ἵνα τί ἡ ὑμῶν ἀρετὴ καὶ φιλόσοφος γνώμη βουλῇ κακῇ χρωμένη ἐν ἀπωλείᾳ γενέσθαι
25 σπεύδει, μὴ πειθομένη ὀρθοδόξῳ συνόδῳ τῇ καθελούσῃ καὶ ἐξεωσάσῃ ἐκ τῆς τοῦ Θεοῦ ἐκκλησίας τὴν τῶν εἰδώλων προσκύνησιν; Ἢ οὐκ ἀκηκόατε τοῦ Δαυὶδ λέγοντος περὶ τῶν τοιούτων εἰδώλων, ὅτι *στόμα ἔχουσι καὶ οὐ λαλήσουσιν, ὀφθαλμοὺς ἔχουσι καὶ οὐκ ὄψονται, ὦτα*

AG
4. ἐκέλευσε G: -ν A   17. πολλὰ post βασιλέως trsp. G   23. ὄνομα : Χαμοδράκων add. in marg. codd.

12. Michael and his disciples are confined in the Phiale prison

When these words had been read aloud in the hearing of all, the serpent of the sea and beast who bore the name of lion,[98] who was unworthy of the imperial purple, was enraged and commanded that they be beaten severely and confined within the prison of the Phiale.[99] He issued many accusations and subjected to anathemas not only the most holy patriarch and his holy, apostolic council, but even the assembly of holy fathers, as heretics, idolaters and upholders of false beliefs and he added, 'In addition to that they also force us to worship idols.' When the holy and God-inspired fathers were imprisoned, they raised grateful hymns to Christ our God, Who had deemed them worthy to undergo such sufferings on His behalf[100] and on behalf of His icon, and they entreated Him that endurance and freedom of speech might be granted them even until death in order that they might put to shame the harsh and Christ-hating tyrant.

Many days passed and the holy men continued fasting for they did not wish to accept anything edible from the attendants of the unmerciful tyrant[101] since they were heretics and Christ-haters, although the emperor sent them many things, dates, dried figs and whatever he knew to be suitable for the nourishment of ascetics. They did not accept these, repeating to him the saying of David, the holy singer of psalms, which declares, 'Let the oil of the wicked never anoint my head,'[102] as they chose rather to perish of hunger than to taste anything of theirs.

13. Leo's attempts at persuasion

The emperor, through a certain learned man who was clever at both speaking and listening, whose name I shall purposely pass over,[103] declared to them, 'For what purpose do you, sirs, endowed as you are with virtue and philosophic judgment, strive using faulty counsel to be ruined while disobeying the orthodox synod which condemned and cast out from the Church of God the worship of idols? Have you not heard David's words concerning such idols: "They have mouths, but they speak not: eyes have they, but they see not: they

---

19-20. Ps. 140:5 (141:5).

ἔχουσι καὶ οὐκ ἀκούσονται, ῥῖνας ἔχουσι καὶ οὐκ ὀσφρανθήσονται, χεῖρας ἔχουσι καὶ οὐ ψηλαφήσουσι, πόδας ἔχουσι καὶ οὐ περιπατήσουσιν, οὐ φωνήσουσιν ἐν τῷ λάρυγγι αὐτῶν. Οὐχὶ καὶ τὰ ὑμῶν σεβάσματα τοιαῦτά εἰσιν; Ὅθεν παραινῶ ὑμᾶς· πείσθητέ μοι καὶ κοινωνήσατε τῇ
5 καθολικῇ ἐκκλησίᾳ, καὶ τιμὰς οὐ τὰς τυχούσας λήψεσθε, καὶ ποιήσω ὑμᾶς ἀρχιερεῖς εἰς ὑπερέχοντας θρόνους. Καὶ μὴ κακῶς ἀπολέσθαι θελήσητε.'
 Ὡς δὲ τοῦτο ἤκουσαν οἱ ἀληθῶς ὀρθόδοξοι καὶ ὁμολογηταὶ ἡμῶν πατέρες, ἠλάλαξαν φωνῇ μεγάλῃ καὶ εἶπον· 'Μὴ γένοιτο ἡμῖν ἀρνήσασθαι
10 ἐν εἰκόνι περιγραπτὸν τὸν Κύριον ἡμῶν Ἰησοῦν Χριστὸν ἢ τὴν αὐτοῦ μητέρα ἢ τοὺς αὐτοῦ ἁγίους.' Τὰς δὲ χεῖρας αὐτῶν ὑπολακήσαντες εἶπον· 'Εἰς τοσοῦτον ἐκχεθήτω ἡμῶν τὸ αἷμα. Οὕτως εἰπὲ τῷ ἀποστείλαντί σε αἱρετικῷ καὶ ἀπηνεῖ τυράννῳ· τύπτε, ἐξόριζε, σφάττε, ποίει ὅ τι ἂν θέλῃς καὶ βούλῃ· οὐδὲν ἄλλο ἐξ ἡμῶν ἀκούεις ἢ ὅτι προσκυνοῦμεν καὶ
15 σεβόμεθα καὶ ἀσπαζόμεθα καὶ τιμῶμεν τὴν εἰκόνα Χριστοῦ τοῦ Θεοῦ ἡμῶν καὶ τῆς αὐτοῦ μητρὸς καὶ τῶν αὐτοῦ ἁγίων, καὶ ὑπὲρ αὐτοῦ προθύμως ἀποθανούμεθα.' Ὁ δὲ κάκιστος ὑπηρέτης τοῦ παμπονήρου βασιλέως ἀπελθὼν λέγει τῷ βασιλεῖ· 'Ἡττήμεθα, βασιλεῦ, ἡττήμεθα· μείζους γὰρ τῶν ἀπειλῶν οἱ ἄνδρες.'
20 (14) Ὁ δὲ βασιλεὺς ταῦτα ἀκούσας ἐκέλευσε τὸν μὲν ἅγιον Μιχαὴλ μετὰ καὶ Ἰὼβ ἐναποκλείστους μεῖναι ἐν τῇ εἱρκτῇ, τοὺς δὲ ἁγίους Θεόδωρον καὶ Θεοφάνην, τοὺς αὐτοῦ μαθητάς, ἐξορίστους γενέσθαι ἐν τῇ νήσῳ Ἀφουσίᾳ. Τούτου δὲ γενομένου καὶ ἐν ἐξορίᾳ παραπεμφθέντων τῶν ἁγίων καὶ τὴν νῆσον καταλαβόντων μηνὶ αὐγούστῳ ἰνδικτιῶνος
25 ἑβδόμης, παρεδόθησαν τῷ ἄρχοντι τῆς νήσου ὥστε φυλάττεσθαι αὐτούς, πάμπολλα παραγγείλαντες αὐτῷ, ὥστε παντοίαις θλίψεσι θλῖψαι αὐτούς, ὅπως τάχιον τοῦ ζῆν ἀπαλλαγῶσιν. Ὁ δὲ Θεός, ὁ μὴ παρορῶν τοὺς εἰς αὐτὸν ἐλπίζοντας, ἔδωκεν αὐτοὺς εἰς οἰκτιρμοὺς ἐνώπιον τοῦ προλεχθέντος ἀρχηγοῦ τῆς νήσου, καὶ ἦσαν ἐν ἀνέσει διάγοντες καὶ τῆς
30 αὐτῶν ὁδοῦ ἤγουν ἀσκήσεως ἐχόμενοι. Ὅθεν καὶ ἐν τῇ νήσῳ ὄντων

AG
14. θέλῃς καὶ βούλῃ : θέλεις καὶ βούλει G | βούλῃ : βούλεσαι A   24. καταλαβόντων A: καταλαβόντος G   27. τάχιον A: τάχειον G

have ears, but they hear not: noses have they but they smell not: they have hands, [237] but they handle not: feet have they, but they walk not: neither speak they through their throat?" And are not your worshipped objects such things as these? For this reason I advise you to obey me and communicate in the catholic Church and you will receive uncommon honours: I shall appoint you as bishops in high thrones. Do not insist on perishing wretchedly.'[104]

When our truly orthodox fathers and confessors heard this, they shouted aloud in a great voice, and said, 'May it not come to pass that we should deny our Lord Jesus Christ Who is circumscribed in an icon, or His Mother or His saints.' They wrung their hands[105] and said, 'To this extent may our blood be poured out.[106] Say this to the heretical and cruel tyrant who dispatched you: "Beat, banish, slaughter; carry out whatever you wish and desire. You will hear nothing else from us but that we worship, revere, embrace, and honour the icon of Christ our God, His Mother and His saints, and we will lay down our lives willingly on His behalf."' The evil servant of the wholly depraved emperor departed and said to him, 'We are defeated, emperor, we are defeated. For the men are above threats.'

14. Michael and Job remain imprisoned while Theodore and Theophanes are exiled

When the emperor learned of these matters, he commanded that the holy Michael and Job remain confined in prison, and that the holy Theodore and Theophanes, his disciples, be banished to the island of Aphousia.[107] When this had taken place and the saints had been sent into exile, reaching the island in the month of August in the seventh indiction,[108] they were handed over to the man who ruled the island so that he might guard them. He was commanded to use every means to subject them to all manner of afflictions in order that they might die the more swiftly. But God, Who does not overlook those who put their trust in Him, gave them compassion before the aforesaid governor of the island, and they lived without constraint, carrying out their way of life, that is to say of spiritual training. Thus while they remained on the island they

---

p.68, 27- 70,3. Ps. 113:13-5 (115:5-7)   6. 'in high thrones': cf. Ge. 41:40   27-8. 'Who does not overlook...Him': cf. Ps. 32:18 (33:18)   28. cf. III Kings 8:50 (I Kings 8:50); Ne. 1:11; 9:27

αὐτῶν, οὐκ ἐπαύσαντο δι᾿ ἐπιστολῶν γράφοντες καὶ ἐπιστηρίζοντες τοὺς ὀρθοδόξους, ὥστε θάνατον μὲν καταδέξασθαι, τὴν δὲ ἑαυτῶν πίστιν μὴ ἀθετῆσαι, μήτε μὴν ἀρνήσασθαι ἐν εἰκόνι περιγραπτὸν τὸν Κύριον ἡμῶν καὶ Θεὸν Ἰησοῦν Χριστὸν ἢ τοὺς ἁγίους, καθὼς αὐτὸς ὁ Κύριος ἡμῶν διδάσκει ἡμᾶς ἐν τοῖς θείοις εὐαγγελίοις, λέγων· 'γίνεσθε φρόνιμοι ὡς οἱ ὄφεις καὶ ἀκέραιοι ὡς αἱ περιστεραί.'

(15) Ἓξ δὲ χρόνων διιππευσάντων καὶ τοῦ τυράννου τελευτήσαντος καὶ αἰωνίᾳ κολάσει παραδοθέντος, ἀνέστη ἕτερος βασιλεὺς Μιχαὴλ τοὔνομα, τῆς αὐτῆς αἱρέσεως καὶ θεομάχου γνώμης ἀνάπλεως ὑπάρχων. Οὗτος ἐκέλευσε τὸν ἅγιον Μιχαὴλ ἐκβληθῆναι ἐκ τῆς προλεχθείσης εἱρκτῆς καὶ ὑπερορίᾳ παραπεμφθῆναι ἔν τινι τῶν τοῦ Ὀλύμπου μοναστηρίων τῆς πόλεως Παρουσιάδος μετὰ καὶ Ἰὼβ τοῦ ὁσιωτάτου ἁλύσεσι δεδεμένους. Τούτου δὲ γεγονότος καὶ τῶν ἁγίων τῇ ἐξορίᾳ παραπεμφθέντων, οὐκ ἐπαύετο ὁ μέγας τῆς εὐσεβείας ἀγωνιστής, ὁ πανόσιος Μιχαήλ, δι᾿ ἐπιστολῶν γράφων καὶ ἐπιστηρίζων τοὺς ὀρθοδόξους πρὸς τὸ ὑποφέρειν τὰς παρὰ τῶν ἀσεβῶν καὶ μισοχρίστων αἱρετικῶν καὶ ἀθέων εἰκονοκαυστῶν ἐπαγομένας αὐτοῖς τιμωρίας.

(16) Τελευτήσαντος δὲ καὶ τούτου παμβεβήλου ἄνακτος Μιχαήλ, ἀνέστη ἀντ᾿ αὐτοῦ ἕτερος βασιλεύς, Θεόφιλος τοὔνομα, γνήσιος υἱὸς ὑπάρχων αὐτοῦ, ὠμὸς τοῖς τρόποις, ἀπηνὴς τῷ φρονήματι, πνέων χριστομάχου θυμοῦ καὶ ὀργῆς, πονηρότατος ὑπὲρ τοὺς πρὸ αὐτοῦ βεβασιλευκότας, θυμῷ ἀσχέτῳ κρατούμενος κατὰ τῶν ὀρθοδόξων τῶν ἀνθισταμένων τῇ αὐτοῦ ἀσεβείᾳ καὶ ἀνατρεπόντων τὸ αὐτοῦ ἄθεον καὶ ἀσεβὲς δόγμα. Οὗτος ὁ προλεχθεὶς βέβηλος ἄναξ τῷ πέμπτῳ ἔτει τῆς αὐτοῦ βασιλείας ἐκέλευσεν ἀνακληθῆναι τὸν ἐν ἁγίοις πατέρα ἡμῶν καὶ μέγαν Μιχαὴλ ἐκ τῆς προλεχθείσης μονῆς. Τούτου δὲ γεγονότος καὶ τοῦ ἁγίου καταλαβόντος τὴν πανευδαίμονα Κωνσταντινούπολιν, ἐκέλευσεν αὐτὸν ἐναπόκλειστον γενέσθαι ἔν τισι θόλοις τῆς εἱρκτῆς, τῆς οὕτω λεγομένης Πραιτώριον, πάνυ ἀφεγγέσι καὶ σκοτεινοῖς καὶ χειμῶνος μὲν λιμνώδεσι καὶ κρυμώδεσι, θέρους δὲ πνιγηροῖς καὶ καυσώδεσιν. Ὃς εἰσελθὼν ἐν τῇ τοιαύτῃ εἱρκτῇ καὶ μηδαμόθεν ἀνάπαυσιν κεκτημένος,

---

AG
2-3. μὴ ἀθετῆσαι δὲ ante τὴν ἑαυτῶν πίστιν trsp. G   18. καὶ A: om. G   20. ἀπηνὴς G: ἀπεινὴς A   21. πρὸ A: om. G   30. πνιγηροῖς : πνηγηροῖς codd.

did not cease writing letters[109] and encouraging those of orthodox faith to accept death, but not to deny their faith or repudiate our Lord and God Jesus Christ as He is circumscribed in an icon, or His saints, even as our Lord Himself taught us in the divine gospels, saying, 'Be ye therefore prudent as serpents and harmless as doves.'

15. The reign of Michael II: the exile of Michael and Job to Bithynia

When six years had elapsed and the tyrant had died and passed into eternal punishment, there arose[110] another emperor by the name of Michael, who was full of the same heretical and God-opposing opinion.[111] He commanded that the holy Michael be taken out of the aforesaid prison and sent into banishment with the most holy Job to one of the monasteries of Olympos in the city of Parousias,[112] bound in chains. When this had come to pass and the saints had been sent into exile, the great and all-holy champion of piety Michael did not cease writing letters and encouraging those of orthodox faith to endure the punishments laid upon them [238] by the impious and Christ-hating heretics and godless icon-burners.

16. The accession of Theophilos and the return of Michael and Job to the Praetorium prison in Constantinople

When this wholly profane ruler[113] Michael had also died, there arose after him another emperor by the name of Theophilos, who was his very own son.[114] He was savage in ways and harsh in mind, breathing forth Christ-hating anger and fury. He was far more wicked than those who ruled before him, for he was possessed by unbridled anger against those of orthodox faith who opposed his impiety and who refuted his godless and impious doctrine. In the fifth year of his reign this aforesaid profane ruler commanded that our great father Michael of saintly memory be recalled from the aforesaid monastery. When this had come to pass and the saint had reached all-fortunate Constantinople, he commanded that he be imprisoned within certain vaults in the prison called the Praetorium,[115] which were completely unlit and gloomy, dank and ice-cold in winter, and stifling and parched in summer. He entered this prison and obtained respite from no quarter as he had no one to serve and assist him (for

---

5-6. Mt. 10:16

ΒΙΟΣ ΤΟΥ ΜΙΧΑΗΛ ΤΟΥ ΣΥΝΚΕΛΛΟΥ

μήτε μὴν τὸν περιποιούμενον καὶ συγκροτοῦντα αὐτὸν ἔχων (οὐ γὰρ εἴων τινὰ τούτῳ καθομιλῆσαι· ὑπὸ γὰρ δύο στρατιωτῶν ὠμῶν καὶ ἀνηλεῶν ἦν φυλαττόμενος, οἵτινες οὔτε τὸν καθυπουργοῦντα αὐτῷ, Ἰὼβ τοὔνομα, εἴων τούτῳ κἂν πρὸς βραχὺ προσβλέψαι ἢ τὸ σύνολον καθομιλῆσαι).
5 Ὅθεν ἐκ τῆς τοιαύτης συνοχῆς τε καὶ στενοχωρίας ὁ ἐν ἁγίοις πατὴρ ἡμῶν καὶ ὁμολογητὴς μέγας Μιχαὴλ περιέπεσε χαλεπωτάτῃ ἀρρωστίᾳ ἐπὶ δυσὶν ἔτεσιν, ἔκ τε τοῦ γήρως καὶ τῶν πολλῶν θλίψεων, καὶ ἀμβλυωπίᾳ κατεσχέθη καὶ κυφότητι.
Εὐφροσύνη δέ τις μονάζουσα πιστὴ καὶ ὀρθόδοξος πάμπολλα τούτῳ
10 τῷ πανοσίῳ παρεμυθεῖτο καὶ ἐν ταῖς σωματικαῖς χρείαις ἀντελαμβάνετο. Ὅσους γὰρ χρόνους πεποίηκεν ἐν τῇ ἑτέρᾳ εἱρκτῇ μετὰ τὸ ἀναστῆναι αὐτὸν ἐκ τῆς χαλεπωτάτης ἐκείνης ἀσθενείας καὶ ἐκβληθῆναι αὐτὸν ἐκ τῆς ζοφωτάτης καὶ ὀζώδους εἱρκτῆς καὶ ἐν ἑτέρᾳ διαφερούσῃ ἐγκλεισθῆναι, οὐ διέλειπε διακονοῦσα καὶ ἀποστέλλουσα αὐτῷ διὰ τοῦ
15 αὐτὸν καθυπουργοῦντος τήν τε βρῶσιν καὶ πόσιν καὶ τὴν τοῦ σώματος περιβολήν. Μετὰ γὰρ δύο ἔτη ἐκέλευσεν αὐτὸν ὁ βασιλεὺς ἐξενεχθῆναι, καθὼς προλέλεκται, ἐκ τῆς πανζόφου καὶ κρυμώδους ἐκείνης εἱρκτῆς καὶ ἐναπόκλειστον γενέσθαι, δεδεμένον τὸν αὐχένα ἁλύσει καὶ τοὺς πόδας ἐν ξύλῳ ἠσφαλισμένον, ἐν ἑτέρᾳ διαφερούσῃ εἱρκτῇ τοῦ αὐτοῦ
20 Πραιτωρίου.
(17) Μετὰ δὲ τέσσαρας μῆνας τῆς αὐτοῦ καθείρξεως ἐν τῇ τοιαύτῃ εἱρκτῇ, ἐν ὑπομνήσει γέγονεν ὁ προλεχθεὶς ἀσεβὴς ἄναξ περὶ τῶν αὐτοῦ μαθητῶν, Θεοδώρου λέγω καὶ Θεοφάνους. Τίς δὲ ἡ αἰτία τῆς τοιαύτης ὑπομνήσεως περὶ τῶν αὐτοῦ μαθητῶν πρὸς τὸν βασιλέα γέγονεν, ἔνθεν
25 ἐρῶ. Στέφανός τις ὑπῆρχεν, ἀσηκρῆτις τῇ ἀξίᾳ· οὗτος ἐν γνώσει ἦν τῷ θεράποντι τοῦ Χριστοῦ Μιχαὴλ καὶ τοῖς αὐτοῦ μαθηταῖς, καὶ ἦν ὑπ' αὐτῶν νουθετούμενος τὰ τῆς ὀρθοδοξίας διδάγματα. Ὅστις καὶ μικρὸν ὕστερον ὑποβληθεὶς παρά τινων μισοχρίστων τῷ τυράννῳ ὡς ἄτε ὀρθόδοξος καὶ ἔμπροσθεν αὐτοῦ ἀχθείς, πολλάς τε τιμωρίας καὶ θλίψεις
30 ὑπ' αὐτοῦ παθὼν καὶ μὴ δυνηθεὶς καρτερῆσαι συνέθετο καὶ καθυπέγραψε τῇ αὐτοῦ εἰκονομάχῳ αἱρέσει. Πρὸς ὃν ὁ ἐν ἁγίοις πατὴρ ἡμῶν Μιχαὴλ

AG
6. περιέπεσε G: -ν A   14. διέλειπε G: -ν A   17. πανζόφου G : πανζόφους A | κρυμώδους G: κρυμνώδους A   30. καθυπέγραψε G: -ν A

they did not permit anyone to converse with him, and he was guarded by two savage and unmerciful soldiers who did not allow the monk named Job who attended to him to see him even for a short time or to converse with him at all). As a result of such oppression and constraint, our father and confessor of saintly memory, the great Michael, fell victim to a most grievous illness for a period of two years, as a consequence of old age and his many afflictions, and he was hindered by dim-sightedness and a bent back.[116]

Nevertheless, a certain Euphrosyne, a faithful and orthodox nun, comforted this all-holy man greatly and provided for his bodily needs.[117] Through the years which he spent in the other cell after he had recovered from that most grievous illness and had been taken from that utterly dim, odorous cell and enclosed within a different one, she did not cease serving him and sending him food, drink and a covering for his body with the help of the man who attended him. For after two years the emperor commanded that he be removed from that extremely dark and icy cell, as has been said before, and enclosed within a different one in the same Praetorium, bound and secured with his neck in chains and his feet in stocks.

17. Theophilos hears of the proselytizing activities of the four monks

After four months of his confinement in this prison, the aforesaid impious ruler received a report about Michael's disciples Theodore and Theophanes. The reason for this report to the emperor concerning Michael's disciples was as follows: [239] there was a certain Stephen who belonged to the rank of *asekretis*.[118] He was acquainted with the servant of Christ Michael and with his disciples, and was advised by them concerning the orthodox teachings. After a short time he was denounced to the tyrant by some Christ-haters as being orthodox. After being summoned before the emperor, he suffered many punishments and afflictions at his hands and as he was unable to endure these, he accepted and subscribed to the tyrant's icon-fighting heresy. When our father Michael of saintly memory learned of this affair he sent him

ταῦτα μαθὼν παρακλητικαῖς ἐπιστολαῖς ἐχρήσατο, τοῦτον ἀνακαλούμενος καὶ ἀποστρέψαι παραινῶν ἐκ τῆς τοιαύτης αἱρέσεως. Ὅ δὴ καὶ πεποίηκεν, εἰ καὶ μικρόν τι, ὡς ἄνθρωπος δειλανθεὶς τὰς πικρὰς τιμωρίας τοῦ ἀνηλεοῦς τυράννου ὑπέκυψε τῇ αὐτοῦ ἀθέσμῳ καὶ
5 παρανόμῳ αἱρέσει. Ἔσχατον δὲ ταῖς τοῦ ἁγίου διδασκαλίαις καὶ παραινέσεσι πεπαρρησιασμένῃ τῇ φωνῇ ἐκήρυξέ τε καὶ ὡμολόγησεν ἐν εἰκόνι περιγραπτὸν προσκυνεῖν καὶ σέβεσθαι τὸν Κύριον ἡμῶν Ἰησοῦν Χριστόν. Ὅντινα Στέφανον, πολλὰς τιμωρίας προσαγαγὼν ὁ μισόχριστος τύραννος καὶ μὴ ἰσχύσας τούτου τὴν κατὰ Θεὸν ἔνστασιν νικῆσαι,
10 ὑπερορίᾳ κατεδίκασε, τὰ δὲ αὐτοῦ χρήματα τῷ βασιλικῷ ταμιείῳ προσενεχθῆναι ἐκέλευσεν.

Οὐ μόνον δὲ τοῦτον τὸν προλεχθέντα Στέφανον ὁ ἐν ἁγίοις πατὴρ ἡμῶν καὶ ὁμολογητὴς Μιχαὴλ ὑπὲρ Χριστοῦ καὶ τῆς αὐτοῦ εἰκόνος μαρτυρῆσαι πέπεικεν, ἀλλὰ καὶ ἕτερόν τινα, Καλλονᾶν τοὔνομα, τῇ ἀξίᾳ σπαθάριον,
15 ὅστις καὶ γνώριμος αὐτοῦ ὑπῆρχεν, ταῖς νουθετικαῖς αὐτοῦ καὶ στερροποιαῖς ἐπιστολαῖς ἐναποθανεῖν τῇ ἀθλήσει καὶ ὁμολογίᾳ τοῦ Χριστοῦ πεποίηκεν. Ἅτινα μαθὼν ὁ προλεχθεὶς μισόχριστος ἄναξ τοσοῦτον ἐξήφθη τῷ θυμῷ, ὡς ὑπερζέσαι αὐτόν.

Τούτων ἕνεκα τῶν αἰτιῶν ἡ ὑπόμνησις τούτων πρὸς τὸν ἀλιτήριον καὶ
20 παμβέβηλον ἄνακτα παρὰ τῶν μισοχρίστων αὐτοῦ ὑπασπιστῶν γέγονεν, οὑτωσὶ λεγόντων · Δέσποτα αὐτοκράτορ, ἥκασί τινες τέσσαρες μοναχοὶ ἐκ τῆς ἁγίας πόλεως, ὡς αὐτοὶ λέγουσιν, ὄντες, ἐπὶ τοῦ πρό σου βεβασιλευκότος ἀποσταλέντες παρὰ τοῦ αὐτῶν ἀρχιεράρχου μετὰ καὶ ἐπιστολῶν τινων, τὴν πάροδον ποιούμενοι πρὸς τὴν μεγαλόπολιν Ῥώμην,
25 πρὸς τὸ διαστρέψαι τὸν ὀρθοδοξότατον καὶ πιστότατον βασιλέα Λέοντα καὶ πεῖσαι τοῦτον τοῦ προσκυνεῖν τὰ εἴδωλα, ἃ αὐτοὶ ἁγίας εἰκόνας λέγουσιν εἶναι, ἀνάπλεοι ὄντες τῆς αὐτῶν εἰδωλολάτρου πίστεως. Ὅθεν καὶ ὡς πρὸς ἀρραγῆ πέτραν τῆς αὐτοῦ ὀρθοδόξου πίστεως προσκόψαντες, οὐ μόνον τοῦτον τῆς ὀρθοδόξου πίστεως καθελεῖν οὐκ ἴσχυσαν, ἀλλὰ
30 καὶ αὐτοί, πολλὰ ὑπ' αὐτοῦ διδαχθέντες καὶ νουθεσίαις καὶ παρακλήσεσι παντοίαις ὑποβληθέντες οὐδὲν ἐκ τῶν τοιούτων νουθεσιῶν καὶ παρακλήσεων ἐκαρπώσαντο ὄφελος. Καίπερ τοῦ βασιλέως τιμὰς

AG
10. κατεδίκασε G: -ν A   14. ἕτερόν G: ἕτετερον A | Καλλονᾶν A: Καλωνὰν G   15. γνώριμος G: σύντεκνος A   26. ἃ : ἃς codd.

hortatory letters and he called on him and exhorted him to turn away from such heresy. Which indeed Stephen did, but only for a short time since being human he was frightened by the relentless punishments of the unmerciful tyrant and submitted to the emperor's wicked and unlawful heresy. Finally, moved by the saint's teachings and admonishments, he proclaimed and confessed outspokenly that he worshipped and revered our Lord Jesus Christ as He is circumscribed in an icon.[119] The Christ-hating tyrant, inflicting many punishments on this same Stephen yet failing to overcome his godly resistance, condemned him to exile and commanded that his possessions be delivered up to the imperial treasury.

Not only did our father and confessor Michael of saintly memory persuade the aforesaid Stephen to bear witness on behalf of Christ and His icon, but with his admonishing and strengthening letters he also caused another man, Kallonas by name, a *spatharios* by rank,[120] who was an acquaintance of his, to remain in the contest and confession of Christ until his very death. When the aforesaid Christ-hating ruler learned of these matters he boiled over, so enflamed was he with anger.[121]

For all these reasons, the criminal and wholly depraved ruler received a report about the monks from his Christ-hating bodyguards[122] who addressed him in the following manner: 'Lord and absolute ruler, four monks arrived hailing, so they themselves say, from the holy city. In the lifetime of the emperor who preceded you, they were dispatched by their prelate with certain letters as they journeyed to the great city of Rome, in order to lead astray the wholly orthodox and faithful emperor Leo and to persuade him to worship idols which they call holy images, since they were full of their idolatrous faith. When they stumbled on the unbreakable rock of his orthodox faith, not only were they powerless to sway him from his orthodox faith, but they themselves, though they were taught many things by him and exposed to all manner of admonitions and exhortations, derived no profit from these admonitions and exhortations. Although the emperor promised them manifold honours and the

---

28. 'they stumbled on the unbreakable rock': cf. Ps. 90:12 (91:12); Mt. 4:6; Lu. 4:11; Ro. 9:32

παντοίας καὶ ὑπερβαλλούσας ὑποσχέσεις ὑποσχομένου καὶ θρόνων μεγίστων, εἰ ἐπιστρέψαντες ἐκ τῆς μυσαρᾶς τῶν εἰκονολατρῶν, μᾶλλον δὲ εἰδωλολατρῶν, αἱρέσεως συνθῶνται τῇ καθολικῇ ἐκκλησίᾳ, οὐχ εἵλοντο οὔτε μὴν ὑπήκουσαν ταῖς ὀρθοδόξοις αὐτοῦ διδασκαλίαις.
5 Ὅθεν καὶ ἀσχέτῳ θυμῷ κατ᾽ αὐτῶν ληφθεὶς παντοίαις θλίψεσι καὶ τιμωρίαις καθυπέβαλεν, ἴσως πεῖσαι αὐτοὺς καραδοκῶν διὰ τῶν τοιούτων θλίψεων συνθέσθαι τῇ ἀληθείᾳ. Ὡς δὲ εἶδεν ἑαυτὸν καθυστεροῦντα καὶ μεταστῆσαι μὴ δυνάμενον, τὸν μὲν ἔξαρχον αὐτῶν καὶ διδάσκαλον, ὃν καὶ σύγκελλον διαβεβαιοῦνται εἶναι τοῦ
10 ἀρχιεράρχου τῆς ἁγίας Χριστοῦ τοῦ Θεοῦ ἡμῶν πόλεως, μετὰ καὶ ἑτέρου τινὸς γηραιοῦ ἐν τῇ τῆς Φιάλης εἱρκτῇ ἐναποκλείστους γενέσθαι ἐκέλευσεν, τοὺς δὲ αὐτοῦ δύο μαθητὰς ὑπερορίᾳ κατεδίκασεν ἐν τῇ νήσῳ Ἀφουσίᾳ. Διὸ καὶ ἔκτοτε οὐκ ἐπαύσαντο δι᾽ ἐπιστολῶν γράφειν καὶ ἀναπείθειν τοὺς ὀρθοδόξως βιοῦν ἐθέλοντας, καὶ ἐκταράσσουσι
15 τοῖς αὐτῶν ἀθέοις δόγμασι τὸ τῶν ὀρθοδόξων ἱερέων τε καὶ βασιλέων δόγμα, καὶ οὐκ ἐῶσιν ἠρεμεῖν καὶ ἐν γαλήνῃ διάγειν τὸ τῶν ὀρθοδόξων σύστημα. Ὅθεν καὶ τοὺς προσφιλεῖς σου καὶ συγγνώμονας Στέφανόν τε τὸν ἀσηκρῆτις καὶ Καλλονᾶν τὸν σπαθάριον, τοὺς εὐγενεστάτους καὶ λογιμωτάτους ἄνδρας, ἔπεισαν ἀρνήσασθαι τὸ σὸν ὀρθόδοξον καὶ
20 ἀποστολικὸν καὶ βασιλικὸν δόγμα, καὶ μέχρι θανάτου ποινὰς καὶ μάστιγας καὶ ὑφαιρέσεις πραγμάτων καθυπομεῖναι καὶ μὴ συνθέσθαι τῇ ἀληθείᾳ.᾽
(18) Ταῦτα ἀκούσας ὁ βασιλεὺς Θεόφιλος καὶ μέγα στενάξας καὶ λεοντιαῖον βρύξας καὶ τὼ χεῖρε τὰς ὄψεις παίων καὶ τὸ ᾽οὐαὶ᾽ ἀναβοῶν
25 ἐκέλευσε τοὺς αὐτοῦ μαθητάς, τοῦ θεσπεσίου λέγω Μιχαήλ, τοὺς ἁγίους Θεόδωρον καὶ Θεοφάνην, ἐκ τῆς νήσου Ἀφουσίας διὰ ταχυδρόμου ἐπανελθεῖν, τὸν δὲ ἅγιον Μιχαὴλ σὺν τῷ πανοσίῳ Ἰώβ, ὡς ἄτε γηραιοὺς καὶ ἐκ τῶν πολλῶν θλίψεών τε καὶ ἀσθενειῶν τετρυχωμένους καὶ ἀμβλυωπίᾳ καὶ κυφότητι κεκρατημένους καὶ τεταλαιπωρημένους ἔκ τε
30 πείνης καὶ δίψης καὶ γυμνότητος, ἁλύσεσι δεθῆναι προσέταξε τοὺς αὐτῶν τιμίους αὐχένας καὶ τοὺς πόδας ἐν ξύλῳ ἀσφαλισθῆναι καὶ μὴ ἐᾶν τινα τούτοις προσομιλεῖν, ὅπως μὴ διαστρέφωνται παρ᾽ αὐτῶν πρὸς

AG
3-4. οὐχ εἵλοντο A: οὐκ εἵλαντο G 6. καραδοκῶν A: δοκῶν G 9. διαβεβαιοῦνται G: διαβεβαιοῦντα A 11. Φιάλης : Φιάλεως A Φιάλεος G 14. βιοῦν: βιοῖν codd. 18. Καλλονᾶν A: Καλωνᾶν G

surpassing promise of high thrones if they should turn away from the abominable heresy of the image worshippers, or rather the idolaters, and obey the catholic Church, they did not accept or even [240] heed his orthodox teachings. Seized with ungovernable rage, he subjected them to all sorts of afflictions and punishments, expecting perhaps to persuade them through such afflictions to embrace the truth. When he perceived that he was failing and was unable to sway them, he commanded that their leader, the teacher who they asserted was *synkellos* of the bishop of the holy city of Christ our God, be confined with another old man in the Phiale prison, while he condemned his two disciples to exile on the island of Aphousia. Wherefore they did not cease thereafter writing letters and persuading those who wished to live in an orthodox manner. They are throwing into disarray the doctrine of orthodox priests and emperors with their godless doctrines and they are not allowing the orthodox community to remain undisturbed and to live in peace. They even persuaded Stephen, the *asekretis*, and Kallonas, the *spatharios*, both most noble and learned men, well disposed to you and of like mind with you, to deny your orthodox, apostolic and imperial doctrine and to endure penalties, whippings and the confiscation of property even until death rather than to heed the truth.'[123]

18. The return of Theodore and Theophanes from the island of Aphousia

When the emperor Theophilos heard of these matters he let out great groans, gnashed his teeth like a lion,[124] struck his face with his two hands and cried out, 'Woe is me!'. He commanded by means of a swift messenger that the disciples of the divine Michael, the holy Theodore and Theophanes, return from the island of Aphousia. As for the holy Michael and saintly Job, since they were old,[125] worn down by many afflictions and illnesses, overpowered by dim-sightedness and stooping, and suffering from hunger, thirst and nakedness, he ordered that their venerable necks be bound with chains and their feet made fast in stocks. He also commanded that no one have intercourse with them lest they be led astray by them to idolatrous worship.

τὸ τῆς εἰδωλολατρείας σέβας. Ὦ Χριστέ μου, πῶς ὑμνήσω σοῦ τῆς ἀπεράντου σοφίας καὶ ἀνεξικακίας τὸ πέλαγος, ὅτι βλασφημούμενος παρὰ ἀσεβῶν στομάτων ἀνέχει καὶ μακροθυμεῖς, ὅτι καὶ ἡ τῆς μορφῆς σου εἰκών, ἣν διὰ τὴν ἡμῶν σωτηρίαν ἐκ παρθένου ἁγίας καὶ Θεοτόκου
5 ἀνέλαβες, εἴδωλον παρ' αὐτῶν ὠνομάσθη τε καὶ ἐλέχθη; Ὦ παμμίαροι καὶ ἐχθροὶ τῆς ἀληθείας, ἀχάριστα κτίσματα καὶ τοῦ πονηροῦ πλάσματα, θεολογικῶς εἰπεῖν, ὑπὲρ ὧν Χριστὸς δωρεὰν ἀπέθανεν, ἡ εἰκὼν τοῦ Χριστοῦ, ὃν ὑμεῖς ἀσεβοῦντες διὰ τὴν τῶν ἀνθρώπων ὑφόρασιν θεὸν τῷ δοκεῖν ὁμολογεῖτε, εἴδωλόν ἐστιν ὡς Ἀπόλλωνος, καὶ τῆς αὐτοῦ μητρὸς
10 τῆς εὐλογημένης Θεοτόκου ὡς Ἀρτέμιδος, καὶ τῶν αὐτοῦ ἁγίων ὡς τῶν λοιπῶν ψευδωνύμων θεῶν; εἰς κενὸν ἡ ἐνανθρώπησις αὐτοῦ ἐγένετο; Εἰς κενὸν ἡ τῶν ἀποστόλων διδαχὴ καὶ ἡ τῶν οἰκουμενικῶν συνόδων συνάθροισις; Ἀλλ' ἄπαγε. Οὐκ ἔστιν οὕτως. Οὐκ ἔστιν ὡς ὑμεῖς φατε. Ἡμεῖς δέ, ὁ τοῦ Χριστοῦ λαός, τὸ *βασίλειον ἱεράτευμα*, οἱ ὀρθοδόξως
15 προσκυνοῦντες κατὰ τὴν τῶν ἁγίων ἀποστόλων διδαχὴν ἐν εἰκόνι περιγραπτὸν τὸν Κύριον ἡμῶν Ἰησοῦν Χριστόν, τούτους καταπτύσαντες καὶ τὴν αὐτῶν ληρώδη διδασκαλίαν, προσσχῶμεν τῇ λοιπῇ ἐξηγήσει τῆς ἀθλήσεως τῶν ἁγίων καὶ ὁμολογητῶν πατέρων ἡμῶν, Μιχαὴλ φημὶ καὶ Θεοδώρου καὶ Θεοφάνους, τῶν λαμπρῶν τῆς ἐκκλησίας φωστήρων, τῶν
20 δίκην ἡλίου λαμψάντων καὶ φωτισάντων τὴν ὑφήλιον ἅπασαν τῇ τῶν ὀρθῶν δογμάτων φαιδρότητι.

Εἶτα, καθὼς προλέλεκται, ὅτι παρὰ τῶν αὐτοῦ ὑπηρετῶν ἐν ὑπομνήσει γέγονεν ὁ προλεχθεὶς βέβηλος ἄναξ περὶ τῆς τῶν ἁγίων πατέρων ἡμῶν ἐνστάσεώς τε καὶ ὁμολογίας, οὐ μὴν ἀλλὰ καὶ περὶ τῆς αὐτῶν ὀρθοδόξου
25 διδασκαλίας, ἐκέλευσε διὰ ταχυδρόμου ἐν σπουδῇ πολλῇ εἰσαχθῆναι αὐτοὺς ἐν τῇ πανευδαίμονι Κωνσταντινουπόλει. Ὁ τοῦ παρανόμου δὲ βασιλέως παρανομώτατος ὑπηρέτης, ὁ ἀποσταλεὶς ἀγαγεῖν αὐτούς, καταλαβὼν ἐν σπουδῇ τὴν προλεχθεῖσαν νῆσον, ἐν πολλῷ τῷ τάχει τούτους ἁρπάσας ἦγεν ἐπὶ τὴν πόλιν, τὴν αἰτίαν δι' ἣν αὐτοὺς ἦγεν ἐπὶ
30 τὴν πόλιν, ἀγνοεῖν διαβεβαιούμενος. Εἰσελθόντων δὲ τῶν ἁγίων ἐν τῇ πόλει ἰουλίῳ μηνὶ ὀγδόῃ, ἰνδικτιῶνος τεσσαρεσκαιδεκάτης τότε

AG
8. ὑφόρασιν : ὑφώρασιν codd.   22. ὑπομνήσει A: ὑπομνήμασι G   29-30. τὴν αἰτίαν -- πόλιν A: om. G

O my Christ, how shall I praise the sea of Thy boundless wisdom and forbearance, since Thou endurest and art patient while blasphemed by the mouths of the impious and since even the icon of Thy form which Thou didst assume through the holy Virgin and Mother of God for our salvation has been called and declared an idol by them? O utterly abominable enemies of truth, unthankful creatures and formations of the devil[126] (to speak in the manner of the theologian), on whose behalf Christ died without reward, is the icon of Christ, Whom you, impious as you are, out of respect for men confess in appearance to be God, an idol like one of Apollo? And is the icon of His Mother, the blessed Mother of God, like one of Artemis? Are the icons of His saints like those of the other false-named gods? Was Christ's incarnation then in vain? Was the teaching of the apostles in vain, as well as the gathering of the universal councils? Away with you, it is not so. It is not as you say. Let us, the people of God, the royal priesthood, who [241] worship our Lord Jesus Christ in an orthodox fashion, as He is circumscribed within an icon according to the teaching of the holy apostles, let us spit upon them and their foolish teaching and pass to the remaining narrative of the contest of our saintly confessors and fathers, Michael, Theodore and Theophanes. They were bright luminaries of the Church, who shone in the manner of the sun and illuminated everything under the sun in the brightness of the correct doctrines.[127]

Thereupon since, as has been said, the profane ruler received a report from his servants not only of the resistance and confession of our holy fathers, but also of their orthodox teaching, he sent a command by means of a swift messenger that they should be brought back with all speed to the all-fortunate Constantinople. After the utterly lawless servant of the lawless emperor who was dispatched to fetch them had speedily reached the aforesaid island, he seized them and conducted them with all haste to the city, insisting that he was ignorant of the reason for bringing them to the city.[128] When the saints arrived in the city on the eighth of July of the fourteenth indiction,[129] the man who had

---

6. 'unthankful creatures and formations of the Devil': cf. Lu. 6:35; Greg. Naz. Or. 31 (PG 36, 144D)   14. I Pe. 2:9

κρατούσης, εἰσῆλθεν ὁ ἀγαγὼν αὐτοὺς μονώτατος, καὶ δῆλα τὰ κατ᾽ αὐτοὺς τῷ βασιλεῖ πεποίηκεν. Ὅθεν καὶ προσετάγη παρ᾽ αὐτοῦ καθεῖρξαι αὐτοὺς ἐν τῇ δημοσίᾳ εἱρκτῇ, τῇ οὕτω λεγομένῃ Πραιτώριον. Μετὰ δὲ τὸ πρωῒ ἐκέλευσεν αὐτοὺς παραστῆναι ἔμπροσθεν αὐτοῦ.

5 Τῆς δὲ ἀφίξεως αὐτῶν ἐν ταῖς διανοίαις πάντων προεγνωσμένης ἤδη καὶ προσδοκωμένης, ὡς τῷ βασιλεῖ παραστησομένους καὶ δίκας ὑφέξοντας, οὐδὲν ἦν ἄλλο ἰδεῖν καὶ ἀκοῦσαι ἀλλ᾽ ἢ φόβους καὶ ἀπειλάς, ἃς οἱ ὑπηρέται τοῦ παμπονήρου βασιλέως προσῆγον αὐτοῖς, οἱ μὲν ἀπηνῶς λέγοντες πρὸς αὐτούς· Συντόμως καὶ ἄνευ πάσης ἀντιλογίας
10 ὑποκύψατε τοῖς βασιλικοῖς θεσπίσμασιν, ὦ δυστυχέστατοι, καὶ μὴ θελήσητε τῇ ὑμῶν ἀπονοίᾳ κακῶς ἀπολέσθαι, τῶν δὲ ἀνήκεστα παθεῖν λεγόντων, εἰ παρακούσωσι τοῦ βασιλέως διαμαρτυρόμενοι, ἑτέρων δὲ φασκόντων·· Δαιμόνιον ἔχετε· μὴ ὑμεῖς σοφώτεροί ἐστε τῶν τῆς ἐκκλησίας ἀρχιερέων καὶ τοῦ θεοστέπτου ἄνακτος; Καὶ ἕτερα πάμπολλα καὶ χείρονα
15 τούτων οἱ τοῦ βασιλέως κάκιστοι ὑπηρέται προσῆγον αὐτοῖς, τοῦτο μὲν παραινοῦντες, τοῦτο δὲ καὶ ἐκφοβοῦντες. Καὶ ταῦτα μὲν πρὶν τῷ Χρυσοτρικλίνῳ, ἐν ᾧ ὁ βασιλεὺς ἐκαθέζετο, προσκαλεῖν αὐτοὺς ἤκουον. (19) Εἰσελθόντες δὲ καὶ τῆς πύλης ἐπιβάντες, προάγοντος αὐτῶν τοῦ ἐπάρχου, ὤφθη αὐτοῖς ὁ βασιλεὺς πολλοῦ θυμοῦ καὶ ὀργῆς πνέων,
20 ἱκανῶν αὐτῷ τῶν τῆς συγκλήτου βουλῆς τῶν ἀρχόντων παρισταμένων. Ὡς δὲ μέχρι τούτου ἦλθεν ὁ ἔπαρχος, ἀπέστη ἀπ᾽ αὐτῶν μόνους αὐτοὺς καταλείψας ἐνώπιον τῶν τοῦ βασιλέως ὀφθαλμῶν. Εἰσῆλθον δὲ οἱ ἅγιοι μετὰ πολλοῦ τοῦ θάρσους μηδὲν δειλιῶντες, ἔχοντες ἐν ἑαυτοῖς τὸν τοῦ Θεοῦ φόβον τοῦ εἰπόντος· *Μὴ φοβεῖσθε ἀπὸ τῶν ἀποκτεινόντων τὸ*
25 *σῶμα, τὴν δὲ ψυχὴν μὴ δυναμένων ἀποκτεῖναι· φοβήθητε δὲ μᾶλλον τὸν δυνάμενον μετὰ τὸ ἀποκτεῖναι ἐμβαλεῖν εἰς γέενναν,* ὥστε ἐκ τῆς ὄψεως αὐτῶν ἔκθαμβον γενέσθαι τὸν βασιλέα. Εἰσῆλθον γὰρ οὐχ ὡς εἰς ἆθλον ἢ παγκράτιον, ἀλλ᾽ ὡς εἰς γάμον κληθέντες. Ὡς δὲ παρέστησαν τῷ βασιλεῖ, προσεγγίσαι αὐτοὺς αὐστηρᾷ καὶ
30 θρασείᾳ φωνῇ παρεκελεύσατο καὶ μέχρις αὐτοῦ ἐλθεῖν. Καὶ λέγει

AG
6. προσδοκωμένης A: προσδοκομένης G   8. αὐτοῖς A: αὐτοὺς G   12. διαμαρτυρόμενοι: -- μένων codd.   20-p.84, 25. -- κλήτου -- πάντων προ -- A: om. G   24. ἀποκτεινόντων G: ἀποκτεννόντων A   26. ὥστε G: ὡς A

fetched them entered entirely alone and reported to the emperor about them. He was commanded by him to confine them in the public prison called the Praetorium. After daybreak the emperor commanded them to appear before him.[130]

When their arrival was known in advance and expected in the minds of all and it was understood that they were to be brought before the emperor and to undergo punishment, all that was to be seen or heard were the terrors and threats to which the servants of the wholly depraved emperor subjected them. Some said harshly to them, 'Bow before the imperial decrees at once and without any dispute, O unfortunate ones, and do not choose to perish wretchedly in your madness.' Some said that they would suffer irreparably if they should disobey the emperor and protest,[131] and others said, 'You are possessed of a devil; do you mean to say that you are wiser than the bishops of the Church and the God-crowned ruler?' The evil servants of the emperor added many other and worse threats to these, at times counselling and at others intimidating them. They heard these threats until they were summoned to the Golden Triclinium[132] where the emperor was sitting.

19. The first audience with the emperor Theophilos

With the prefect preceding them they entered and crossed the threshold and beheld the emperor breathing forth great anger and fury, while a fair number of officials of the senate were in attendance. After accompanying them this far, the prefect stepped back leaving them alone before the eyes of the emperor.[133] But the saints entered courageously, fearing nothing, as they possessed [242] within themselves the fear of God, Who said: 'And fear not them which kill the body, but are not able to destroy the soul: but rather fear him which is able to destroy both soul and body in hell.' The emperor was struck with amazement at their appearance. For they entered not as if summoned to a contest or a wrestling match, but as if to a marriage feast.[134]

When they stood before the emperor, he commanded them in a harsh and arrogant voice to approach and come before him. He said to them, 'What is

---

13. cf. Mt. 11:18; Lu.7:33; Jn. 7:20, 8:48, 52   24-6. cf. Mt. 10:28; Lu. 12:4-5

αὐτοῖς· 'Ποίας χώρας ἐστέ;' Λέγουσιν αὐτῷ οἱ ἅγιοι· 'Τῆς Μωαβίτιδος.' Πάλιν σκληροτέρως ἀποκριθεὶς ἔφη αὐτοῖς· 'Καὶ διὰ τί ἤλθετε ἐνταῦθα;' καὶ πρὶν τούτους ἀπολογίσασθαι, ἐπέτρεψεν ἄνδρας ἰσχυροὺς τῇ ῥώμῃ παίειν αὐτῶν τὰς ὄψεις. Ῥαπιζομένων δὲ τῶν ἁγίων ἀνηλεῶς ἐπὶ πολλὴν
5 ὥραν καὶ μὴ δυναμένων αὐτῶν ἵστασθαι ἐκ τῶν ἀφορήτων πληγῶν (ἐσκοτίζοντο γὰρ τῇ φορᾷ τῶν μαστίγων, ὥστε πίπτειν αὐτοὺς καὶ ἀνίστασθαι κατὰ τὸν θεῖον Ἐλεάζαρον, ὃν λάξ γέ τοι κατὰ τῶν κενεώνων ἔτυπτον, ὅπως ἐξανίστατο πίπτων) ἐκράτησεν ἕκαστος αὐτῶν τοῦ στήθους τοῦ παίοντος αὐτόν, καὶ οὕτως ἑδραίως ἱστάμενοι ἐδέχοντο τὰς διὰ
10 Χριστὸν μάστιγας ἀμετάστρεπτοι, ἕως ἂν παύσασθαι τοὺς παίοντας ὁ βασιλεὺς ἐκέλευσεν.

Τί τούτου κοσμιώτερον καὶ παραδοξότερον, ὥστε ἐξισωθῆναι τῇ ἀθλήσει τῷ ἑαυτῶν ποιητῇ; Ὡς γὰρ ὁ ἐμὸς Χριστὸς κατὰ πρόσωπον Πιλάτου ἑστὼς ἐρραπίσθη, οὕτω καὶ οἱ αὐτοῦ γνήσιοι θεράποντες δι'
15 αὐτὸν καὶ τὴν αὐτοῦ εἰκόνα τὰς ὄψεις χαίροντες ἐπαίοντο. Παυσαμένων δὲ τῶν παιόντων, λέγει πρὸς αὐτοὺς ὁ βασιλεύς· 'Τίνος χάριν ἐληλύθατε ἐνταῦθα, ἀνόσιοι;' Ἐβούλετο δὲ αὐτῶν ἀκοῦσαι· ''Ὅτι τὴν αὐτὴν ὑμῖν ἀσπάσασθαι πίστιν βουλόμενοι τὴν μεθ' ὑμῶν οἴκησιν ἠσμενίσαμεν.'

Τῶν δὲ ἁγίων σιωπησάντων καὶ μηδ' ὅλως αὐτῷ ἀποκριναμένων καὶ εἰς
20 γῆν νενευκότων, ἔφη πρὸς τὸν ὕπαρχον ὁ βασιλεύς· 'Ἆρον τοὺς ἀνοσίους τούτους καὶ γράψον τὰ πρόσωπα αὐτῶν, ἐγκολάψας τούσδε τοὺς ἰάμβους, καὶ παράδος αὐτοὺς δύο τῶν τῆς Ἅγαρ υἱῶν, καὶ ἀπαγαγέτωσαν αὐτοὺς εἰς τὴν ἰδίαν πατρίδα.' Ἵστατο δὲ πλησίον τοῦ βασιλέως ὁ ἔχων τοὺς ἰάμβους, Χριστόδουλος τοὔνομα ὁ τούτους σκεψάμενος, ᾧ καὶ
25 ἐπαναγινώσκειν εἰς ἐπήκοον πάντων προσέταξεν, προσθεὶς καὶ τοῦτο· 'Κἂν οὔκ εἰσι καλοὶ κατὰ σύνταξιν, μή σοι μελέτω.' Τοῦτο δὲ εἴρηκεν εἰδὼς ὡς ἄριστα τούτοις ἤσκηται ἡ τῶν ποιητικῶν σκεμμάτων ἀκρίβεια καὶ εἰς ὅσον καταγελασθῶσιν παρὰ τῶν τοῦ Χριστοῦ ἀθλοφόρων. Καί τις παρὼν χαριζόμενος τῷ βασιλεῖ ἔφη· 'Οὐδέ εἰσιν ἄξιοι, ὦ δέσποτα,
30 οὗτοι, ἵνα κάλλιον ὦσιν οἱ ἴαμβοι.'

(20) Καὶ ταῦτα μὲν εἰς τοσοῦτον ἐκεῖνοι οἱ θρυλλολέκται εἶπόν τε καὶ πεπράχασιν. Ἡμεῖς δέ, εἰ μηδὲν κωλύει (καὶ γὰρ οἶδ' ὅτι βλάβην ἐκ

AG
8. ἐκράτησεν G: ἐκράτισεν A 10. ἀμετάστρεπτοι G: ἀμεταστρεπτὶ A 32. Ἡμεῖς: Ἡμᾶς codd.

your country?' and the holy men answered, 'The land of the Moabites.'[135] The emperor answered even more harshly and said to them, 'And why did you come here?'[136] and before they had explained, he ordered strong men to strike their faces forcefully. After the saints had been harshly beaten for a long time and were unable to stand on account of the unendurable blows (for they were made dizzy by the force of the whips so that they fell and were made to stand again in the manner of the divine Eleazar, who was beaten on the flanks even while underfoot, so that he arose again after falling),[137] each of the saints held on to the chest of the man who was beating him, and thus they stood steadfastly and unflinchingly received the whips for the sake of Christ until the emperor commanded the men who beat them to stop.[138]

What is more fitting and marvellous than this, that they were made equal to their Creator in contest?[139] Just as my Christ was smitten as He stood in the presence of Pilate,[140] so His true servants rejoiced as their countenances were struck for His sake and for the sake of His icon. When the men beating them had stopped, the emperor said to them, 'For what reason have you come here, impious ones?' He wished to hear them say, 'We have gladly chosen to dwell with you because we wish to embrace the same faith as yours.' But when the saints remained silent, returned no answer and bent their heads towards the ground, the emperor said to his prefect, 'Raise up these impious men and inscribe[141] their foreheads, incising these iambics, and hand them over to two of the sons of Hagar[142] that they may conduct them to their own country.' Near the emperor there stood a man named Christodoulos with the iambics which he had composed. The emperor commanded him to read them aloud in everyone's hearing and he added, 'Even if they are badly composed, never mind.' He said this, knowing how excellently the saints themselves practised accuracy in poetical composition and how much these verses would be ridiculed by the champions of Christ. One of those present, wishing to please the emperor, said, 'But they are not worthy, O lord, of better iambics.'[143]

20. The iambic verses

So much did those babblers[144] say and do. But as for us, if there is no objection, as indeed I know that we shall in no way sustain harm from these things, let

τούτων οὐδ' ὅλως ὑποστησόμεθα) καὶ τοὺς ἰάμβους ἐπεξέλθωμεν καὶ τούτους τῇ διηγήσει ἐνθήσωμεν. Εἰσὶ δὲ στίχοι ἴαμβοι δώδεκα, οἳ καὶ ἐγράφησαν ἐν τοῖς προσώποις τῶν ἁγίων καὶ ὁμολογητῶν Θεοδώρου καὶ Θεοφάνους, ἐπὶ βασιλέως Θεοφίλου ἐν τῷ Πραιτωρίῳ, ἔχοντες τὸν τύπον
5 τοῦτον·
πάντων ποθούντων προστρέχειν πρὸς τὴν πόλιν,
ὅπου πάναγνοι τοῦ Θεοῦ Λόγου πόδες
ἔστησαν εἰς σύστασιν τῆς οἰκουμένης,
ὤφθησαν οὗτοι τῷ σεβασμίῳ τόπῳ,
10 σκεύη πονηρὰ δεισιδαίμονος πλάνης.
Ἐκεῖσε πολλὰ λοιπὸν ἐξ ἀπιστίας
πράξαντες αἰσχρὰ δεινὰ δυσσεβοφρόνως,
ἐκεῖθεν ἠλάθησαν ὡς ἀποστάται.
Πρὸς τὴν πόλιν δὲ τοῦ κράτους πεφευγότες,
15 οὐκ ἐξαφῆκαν τὰς ἀθέσμους μωρίας.
Ὅθεν γραφέντες ὡς κακοῦργοι τὴν θέαν
κατακρίνονται καὶ διώκονται πάλιν.
Ἡμεῖς δέ, ὁ τοῦ Χριστοῦ λαός, τὸ φιλόχριστον ποίμνιον, ἀνατρέποντες αὐτοῦ τὴν τοιαύτην ληρωδίαν ἐροῦμεν πρὸς αὐτόν· ὦ ἀνόσιε καὶ πάσης
20 ἀληθείας ἐχθρέ, πάναγνον καλεῖς τὸν τοῦ Θεοῦ υἱόν, οὕτινος τὴν μορφὴν ἐν τῇ ἐκκλησίᾳ εἰκονιζομένην ἐξώρυξας καὶ πυρὶ παραδέδωκας; Καίπερ, εἰ ἦν σοι δυνατόν, καὶ αὐτὸ τὸ τῆς κλήσεως ὄνομα ἐξωλόθρευσας ἂν ἐκ τῆς τῶν χριστιανῶν ὁμηγύρεως, τοῦ μὴ καλεῖσθαι τοῦτον Χριστὸν καὶ Θεοῦ υἱόν. Πῶς δὲ καὶ ἁγίαν ὁμολογεῖς πόλιν, παμμίαρε, εἰς ἣν ὁ Υἱὸς
25 καὶ Λόγος τοῦ Θεοῦ διὰ τὴν ἡμῶν σωτηρίαν τὰ τῆς ἐνανθρωπήσεως ὑπέστη μυστήρια; Ἧς τοὺς οἰκήτορας διὰ τὴν εἰς αὐτὸν καὶ τὴν αὐτοῦ εἰκόνα ὁμολογίαν μικροῦ δεῖν κατέσφαξας; Καὶ εἰ πονηρὰ σκεύη κατὰ τὴν σὴν ψευδώνυμον ῥῆσίν εἰσιν οὗτοι οἱ ἅγιοι, τίνι τρόπῳ μετὰ καὶ ἐπιστολῆς θεογράφου πρὸς τὴν σὴν κακότεχνον γνώμην παρὰ τοῦ
30 ἀρχιτελετάρχου καὶ τῆς αὐτοῦ συνόδου καὶ τῶν τῆς ἐρήμου πατέρων, ὡς ἀληθῶς σοφοὶ καὶ τῇ πράξει καὶ γνώσει ἐπέμφθησαν; Καὶ εἰ, ὡς σὺ φῄς, ἐδιώχθησαν οὗτοι ἐκεῖθεν, ἡ ἐπιστολὴ πῶς ἐπεδόθη αὐτοῖς παρὰ τῆς

AG
2. Εἰσὶ G: -ν A   21. ἐξώρυξας A: ἐξόρυξας G   22. ἐξωλόθρευσας: ἐξολόθρευσας codd.   30. ἀρχιτελετάρχου A: ἀρχιτελετάρτου G

us quote and include in the narrative the iambics. The number of these iambic verses is twelve; they were inscribed on the foreheads of the saints and confessors Theodore and Theophanes in the Praetorium prison during the reign of emperor Theophilos and have the following form:

[243] When all men long to speed towards the town,
Wherein the Word of God's all-holy feet
Once stood to succour and preserve the world,
These men were seen within the sacred place,
Foul vessels of perverted heresy.
There many shameful deeds the villains wrought,
In lack of faith and impiousness of mind,
Till driven forth they were as apostates.
But fleeing to our city, seat of power,
They laid not down their lawless foolishness.
Thence branded criminals upon the brow
They are condemned and hunted back once more.[145]

But we the people of Christ, the Christ-loving flock, shall refute such nonsense of his and say to him: 'O impious one and enemy of all truth, do you call the Son of God "all-holy" even while obliterating and casting to the fire His form as it is depicted in the Church? And yet if it had been in your power you would have banished His very name and title from the community of the Christians so that He would not be called Christ and Son of God. How also do you confess that holy city, utterly abominable one, in which the Son and Word of God submitted to the mystery of incarnation for the sake of our salvation? Did you not all but slaughter its two citizens on account of their confession in Him and His holy icon? And if these saints are "foul vessels" according to your false expression, how is it that they were sent as truly wise both in actions and in mind to you who have wicked intentions with the divinely written letter from the chief priest and his synod and the fathers of the desert?[146] And if they were expelled from there as you say, how is it that this letter was given to them by the holy synod and the divine fathers? When

ἁγίας συνόδου καὶ τῶν θείων πατέρων; Ὅτε δὲ καὶ ἐν τῇ τοῦ κράτους πόλει εἰσῆλθον, τί πονηρὸν διεπράξαντο; Ἢ τί δεινὸν τίνι πεποίηκαν; Ὅτι ἐκ τοῦ τῆς αἱρέσεως σκότους πρὸς τὸ τῆς ἀληθείας φῶς ἐχειραγώγησαν πολλοὺς τῶν πιστῶν τῷ καθ᾽ ἑαυτῶν ὑποδείγματι καὶ διὰ τῶν αὐτῶν ὀρθοδόξων καὶ ἁγίων ἐπιστολῶν, τοῦτό σοι καταφαίνεται πονηρὸν καὶ μωρόν; Καὶ πῶς οὐκ ἂν εἶ καταγέλωτος ἄξιος ὁ τῆς ἀλουργίδος ἀνάξιος; Ὅτι δὲ καὶ γραφῆναι τούτων τὰς ὄψεις ἐκέλευσας, οὐδὲν ξένον τῆς σῆς ἀπονοίας καὶ παρανόμου γνώμης πεποίηκας, καὶ τούτους μὲν ἄκων καὶ μὴ βουλόμενος ἀπέδειξας Χριστοῦ μάρτυρας, σεαυτῷ δὲ ἐθησαύρισας αἰωνίαν κόλασιν, εἰς ἣν καταδικασθήσει παρὰ Χριστοῦ τοῦ Θεοῦ, οὕτινος τὴν σαρκομοιόμορφον εἰκόνα ἠθέτησας μετὰ τοῦ πατρός σου τοῦ Σατανᾶ. Τούτων δὲ τῶν ἁγίων μαρτύρων τὰς ὄψεις ἰδόντα τὰ χερουβὶμ καὶ ἡ φλογίνη ῥομφαία οὕτως ἐγγεγραμμένας, αἰδεσθήσονται καὶ τὰ νῶτα δώσουσι καὶ τὴν τοῦ παραδείσου εἴσοδον παραχωρήσουσιν. Ὅτι δὲ καὶ διῶξαι τούτους προτεθύμησαι, ὁ δίκαια κρίνων Θεὸς διὰ τῆς αὐτοῦ δικαίας ὀργῆς τοῦ τοιούτου σε σκοποῦ κωλύσειεν, ὅπως ἡ τοῦ Θεοῦ ἁγία καὶ ὑπερένδοξος πόλις, ἡ νέα Ἰερουσαλήμ, τοιούτους μὴ στερηθείη φωστῆρας, ἀλλ᾽ ἐν τῷ τῆς βασιλείας διαδήματι ὡς ὑπερτίμους λίθους ἐγκαταπήξασα κόσμον ἑαυτῇ περιποιήσηται. Καὶ σὲ μὲν οὐ μετὰ πολὺ ὀλέθριος θάνατος καὶ αἰωνία κόλασις παραδέξεται, τούτων δὲ τὰ μὲν ἱερὰ καὶ τίμια λείψανα ἡ τοῦ Θεοῦ ἐκκλησία ὡς θησαυρὸν ἄσυλον καὶ βασιλικὴν ἀλουργίδα παρ᾽ ἑαυτῇ ἐγκατακρύψειε, τὰς δὲ παναγνους αὐτῶν καὶ τιμίας ψυχὰς ἡ ἄνω Ἰερουσαλήμ, ἡ μήτηρ τῶν πρωτοτόκων, ἧς τεχνίτης καὶ δημιουργὸς ὁ Θεός, ὑποδέξεται αἰωνίως μετὰ πάντων τῶν ἁγίων ἀγαλλιωμένας.

(21) Ἀλλ᾽ ἐπὶ τὸ προκείμενον ἐπανέλθωμεν καὶ ἴδωμεν, τί ὁ τῆς ἀληθείας ἐχθρὸς διετάξατο, τί δὲ οἱ τοῦ Χριστοῦ μάρτυρες πεπόνθασιν. Ὡς γὰρ προείπομεν, ὅτι ἐκέλευσεν ὁ βασιλεὺς τῷ τοὺς ἰάμβους σκεψαμένῳ ἐπαναγνῶναι τούτους εἰς ἐπήκοον τῶν ἁγίων, τούτων ἀναγνωσθέντων ἐκέλευσεν ἐν τῷ Πραιτωρίῳ τούτους ἀπαχθέντας γραφῆναι τὰς ὄψεις. Ὡς δὲ ἐξῆλθον οἱ ἅγιοι ἐκ προσώπου τοῦ βασιλέως, ἀπαγόμενοι πρὸς τὸ

AG
1. Ὅτε : Ὅτι codd.   4. ἑαυτῶν G: ἑαυτὸν A   10. καταδικαθήσει G: καταδικαθήση A   14. δώσουσι G: -ν A   18. στερηθείη G: στερηθήει A   20. μετὰ A: μετ᾽ οὐ G   23. ἐγκατακρύψειε G: -ν A   26. καὶ A: ἵνα G   28. προείπομεν A: προείπωμεν G   29. ἐπαναγνῶναι : ἐπαναγνῶσαι codd.

they entered the imperial city, what evil did they commit? What dreadful thing have they done and to whom? Does it seem to you evil and foolish that they led by the hand many of the faithful from the darkness of heresy to the light of the truth through their personal examples or through those orthodox and holy letters? And why should you not be worthy of derision, you who are unworthy of the purple? In commanding that their faces be inscribed you did nothing which was alien to your madness and your lawless mind, and you involuntarily and unwillingly revealed them to be martyrs of Christ, treasuring up for yourself everlasting punishment to which you will be condemned by Christ our God Whose icon made after the flesh you denied along with your father Satan. The cherubim and flaming [244] sword, beholding the countenances of these holy martyrs thus inscribed, will be overawed, will retreat and yield to them entrance to paradise.[147] But because you were eager to persecute them, God Who judges righteously through His righteous wrath will hinder you from such an aim in order that the holy and exceedingly glorious city of God, the New Jerusalem, may not be deprived of such luminaries, but may place them around herself as an adornment, fixing them as all-precious stones in the diadem of the empire. And while destructive death and eternal punishment will receive you after a short time, the Church of God will hide away within herself their holy and honourable remains as an inviolate treasure[148] and cloak of imperial purple, while the Jerusalem which is above, the mother of the first-born, whose artificer and creator was God, will receive their perfectly pure and venerable souls as they rejoice eternally with all the saints.'

21. The second audience with the emperor: the saints are beaten again

But let us return to the task in front of us and see what the enemy of truth commanded and what the martyrs of Christ suffered. As we said before, the emperor commanded the man who had composed the iambics to read them aloud in the hearing of the saints and when they had been read, he commanded that they be led back to the Praetorium for the inscribing of their faces. As the saints departed from the presence of the emperor and were led back to the

---

9-10. 'treasuring up...punishment': cf. Ro. 2:5; Mt. 25:46   12-5. cf. Ge. 3: 24   17-20. cf. Is. 54: 11-2; Rev. 21:11-9   24. cf. Gal. 4:26-7; Hebr. 12:22

Πραιτώριον, ὡς ἤδη ἔφθασαν εἰς τὴν λεγομένην Θερμάστραν, ἰδοὺ αὖθις φαίνεταί τις τρέχων καὶ ἐπανακάμπτειν τούτους λέγων πρὸς τὸν βασιλέα. Σπουδῇ δὲ πολλῇ παρέστησαν τούτους πάλιν τῷ βασιλεῖ. Ὡς δὲ εἶδεν τούτους, ὁ βασιλεὺς λέγει πρὸς αὐτούς· ' Εἰκὸς ὑμᾶς ἀπελθόντας ἐν τῇ ὑμῶν γαίῃ λέγειν ὅτι τὸν βασιλέα Ῥωμαίων ἐνεπαίξαμεν· ἀλλ᾽ ἐγὼ πρότερον καταπαίξας ὑμᾶς καὶ δεινῶς βασανίσας οὕτως οἴκαδε ἀπολύσω.'

Καὶ κελεύει ἐκδυθῆναι τοὺς ἁγίους τὰς αὐτῶν ἐσθῆτας καὶ γυμνοὺς στῆναι ἔμπροσθεν αὐτοῦ. Ὡς δὲ ἐξεδύθησαν οἱ ἅγιοι τοῦ Χριστοῦ μάρτυρες, ἐκέλευσεν ὁ βασιλεὺς ἄνδρας δυνατοὺς τῇ ἰσχύϊ ἱμᾶσι λεπτοῖς δήσαντας αὐτῶν τὰς χεῖρας τεῖναι ἐπὶ πολὺ ἀνὰ ἓξ ἑκάστῳ αὐτῶν, ὅπως μὴ ἰσχύωσι τυπτόμενοι κλονεῖσθαι ὧδε κἀκεῖσε. Ταθέντων δὲ τῶν ἁγίων σφοδρῶς, ἐκέλευσεν ἕνα ἔμπροσθεν καὶ ἕνα ὄπισθεν σταθέντας βουνεύροις τύπτειν αὐτοὺς ἀφειδῶς. Ἐπὶ τοσοῦτον δὲ αὐτοὺς ἔτυψαν, ὥστε ἀλλαγῆναι ἑνὶ ἑκάστῳ αὐτῶν ἀνὰ τεσσάρων στρατιωτῶν. Τυπτομένων δὲ τῶν ἁγίων τά τε νῶτα αὐτῶν καὶ στήθη, οὐδὲν ἄλλο παρ᾽ αὐτῶν ἠκούετο ἢ τὸ ' Κύριε ἐλέησον' καὶ τὸ '' Ἁγία Θεοτόκε, ἐλθὲ εἰς βοήθειαν ἡμῶν.' Ὁ δὲ βασιλεὺς ταῦτα ἀκούσας εὐχομένων τῶν ἁγίων, θυμομαχῶν καὶ ἀπαύστως βοῶν καὶ καθ᾽ ἑαυτὸν ἐνορκῶν, τοὺς τύπτοντας ἐπέτρεπεν οὕτωσὶ λέγων · '' Ὡς ἔχεις ἐμέ, δὸς καλά.'

Ὡς δὲ κατέτεμον τοὺς ἁγίους ἐπὶ πολύ, ὥστε μὴ ἰσχύειν ἀνταποκρίνεσθαι, καὶ τοῦ αἵματος αὐτῶν οἱονεὶ ποταμίου ῥεύματος τὸ ἔδαφος ἅπαν καταχρώσαντος, συρῆναι ἐκέλευσε τούτους καὶ οὕτως ἀπαχθῆναι ἐν τῇ φυλακῇ. Ἐξελθόντων δὲ τῶν ἁγίων, μόλις ἴσχυον βαδίζειν ἐκ τῶν ἀφορήτων πληγῶν. Καὶ ἰδοὺ πάλιν ἕτερος καταδραμὼν στραφῆναι τούτους ἐκέλευσεν. Ὡς δὲ οὐκ ἴσχυον ἀνθυποστρέψαι οἱ ἅγιοι, ἐξελθών τις ἀπὸ τοῦ βασιλέως ἀποσταλείς, ἐπυνθάνετο παρ᾽ αὐτῶν λέγων· ' Τίνος χάριν τῷ θανάτῳ Λέοντος τοῦ βασιλέως ἐπεχάρητε; Καὶ διὰ τὶ προσφυγόντες αὐτῷ τὴν αὐτὴν αὐτῷ οὐκ ἐκρατήσατε πίστιν;' Πρὸς ὂν οἱ ἅγιοι μόλις ἀποκριθέντες εἶπον· ' Οὔτε τῷ θανάτῳ Λέοντος ἐπεχάρημεν, οὔτε τὴν αὐτοῦ εἱλόμεθα πίστιν, μᾶλλον δὲ θεομάχον αἵρεσιν, κρατῆσαι.' Ὁ λογοθέτης δὲ ἦν ὁ τοῦ δρόμου ὁ ταῦτα αὐτοὺς

AG
1. εἰς A: πρὸς G   4. τούτους A: τούτους πάλιν G | Εἰκὸς A: Εἰκὼς G   25. ἐκ A: ἀπὸ G

Praetorium, just as they reached the so-called Thermastra,[149] behold, someone again appeared running, telling them to return to the emperor. With all haste they presented them once again to the emperor. When the emperor beheld them, he said to them, 'It is likely that when you return to your land you will say, "We have made sport of the emperor of the Romans." But I shall only release you homeward after first mocking and torturing you cruelly.'[150]

He then commanded that the saints be stripped of their clothing and made to stand naked before him. When the holy martyrs of Christ had been stripped, the emperor ordered very strong men to bind their hands with fine thongs and then to stretch six thongs tightly over each of them, so that it would not be possible for them to sway back and forth as they were beaten. When the saints had been firmly stretched out, he commanded one man to stand in front and another behind each of them and he commanded them to strike the saints mercilessly with ox-hide whips. They struck them with so many blows that it was necessary to alternate four soldiers for each one of them. As the saints were being struck both on their backs and on their chests, nothing was heard from them except, 'Lord, have mercy,' and 'Holy Mother of God, come to our aid!'[151] When the emperor heard the saints praying thus he was angry and shouting ceaselessly and swearing to himself, he urged on those striking them, saying, 'As you love me, thrash them well!'[152]

When they had lacerated the saints to the extent that they were powerless to offer a reply and their blood like the stream of a river had stained the whole floor, he commanded that they [245] be dragged and thus taken back to the prison. As the saints departed they were scarcely able to walk after the unendurable blows. Yet behold, once again a man ran after them and ordered them to turn back. As the saints were unable to return, a messenger sent from the emperor went out and enquired of them, 'Why did you rejoice at the death of the emperor Leo? And why after seeking refuge with him did you not adopt his faith?' To which the saints, scarcely able to answer him, said, 'We did not rejoice at Leo's death, nor did we choose to adopt his faith, or rather God-opposing heresy.' The man who asked them these questions was the

---

4-5. 'return to your land': cf. Homer, *Odyssey*, XVI, 206; XIX, 484; XXI, 208; XXIV, 322

ἐρωτῶν. Λέγει δὲ πρὸς αὐτούς· 'Πορεύεσθε οὖν πρὸς τὴν ὑμῖν προσταχθεῖσαν παρὰ τοῦ βασιλέως ὁδόν.' Τότε εἰς τὸ Πραιτώριον εἰσήχθησαν οἱ ἅγιοι, σκοτίας ἤδη γεγονυίας.

(22) Μετὰ δὲ τέσσαρας ἡμέρας προκαθίσας ὁ ὕπαρχος ἐπὶ τοῦ θρόνου
5 αὐτοῦ ἐκέλευσεν ἀχθῆναι τοὺς ἁγίους ἔμπροσθεν αὐτοῦ. Ἤρξατο δὲ ἐκφοβεῖν αὐτοὺς ἀνηκέστοις βασάνοις καὶ ἀπειλαῖς· καὶ κολάζειν μὲν πρότερον μὴ εἴξαντας τῇ αὐτῶν κελεύσει, ὕστερον δὲ καὶ τὰς ὄψεις αὐτῶν γράφειν καὶ Ἀγαρηνοῖς παραδιδεῖν καὶ ἐν τῇ αὐτῶν πατρίδι ἀπολύειν ἔφασκεν. Μὴ εἰξάντων δὲ τῶν ἁγίων ποιῆσαι τὸ τοῦ βασιλέως
10 πρόσταγμα, συγκαθημένων τῷ ὑπάρχῳ τοῦ τε Χριστοδούλου, τοῦ τοὺς ἰάμβους σκεψαμένου, καὶ τοῦ αὐτοῦ πατρός, καὶ τῶν ἁγίων σκληρῶς ἀπαναινομένων καὶ μυρίους θανάτους ὑπομένειν ἑτοίμως ἐχόντων καὶ ὡς 'Οὐ χρανθησόμεθά ποτε τῇ κοινωνίᾳ ὑμῶν' φησάντων 'ἢ κἂν γοῦν τῇ συγκαταθέσει τῶν ἀθετησάντων τὴν τῶν χριστιανῶν πίστιν τε καὶ
15 ὁμολογίαν, εἰ τοὺς ὀφθαλμοὺς ἐξορύξειας καὶ τὸ σῶμα κατακαύσειας πυρί,' ὁ τοῦ Χριστοδούλου πατήρ, ἐν χάριτος μοίρᾳ τὸν λόγον ποιούμενος, ἔφη πρὸς τὸν ὕπαρχον· 'Οὐδέποτε οὗτοι προσεκύνησαν εἰκόνα, καὶ τί πεπόνθασιν ἐνταῦθα ἐλθόντες, οὐκ οἶδα.' Πρὸς ὃν αὐστηρᾷ τῇ φωνῇ ὁ τοῦ Χριστοῦ μάρτυς Θεοφάνης εἶπεν· ' Ἀπόστα ἀφ' ἡμῶν, ἐχθρὲ τῆς
20 ἀληθείας· οὐ γὰρ οἶδας τί λέγεις, οὔτε περὶ τίνων διαβεβαιοῖ· ἡμεῖς γὰρ καὶ ὁμολογοῦμεν καὶ σεβόμεθα καὶ προσκυνοῦμεν τὸν ἀληθινὸν ἡμῶν Θεὸν τὸν Κύριον Ἰησοῦν Χριστὸν καὶ τὴν αὐτοῦ εἰκόνα καὶ τῆς αὐτοῦ μητρὸς καὶ τῶν αὐτοῦ ἁγίων, εὖ εἰδότες, ὅτι ἡ τῆς εἰκόνος τιμὴ ἐπὶ τὸ πρωτότυπον ἀνάγει τὴν τιμήν. Καὶ ὑπὲρ αὐτοῦ καὶ τῆς αὐτοῦ εἰκόνος
25 ἀποθνήσκομεν καὶ τὸ αἷμα ἡμῶν ἐκχέομεν.' Ὡς δὲ τούτων ἀκήκοεν ὁ ἔπαρχος, θωπείαις χρώμενος λέγει πρὸς αὐτούς· 'Μίαν μόνον ἅπαξ κοινωνήσατε, καὶ ἕτερον οὐ θέλω, καὶ ἀπολύω ὑμᾶς, καὶ πορεύεσθε ὅπου φίλον ὑμῖν ἐστιν.' Ἀποκριθεὶς δὲ ὁ τοῦ Χριστοῦ μάρτυς Θεόδωρος ἔφη πρὸς αὐτόν· '"Ομοιόν τι λέγεις, ὦ ὕπαρχε, ὡς εἴ τις ἕτερον παρακαλοίη
30 λέγων· οὐδὲν αἰτοῦμαί σε ἄλλο ἢ τὴν σὴν ἀποκόψαι κάραν, καὶ πορεύου ὅπου θέλεις. Γίνωσκε τοίνυν ὡς ἡμεῖς αἰσχύνην ἡγούμεθα τὸ τολμᾶν τινα πρὸς κοινωνίαν ἡμᾶς προτρέπεσθαι, πρὸς ἣν αὐτὸς ἡμᾶς παραινεῖς

AG
6. ἀνηκέστοις A: ἀνεικέστοις G   9. ἔφασκεν A: ἔφασκε G   10-1. τοῦ² -- σκεψαμένου G: τῷ -- σκεψαμένῳ A   13. φησάντων A: φεισάντων G   20. διαβεβαιοῖ : διαβεβαιοῦσαι codd.   25. ἐκχέομεν A: ἐκχέωμεν G

logothete of the course.[153] He said to them, 'Set out then on the journey which has been appointed for you by the emperor.' Then the saints were led into the Praetorium as it had already become dark.[154]

22. The saints' audience with the prefect of the city

After four days the prefect ascended his throne and commanded that the saints be led before him. He began to intimidate them with frightful tortures and threats. He declared that if they did not give way to their persecutors' command, first he would chastise them, then inscribe their faces and hand them over to the Hagarenes[155] and have them deported to their own country. The saints refused to carry out the emperor's command. As they refused stubbornly and were ready to endure countless deaths saying, 'We shall never be defiled by entering into communion with you or even by agreeing with those who reject the faith and confession of Christians, even if you gouge out our eyes and cast our bodies to the flames,' the father of Christodoulos— for Christodoulos, the author of the iambics, and his father were sitting as assessors with the prefect— made a speech out of kindness and said to the prefect, 'These men never worshipped an icon, and I do not know why on earth they have come here.' But the martyr of Christ, Theophanes, said to him in a stern voice, 'Be gone from us, enemy of truth. You know not what you say nor what you affirm.[156] For we confess, honour and worship our true God, the Lord Jesus Christ, and His icon and those of His Mother and His saints, knowing full well that the honour of the icon brings honour to its prototype. We shall die and shed our blood on behalf of Him and His icon.' When the prefect heard these words, he said to them using flattery, 'If you will partake of communion but once, I desire nothing else. I shall let you go free and you may go wherever you wish.' But the martyr of Christ, Theodore, answered him and said, 'O prefect, you speak just as one might entreat someone saying, "I demand nothing of you but that you cut off your head, and you may go wherever you wish." Understand that we regard it as shameful that anyone should dare to lead us to the communion to which you exhort us to come. I

ἐλθεῖν. Θαυμάζω δὲ ὅτι μὴ πόρρωθεν καὶ ἐξακοῆς πέπεισται ὁ τοιοῦτος ὡς ῥᾷον αὐτῷ τὸν οὐρανὸν γῆν καὶ γῆν τὸν οὐρανὸν γενέσθαι ἢ ἡμᾶς μεταστῆσαι τῆς ἡμῶν ὁμολογίας καὶ πίστεως· καὶ ὥσπερ ἀδύνατόν ἐστιν ἄνθρωπον ὄντα εἰς οὐρανὸν ἱππάσασθαι, οὕτως ἀδύνατόν ἐστιν ποιῆσαι
5 ἡμᾶς ὃ λέγεις. Ποίει οὖν ὃ θέλεις. Τῶν γὰρ σωμάτων κύριος εἶ, τῶν δὲ ψυχῶν ἡμῶν ὁ Χριστὸς ὑπάρχει κύριος.'
(23) Τότε κελεύει ὁ ὕπαρχος τὰς ὄψεις αὐτῶν γραφῆναι. Τῶν δὲ πληγῶν τῶν ἁγίων ἔτι φλεγμαινουσῶν καὶ πόνων ἀφορήτων τούτοις παρεχουσῶν, προσελθόντες οἱ δήμιοι καὶ ἐπὶ σκάμνων τανύσαντες ἕνα ἕκαστον τῶν
10 ἁγίων, ἐκόλαπτον τὰς ὄψεις αὐτῶν. Καὶ ἐπὶ πολλὴν ὥραν κεντοῦντες τὰ πρόσωπα αὐτῶν, ἔγραφον τοὺς ἰάμβους ἐπ᾽ αὐτοῖς. Ὡς δὲ ἐτέλεσαν γράφοντες, ἀνέστησαν αὐτοὺς καὶ ἀπὸ τῆς ἡμέρας ἐκείνης οὐδὲν ἕτερον αὐτοῖς λελάληκαν. Μέλλοντες δὲ ἐξιέναι ἐκ προσώπου τοῦ ἐπάρχου, ἔφησαν οἱ ἅγιοι πρός τε τὸν ὕπαρχον καὶ τοὺς αὐτῷ συγκαθημένους,
15 ὑποδεικνύντες τὰς αὐτῶν ὄψεις·'Ταῦτα τὰ γράμματα, εὖ ἴστε, θεασάμενα τὰ χερουβὶμ ὑποχωρήσειε, καὶ ἡ φλογίνη ῥομφαία τὰ νῶτα δοῦσα ἡμῖν τοῦ παραδείσου τὴν εἴσοδον παραχωρήσειεν, αἰδούμενα τὰς ὄψεις τὰς ὑπὲρ τοῦ ἰδίου αὐτῶν δεσπότου ἀτίμως οὕτως ἐγχαραχθείσας. Καὶ γὰρ ἀπ᾽ αἰῶνος μόνοις ἡμῖν πέπρακται τοῦτο καὶ εὕρηται καινὸν ἐπιτήδευμα.
20 Φιλανθρώπους δὲ ἀπεδείξατε πάντας ὅσοι κατὰ τοῦ θείου ἡμῶν δόγματος ἐμάνησαν, ὠμότεροι τούτων φανέντες. Ἐν δὲ τῷ προσώπῳ τοῦ Χριστοῦ πάντως ἐπιγνώσεσθε πάντα ταῦτα τὰ γράμματα· αὐτὸς γὰρ εἴρηκεν·'Ὅσα ἂν ἐποιήσατε ἑνὶ τούτων τῶν ἐλαχίστων, ἐμοὶ ἐποιήσατε.'
Τούτων δὲ τῶν λόγων ἀκούσας ὁ βασιλεὺς (ὁ γὰρ ὕπαρχος ἀπήγγειλεν
25 αὐτῷ ταῦτα) εἶπεν πρὸς αὐτόν, ὡς οἶμαι, καταβροντηθεὶς τῇ τῶν λόγων δυνάμει·'Εἰ ἠπιστάμην ὅτι ἀληθές ἐστι τοῦτο, ἅπαντα τὸν ὑπ᾽ ἐμὲ λαὸν ἔγραψα ἂν οὕτως.' Καί μοι, παρακαλῶ, μηδεὶς ἀπιστείτω ὥς τι τῆς ἀληθείας προχαράξαντι ἢ ὃ μὴ πρόσεστι πεπονθέναι τοῖς τοῦ Χριστοῦ

AG
1. πέπεισται G: πέπισται A 4. ἱππάσασθαι: ἵππασθαι codd. 9. σκάμνων A: σκάμνου G 16. ὑποχωρήσειε G: -ν A

marvel that such a man has not been convinced [246] for a long time and from hearsay that it would be easier for him to make heaven earth, and earth heaven than to turn us away from our confession and faith.[157] Just as it is impossible for a man to reach heaven on horseback,[158] so is it impossible for us to do what you say. Do then what you will. For whereas you are the master of our bodies, Christ is Lord of our souls.'

23. Theodore's and Theophanes' faces are inscribed with the iambic verses

Then the prefect ordered that their faces be inscribed. While the wounds of the saints were still inflamed and causing them unbearable pain, the executioners approached, stretched out each one of the saints upon a bench and began to engrave their faces. And by pricking their faces for a long time[159] they wrote the iambics on them. When they had finished inscribing them, they made them stand and from that day forth addressed them no further. As they were about to leave the presence of the prefect, the saints displayed their faces and said to the prefect and his coassessors, 'Understand that when they have seen these letters the cherubim will withdraw and the fiery sword, retreating before us, will yield entrance to paradise, revering these countenances which were so ignominiously engraved for the sake of their Master. For in all time, this novel practice has been performed only on us and invented only for us. You have revealed all those who have raged against our divine doctrine as benevolent men for you have appeared more savage than they. You will recognize all these letters in the countenance of Christ, for he said, "Inasmuch as ye have done it unto one of the least of these <My brethren>, ye have done it unto Me."'[160]

When the emperor heard of these words (for the prefect reported these matters to him), he said to him, (for I think he was thunderstruck by the power of those words): 'If I had thought that this were true, I should have branded thus all of my subjects.'[161] And for my part, I beg that no one may believe that I have falsified any of the truth or wished to include anything in this narration which was not suffered by the martyrs of Christ. The faces of the holy

---

8. cf. Is. 1:6   23. Mt. 25:40

μάρτυσι ταύτη μου τῇ διηγήσει ἐνθεῖναι θελήσαντι. Ἐγράφησαν δὲ τὰ πρόσωπα οἱ ἅγιοι τοῦ Χριστοῦ ὁμολογηταὶ καὶ μάρτυρες Θεόδωρος καὶ Θεοφάνης, μηνὶ ἰουλίῳ ὀκτωκαιδεκάτῃ, ἰνδικτιῶνος τεσσαρεσκαιδεκάτης.

5 (24) Μετὰ δὲ τὸ ἐξελθεῖν τοὺς ἁγίους μάρτυρας, καθὼς ἔφαμεν, ἐκ προσώπου τοῦ ἐπάρχου ἐκέλευσεν αὐτοὺς ὁ βασιλεὺς ἐναποκλείστους γενέσθαι ἐν τῇ τοιαύτῃ εἱρκτῇ πλησίον τοῦ αὐτῶν καθηγουμένου καὶ ποιμένος, τοῦ θεοφόρου λέγω Μιχαήλ. Ὡς δὲ ταῦτα ἔγνω ὁ ὁμολογητὴς τοῦ Χριστοῦ, ἐχάρη λίαν, ἀκούσας ὅτι ὑπὲρ τοῦ Χριστοῦ καὶ τῆς αὐτοῦ
10 εἰκόνος τά τε νῶτα καὶ στήθη τυφθέντες καὶ τὰς ὄψεις γραφέντες μετὰ παρρησίας ἐκήρυττον τὸ τῆς οἰκονομίας μυστήριον, καὶ ὡς οὐχ ὑπεβλήθησαν ἢ ἡττήθησαν τοσαύτας βασάνους ὑπὸ τοῦ τυράννου δεξάμενοι. Ὅθεν καὶ δι᾽ ἐπιστολῶν ἐδήλωσεν αὐτοῖς οὑτωσὶ λέγων (οὐ γὰρ ἔβλεπον ἀλλήλους πρὸς πρόσωπον, εἰ μή τί γε δι᾽ ἐπιστολῶν, καὶ
15 τοῦτο μόλις συγχωρούμενον)· Γέγηθα, τέκνα μου πνευματικά, τῇ ὑμῶν παρρησίᾳ, ἀκούσας καὶ τὰς ὑμῶν ἀριστείας καὶ διὰ Χριστὸν μαρτυρίας. Καὶ μακαρίζω ὑμῶν τὰ μέλη, τὰ καταξανθέντα μάστιξιν ὑπὲρ τοῦ πλαστουργοῦ καὶ Κυρίου ἡμῶν Ἰησοῦ Χριστοῦ, τοῦ τὰ νῶτα δεδωκότος ὑπὲρ ἡμῶν εἰς μάστιγας. Ὑπερεπαινῶ δὲ καὶ περιπτύσσομαι τὰ στήθη
20 καὶ νῶτα τοῖς αἵμασι καταρραντισθέντα διὰ τὸ δι᾽ ἡμᾶς ἐκ τῆς λόγχῃ τρωθείσης ζωοποιοῦ πλευρᾶς ῥεῦσαν θεῖόν τε καὶ σωτήριον αἷμα. Ἀσπάζομαι τὰ τίμιά μοι καὶ φίλτατα πρόσωπα ἐκεῖνα, τὰ διὰ τὸν σεπτὸν τοῦ Κυρίου χαρακτῆρα κατασημανθέντα χαράγμασιν. Καταφιλῶ τὰς ἐμψύχους εἰκόνας καὶ μορφάς, τὰς ὑπὲρ τῆς ἀναστηλουμένης καὶ
25 γραφομένης εἰκόνος καὶ μορφῆς τοῦ Λυτρωτοῦ μου καὶ Σωτῆρος σιδήρῳ κατακεντηθείσας καὶ μελανθείσας. Χαίρετε τοίνυν ἐπὶ τούτοις, τεκνία μου, καὶ κραταιούσθω ὑμῶν ἡ καρδία, ὅτι ἀληθῶς ἑαυτοὺς ἀπεδείξατε οἰκήτορας ὄντας τῆς ἁγίας πόλεως Ἱερουσαλὴμ καὶ ἀπογόνους καὶ ὁμοχώρους τῶν ἁγίων τριῶν παίδων, τῶν τὴν Βαβυλωνίαν
30 κατασβεσάντων κάμινον, καὶ τῶν λοιπῶν ἑπτὰ τῶν Μακκαβαίων λέγω παίδων σὺν τῷ γηραιῷ Ἐλεάζαρ τῶν καταισχυνάντων τὸν

AG
5. Μετὰ δὲ G: Ὡς δὲ μετὰ A   12. ὑπεβλήθησαν : ὑπεβεβλήθησαν A ὑπεκλήθησαν G   13. post ἐπιστολῶν add. χρησάμενος A   15. συγχωρούμενον : -- μενοι codd.   21. τρωθείσης A: τροθείσης G   23. χαράγμασιν A: --σι G   31. τῷ γηραιῷ : τοῦ γηραιοῦ codd.

confessors and martyrs of Christ, Theodore and Theophanes, were inscribed on the eighteenth of July in the fourteenth indiction.[162]

24. Michael's letter of encouragement to Theodore and Theophanes

After the departure of the holy martyrs from the presence of the prefect as I have described, the emperor commanded that they be confined within the same prison near their leader and shepherd, I mean the God-inspired Michael. When the confessor of Christ learned of these matters, he rejoiced greatly on hearing that while their backs and chests were beaten and their faces inscribed on behalf of Christ and His icon, they had outspokenly proclaimed the mystery of the dispensation and that they had not submitted nor had they been defeated by such trials as they had received from the tyrant. And this he made clear to them by means of a letter, saying the following words (for they did not see each other face to face [247] and only communicated after a fashion through letters, and even this was scarcely allowed): 'I rejoiced in your outspokenness, my spiritual children, when I heard of your valour and testimony on behalf of Christ. I bless your limbs which have been lacerated by whips on behalf of our Maker and Lord, Jesus Christ, Who offered His back to whips on our behalf. I praise above measure and embrace the breasts and backs which were sprinkled with blood on account of the divine and saving blood which flowed on our behalf from the life-giving side which was pierced with a lance. I salute those honourable and most beloved countenances which were marked with letters on account of the sacred image of Christ.[163] I caress the living icons and forms[164] which were pricked with iron and blackened on behalf of the erected and painted icon and form of my Redeemer and Saviour. Rejoice then in these things, my children, and let your hearts be strengthened, for you truly displayed yourselves as inhabitants of the holy city of Jerusalem and as the descendants and compatriots of the three holy children who quenched the Babylonian furnace[165] and moreover of the other seven children, I mean of the Maccabees, who with the aged Eleazar put to shame the idolater

---

27. 'let your hearts be strengthened': cf. Ps. 26:14 (27:14); 30:24 (31:24)

εἰδωλολάτρην Ἀντίοχον. Εὔχομαι δὲ καὶ μέχρι τέλους τῷ Θεῷ δοθῆναι ὑμῖν καρτερίαν καὶ ὑπομονήν, ὅπως εἰς τέλος καταισχύνωμεν καὶ καταλύσωμεν τὸ τοῦ τυράννου ἄθεον δόγμα οἱ τῆς ἁγίας Ἰερουσαλὴμ πολῖται. Τί δέ εἰσιν τὰ ἐν ταῖς ὑμῶν ὄψεσι γραφέντα, δι᾽ ἐπιστολῆς ὑμῶν
5 διδαχθῶ, καὶ τί προστέταχε καθ᾽ ὑμῶν ὁ παμβέβηλος ἄναξ; Καὶ τί ἐπαπειλοῦσιν ἡμῖν ἢ βουλεύονται ἕτερον κατὰ τῆς ἡμῶν ταλαιπωρίας; Τὴν προσκύνησιν δὲ διὰ ταύτης μου τῆς ἐπιστολῆς ὁ καρτερικώτατος καὶ δεύτερος Ἰὼβ ἀπονέμει τῇ ὑμῶν ἀγάπῃ. Τὰ δὲ καθ᾽ ἡμῶν καὶ οἷα οὐ μὴ διέλαθε τῇ ὑμῶν ἐνθέῳ καὶ θεοφιλεῖ εὐλαβείᾳ. Οὐ μόνον δὲ ἀλλὰ καὶ ὁ
10 μέγας τῆς εὐσεβείας ἀγωνιστὴς καὶ πρόμαχος Μεθόδιος τὴν προσκύνησιν δι᾽ ἐμοῦ ἀπονέμει ὑμῖν, πάμπολλα ὑμῶν ὑπερευχόμενος, μαθὼν τὰ ὑμῶν κατὰ τῆς ἀσεβείας ἀριστεύματα.᾽

Οὗτος γὰρ ὁ πανόλβιος καὶ μέγας τῆς εὐσεβείας ἀγωνιστὴς Μεθόδιος πλείστας ἐπιστολὰς πέπομφε τῷ πανιέρῳ Μιχαήλ, δεσπότην ἀποκαλῶν
15 καὶ πατέρα καὶ κηδεμόνα καὶ ἄξιον πολίτην τῆς τῶν οὐρανῶν βασιλείας· ὁμοίως δὲ καὶ τοῖς αὐτοῦ συναγωνισταῖς, Θεόδωρον λέγω καὶ Θεοφάνην, οὐ διέλειπε γράφων καὶ ἐπιστηρίζων, καὶ ὄντων αὐτῶν ὑπερορίων ἐν τῇ νήσῳ Ἀφουσίᾳ. Ὁ γὰρ ἐν ἁγίοις καὶ μέγας Μεθόδιος πολλὰς καὶ διαφόρους ὑπερορίας καὶ μάστιγας διὰ Χριστὸν καὶ τὴν αὐτοῦ ἁγίαν καὶ
20 προσκυνητὴν εἰκόνα παρὰ τῶν ἀσεβῶν εἰκονοκαυστῶν ὑπέστη, καὶ ἐν τῷ αὐτῷ Πραιτωρίῳ, ἐν ᾧ καὶ οἱ ἅγιοι καὶ θεοφόροι ἡμῶν πατέρες ὑπῆρχον ἐναπόκλειστοι, οὐκ ὀλίγους διετέλεσεν ἐγκεκλεισμένος χρόνους. Ὅθεν καὶ ἀλλήλοις δι᾽ ἐπιστολῶν γράφειν καὶ ἐπιστηρίζειν πρὸς τὸν τῆς εὐσεβείας ἀγῶνα οὐ διελίμπανον.

25 Τούτων δὲ οὕτως ἐχόντων καὶ τῶν ἁγίων καὶ ὁμολογητῶν ἡμῶν πατέρων ὄντων ἑβδομάδος χρόνῳ ἐναποκλείστων ἐν τῇ τοῦ Πραιτωρίου εἱρκτῇ, τί θαυματουργεῖ ὁ τῶν ὅλων Θεός, ὁ μὴ ἐῶν *τὴν ῥάβδον τῶν ἁμαρτωλῶν ἐπὶ τὸν κλῆρον τῶν δικαίων ἐπὶ πολὺ ἐγκαρτερῆσαι πρὸς τὸ μὴ ἐκτεῖναι τοὺς δικαίους τὰς ἑαυτῶν ἐν ἀνομίαις χεῖρας*, ὁ λυτρούμενος τὴν αὐτοῦ
30 ἐκκλησίαν ἐκ τῶν αὐτῆς πολεμίων; Αὐτὸς γὰρ εἴρηκε τῷ Πέτρῳ, ὅτι ᾽ἐπὶ

AG
1. εἰδωλολάτρην G: -ιν A 6. ἡμῖν codd.: ὑμῖν Šev. | ἡμῶν codd.: ὑμῶν Šev. 11. ὑμῶν¹ A: ὑμῖν G 13. τῆς εὐσεβείας A: om. G 16. ante συναγωνισταῖς add. καὶ A 17. διέλειπε A: διέλιπε G

Antiochus.[166] I pray to God that patient endurance and perseverance may be granted to you until the end, so that we the citizens of the holy Jerusalem may put to utter shame and abolish the godless doctrine of the tyrant. Let me be instructed by letter as to what these words are which were written upon your faces, and what the wholly profane ruler enjoined against you and further with what else they are threatening us or what else they are devising against us in our misery. The most steadfast Job, that second Job, venerates your charity with this letter of mine. As for the measures taken against us and what they are, these have not escaped your God-inspired and God-loving piety. Not only this, but also the great contender and champion of piety Methodios[167] venerates you through me and is praying much on your behalf, having learned of your deeds of prowess against impiety.'

This wholly blessed and great champion of piety Methodios had sent a great many letters to the all-holy Michael, calling him lord, father, guardian and worthy citizen of the heavenly kingdom. Likewise he did not cease writing to Michael's fellow-contenders, Theodore and Theophanes, and encouraging them even when they were exiled on the island of Aphousia. For the great Methodios of saintly memory underwent many and varied exiles and whippings on behalf of Christ and His holy and venerable icon at the hands of the impious icon-burners, and he spent many years enclosed in the same Praetorium prison in which our holy and God-inspired fathers were confined.[168] Thus they did not cease writing and encouraging each other towards the contest of piety.

[248] In these circumstances, when our holy fathers and confessors had thus been confined for seven years in the Praetorium prison,[169] what did the God of all creation marvellously bring about, Who suffers not 'the rod of the wicked to remain long upon the lot of the righteous, lest the righteous put forth their hands into iniquity,' and Who delivers His Church from her enemies?

27-9. cf. Ps. 124:3 (125:3)

τῇ πεπετρωμένῃ σου πίστει *οἰκοδομήσω μου τὴν ἐκκλησίαν, καὶ πύλαι Ἅιδου οὐ κατισχύσουσιν αὐτῆς,*˙ πύλας Ἅιδου τοὺς ἐπαλλήλους πειρασμοὺς τῆς αὐτοῦ ἐκκλησίας καλέσας.

(25) Οὐ πολὺ τὸ ἐν μέσῳ, καὶ δὴ ὁ προλεχθεὶς ἀσεβέστατος ἄναξ τέλει τοῦ
5 βίου ἐχρήσατο, τῷ αἰωνίῳ καὶ ἀτελευτήτῳ πυρὶ εἰς αἰῶνας κολασθησόμενος. Τούτου δὲ ἡ βασιλεία καὶ τὸ κράτος εἰς Θεοδώραν τὴν αὐτοῦ σύνευνον καὶ Μιχαὴλ τῷ αὐτῶν υἱῷ διέβαινεν. Ὅθεν σπουδαίαν καὶ νεανικὴν ἡ Θεοδώρα τὴν φροντίδα τίθεται πρὸ τῶν ἄλλων ἁπάντων ἀριστευμάτων καὶ φιλοτιμιῶν, ἐξ ὧν βασιλεῖς εὐδοκιμεῖν πεφύκασι, μὴ
10 ἂν ἄλλως ἀσφαλῆ τὴν ἀρχὴν ἑαυτῇ καταστήσασθαι καὶ ἀνδρείαν ἐν θηλείας προσχήματι γενναιότητα ἐπιδείξασθαι, εἰ μὴ ἵλεων τὸν Θεὸν διὰ τῆς τῶν εὐσεβῶν δογμάτων καὶ τῆς τῶν σεπτῶν εἰκόνων φαιδρᾶς ἀνατυπώσεως ἀπεργάσεται καὶ τοὺς ἤδη διασχισθέντας εἰς ἑνότητα μίαν συνάψειεν, ἵνα διὰ τῆς αὐτῶν ἑνώσεως ἡ τῶν ἀποστολικῶν καὶ
15 πατρικῶν δογμάτων βεβαία καὶ ἀστασίαστος ὀρθοτομία τῆς πίστεως διασώζοιτο.

Ταῦτα τοιγαροῦν σοφῇ ἀγχινοίᾳ σκοπήσασα καὶ λελογισμένῃ συνέσει, ἐκέλευσε τοὺς ὑπὲρ τῆς ὀρθοδόξου πίστεως εἴτε ἐν ὑπερορίαις παραπεμφθέντας ἢ ἐν φυλακαῖς ἐναποκλείστους ὄντας ἀνακληθῆναί
20 τε καὶ ἀπολυθῆναι καὶ ἐν τῇ βασιλευούσῃ πόλει πρὸς αὐτὴν παραγενέσθαι. Τῶν δὲ προσταγμάτων πανταχόσε διαθεόντων καὶ ἐπισυναγόντων τοὺς τοῦ Χριστοῦ ὁμολογητὰς καὶ μάρτυρας, ἥκασιν αἱ τοῦ Χριστοῦ ἔμπνοοι στῆλαι ἐκ διαφόρων χωρῶν τε καὶ πόλεων, ὡς ἐκ λειμώνων ἐαρινῶν πάντερπνα ἄνθη. Καὶ ἦν ἰδέσθαι τὸ γραφικὸν ἐκεῖνο
25 πληρούμενον λόγιον τὸ φάσκον · *Ἆρον κύκλῳ τοὺς ὀφθαλμούς σου, Σιών, καὶ ἴδε συνηγμένα τὰ τέκνα σου ἐν σοί. Ἥκασι γὰρ ἀπὸ ἀνατολῶν καὶ δυσμῶν καὶ βορρᾶ καὶ νότου προσκυνῆσαι περιγραπτὸν τῷ βασιλεῖ σου ἐν σοί.*˙ Καὶ δὴ τούτων συναθροισθέντων, προστέταχεν ἡ θεοσεβὴς Θεοδώρα ἔν τινι ἀφωρισμένῳ τῶν ἀνακτόρων οἴκῳ ἅπαν τὸ
30 ἐκκλησιαστικὸν καὶ ἀθλητικὸν στῖφος συναθροισθῆναι, παρούσης καὶ

AG
2. Ἅιδου¹ A: ᾅδου G   3. ἐπαλλήλους A : ἀλλεπαλλήλους G   10. ante ἑαυτῇ add. ἐν A   11. θηλείας A: θηλείαις G   προσχήματι: προσσχήματι codd.   18. ἐκέλευσε G: -v A   19. post ἢ add. καὶ A   22. αἱ A: οἱ G   24. λειμώνων A: λειμόνων G   29. ἀφωρισμένῳ A: ἀφορισμένῳ G | ἀνακτόρων οἴκῳ G: ἀνακτορικῶν οἴκων A

For He said to Peter, 'Upon thy faith of rock I will build My Church; and the gates of hell shall not prevail against it,' meaning by the gates of hell the continuous temptation of His Church.

25. The accession of Michael III and his mother Theodora: the restoration of icons

A short time elapsed and the aforesaid, utterly impious ruler expired, to be punished with eternal and everlasting fire through the ages. His empire and power passed to Theodora his wife and to their son Michael.[170] Theodora took zealous and vigorous thought before all other good deeds and displays of munificence from which emperors naturally acquire high reputation to render her reign sound and to display her manly nobility in feminine garb[171] and she achieved this in no way more than by propitiating God through the splendid representation of pious doctrines and of sacred icons and by reuniting into one unity those who had been in schism, in order that the firm and undisputed correctness of the faith of the doctrines of the apostles and fathers might be preserved through their union.[172]

Thus when she had contemplated these matters with wise sagacity and considered intelligence, she commanded that those who had been sent into exile or who were confined in prisons on behalf of the orthodox faith should be recalled and released, and that they should wait on her in the imperial city. When her orders had gone forth everywhere and had collected the confessors and martyrs of Christ, the living monuments[173] of Christ returned from various districts and cities, just as wholly delightful flowers from spring meadows.[174] And one could see the scriptural passage fulfilled which says, 'Lift up thine eyes round about and behold, Sion; all thy children gather themselves together in thee. For they have come from the east, the west, the north, and the south' to venerate thy king in thee in a circumscribed fashion.[175] When they were assembled, the most pious Theodora commanded that the whole ecclesiastical body of spiritual combatants be assembled within a

---

1-2. cf. Mt. 16:18   25-8. cf. Is. 49:18, 60:4; Mt. 8:11; Lu. 13:29

τῆς συγκλήτου πάσης καὶ πολὺ πλῆθος τοῦ λοιποῦ λαοῦ, ὅπως περὶ τοῦ τῶν σεπτῶν εἰκόνων ὀρθοδόξου δόγματος τρανέστατα τῷ λαῷ διαγγεῖλαι. Καὶ δὴ ψήφῳ θείᾳ τῆς προειρημένης βασιλίσσης καὶ τοῦ ταύτης νέου υἱοῦ, Μιχαὴλ φημι τοῦ ἄνακτος, καὶ τῶν τοῦ Θεοῦ ἱεραρχῶν καὶ
5 ὁσιομαρτύρων, τοὺς κατὰ τῶν θείων εἰκόνων λυττήσαντας παντοίοις ἀναθέμασι καθυπέβαλλον, ὥστε τῇ ἀθρόᾳ καὶ ἀδοκήτῳ τῶν πραγμάτων μεταβολῇ παραπληξίᾳ καὶ σκοτώσει λογισμῶν τὸν τηνικαῦτα δυσσεβῶς τῆς ἀρχιερωσύνης ἐπειλημμένον Ἰωάννην μικροῦ δεῖν τὴν παμβέβηλον ψυχὴν ἀπορρῆξαι. Οὕτινος λοιμοῦ καὶ φθορέως προστάξει τῶν εὐσεβῶν
10 βασιλέων καὶ τῆς τῶν θείων πατέρων ἱερᾶς συνόδου καθαιρεθέντος καὶ τελείῳ ἀναθέματι ὑποβληθέντος καὶ ἀτίμως ἐξεωθέντος τοῦ τε ἀποστολικοῦ θρόνου καὶ τῆς πόλεως, φροντὶς ἦν μία κοινὴ πᾶσι, τὸ τίνα ἀποκαλύψειε Κύριος ὁ Θεὸς ἰθύνειν καὶ διέπειν τὸν ἀρχιερατικὸν τῆς ἐκκλησίας θρόνον. Ἅπαντες γὰρ ἀπέβλεπον πρὸς τὸν μέγαν τῆς εὐσεβείας
15 ἀγωνιστήν, τὸν πάνσοφον λέγω Μιχαήλ, ὡς ἅτε συγκέλλου αὐτοῦ ὄντος τῆς ἁγίας Χριστοῦ τοῦ Θεοῦ ἡμῶν πόλεως καὶ σοφοῦ τὰ θεῖα καὶ πολλὰς ὑπομεμενηκότος ποινάς τε καὶ μάστιγας ὑπὲρ Χριστοῦ καὶ τῆς αὐτοῦ εἰκόνος ὥστε τούτῳ προχειρισθῆναι τοὺς τῆς ἐκκλησίας οἴακας.

(26) Ὁ δὲ πατὴρ ἡμῶν καὶ μέγας Μιχαὴλ τοῦτο μὴ ἀνασχόμενος (τὴν γὰρ
20 ἀψευδῆ ταπείνωσιν τοῦ Χριστοῦ ἠσπάζετο πάντοτε), εὐτελῆ ἑαυτὸν καὶ ἀνάξιον λέγων εἶναι τοῦ τοιούτου ἐγχειρήματος, σὺν τούτῳ τοίνυν τῷ πανσόφῳ Μιχαὴλ βουλῇ καλῇ χρησαμένη ἡ τοῦ Θεοῦ σύνοδος σὺν τῇ προλεχθείσῃ βασιλίσσῃ ἀποστεῖλαι διέγνωσαν πρὸς τὸν μέγαν Ἰωαννίκιον, φωστῆρος δίκην λάμποντος τότε ταῖς κατὰ Θεὸν ἀρεταῖς τῇ
25 τε προοράσει καὶ τοῖς θαύμασιν ἐν τῷ τοῦ Ὀλύμπου ὄρει σὺν τῷ αὐτοῦ συναγωνιστῇ Εὐστρατίῳ τῷ θαυματουργῷ καὶ ἡγουμένῳ τῆς τῶν Ἀγαύρων μονῆς. Τοῦτο δὴ καὶ πεποιήκασιν, ἀποστείλαντες δύο μὲν ἐκ τῆς ἱερᾶς συνόδου καὶ ἐκ τῶν βασιλικῶν αὐλῶν σπαθάριον οὕτω λεγόμενον. Οἵτινες ἀπελθόντες καὶ τῷ ὄρει προσβαλόντες καὶ εὑρόντες
30 τὸν ἅγιον ἐν τῇ Λαύρᾳ τοῦ ἁγίου προφήτου Ἠλίου διὰ τὴν τῶν αἱρετικῶν ἄμυναν, δῆλα τούτῳ ἐποίησαν τὰ δόξαντα τῇ τε ἁγίᾳ συνόδῳ καὶ τοῖς φιλοχρίστοις βασιλεῦσιν.

AG
9. ἀπορρῆξαι G: ἀπορρῖξαι A   12. πᾶσι G: -ν A   29. προσβαλόντες : προσβαλλόντες codd.

certain separate chamber of the palace, with the entire senate and a great multitude of the rest of the people present, in order that she might proclaim to the people with all clarity regarding the orthodox doctrine of the sacred icons. And by the divine decision of the aforementioned empress and her young son, I mean the ruler Michael, and of the prelates and holy martyrs of God, they condemned with all sorts [249] of anathemas those who had raged against the divine icons so that John, who impiously occupied the office of bishop at that time, was so deranged and his wits so obscured that he almost gave up his utterly profane spirit on account of the sudden and unexpected reversal in his affairs.[176] When this pestilential and corrupting man was deposed by the command of the pious emperors and the holy synod of divine fathers and delivered to utter anathema and dishonourably expelled from the apostolic throne and from the city, there remained one care which was shared by all: whom would the Lord God reveal to guide and direct the high-priestly throne of the Church? They all turned their eyes to the great, all-wise champion of piety, I mean Michael, that they might hand the helm of the Church over to him since he was *synkellos* of the holy city of Christ our God, wise in divine matters, and had endured many tribulations and whippings on behalf of Christ and His icon.

26. The guidance of St Ioannikios in selecting a new patriarch

But our great father Michael did not agree to this[177] (for he was always eager to embrace the true humility of Christ), and he declared that he was lowly and unworthy of so great an undertaking. The synod of God, having consulted with the all-wise Michael and with the aforesaid empress made a commendable resolution and determined to send to the great Ioannikios who then shone as a luminary on Olympos[178] with virtues according to God and with the gift of foresight and miracles,[179] in company with his fellow contender Eustratios,[180] the worker of miracles and abbot of the monastery of Agauroi.[181] And so this was done: they sent two men from the holy synod and the so-called *spatharios* of the imperial court. When these men had departed, had reached the mountain and found the saint within the *laura* of the holy prophet Elias[182] where he was staying for protection against the heretics, they explained to him what had been resolved by the holy synod and by the Christ-loving emperors.

Ὁ δὲ τοῦ Θεοῦ ἄνθρωπος ὁ μέγας Ἰωαννίκιος τούτων ἀκούσας ἐχάρη λίαν καὶ μηδὲν μελλήσας προσάγει δέησιν Κυρίῳ τῷ Θεῷ ἐλεῆσαι τὴν αὐτοῦ ποίμνην καὶ ἀναδεῖξαι τὸν μέλλοντα ἀξίως ποιμᾶναι τὴν αὐτοῦ ὀρθόδοξον καὶ ἱερὰν ποίμνην, ἣν περιεποιήσατο τῷ ἰδίῳ αἵματι. 5 Ἀποκλείσας γὰρ κατὰ τῶν προλεχθέντων ὁσίων ἀνδρῶν τοῦ σπηλοειδοῦς ἐκείνου καὶ βραχυτάτου οἰκήματος θύραν ἐκέλευσεν αὐτοὺς συναγωνίσασθαι αὐτῷ ταῖς εὐχαῖς, ὅπως τὸ συμφέρον Κύριος φανερώσῃ. Μετὰ δὲ ἑβδόμην ἡμέραν τῆς πρὸς τὸν Θεὸν αὐτοῦ δεήσεως ἀνοίξας τὴν προλεχθεῖσαν θύραν καὶ ἐξελθὼν ἐπιδίδωσιν αὐτοῖς ῥάβδον, τοῦτο 10 πρὸς αὐτοὺς λέξας· ''Ἀπέλθετε, τέκνα, καὶ ἐπίδοτε τὴν ῥάβδον ταύτην Μεθοδίῳ μοναχῷ καὶ πρεσβυτέρῳ, τῷ ὄντι ἐξορίστῳ ἐν τῇ τῶν Ἐλεοβωμητῶν μονῇ.' Καὶ ἀπέλυσεν αὐτοὺς ἐπευξάμενος.

Οἱ δὲ προλεχθέντες εὐλαβεῖς ἄνδρες, οἵ τε ἀρχιερεῖς καὶ ὁ σπαθάριος, καταλαβόντες τὴν πανευδαίμονα Κωνσταντινούπολιν δῆλα ταῦτα 15 πεποιήκασιν τῇ τε συνόδῳ καὶ τοῖς βασιλεῦσιν. Οἱ δὲ εὐθέως ἐκέλευσαν διὰ ταχυδρόμου τὸν προλεχθέντα πανόσιον ἄνδρα καταλαβεῖν τὴν βασιλεύουσαν μεγαλόπολιν· τοῦτο γὰρ ἐδήλωσεν ἡ ἐπιδοθεῖσα παρὰ τοῦ ἁγίου ῥάβδος, σημαίνουσα τὸν μέλλοντα ποιμᾶναι τὴν τοῦ Θεοῦ ἁγίαν καὶ ἀποστολικὴν ἐκκλησίαν. Οὗτος γάρ ἐστιν, ἀδελφοί, ὁ 20 προειρημένος Μεθόδιος, περὶ οὗ μνείαν ἀνωτέρω πεποιήμεθα.

(27) Καὶ δὴ τούτου γενομένου καὶ τοῦ ἁγίου Μεθοδίου καταλαβόντος τὴν πανευδαίμονα Κωνσταντινούπολιν, ἐν ᾗ καὶ ὑπὲρ τοῦ Χριστοῦ καὶ τῆς αὐτοῦ ἁγίας καὶ σεβασμίας εἰκόνος πολλῶν βασάνων πεῖραν εἰλήφει, χειροτονεῖται ψήφῳ θείᾳ καὶ τῆς ἁγίας καὶ οἰκουμενικῆς συνόδου καὶ 25 ἀποκαθίσταται εἰς τὸν ἐκ Θεοῦ αὐτῷ ἀποκαλυφθέντα ἀποστολικὸν θρόνον. Τούτων δὲ οὕτως γεγονότων, τοὺς μὲν αἱρετικοὺς καὶ αὐτὸς μυρίοις ἀναθέμασι καθυπέβαλλεν, καὶ τοὺς ἱερεῖς ἅπαντας ἐκκαθάρας τὴν τοῦ Θεοῦ ἐκκλησίαν τῆς αὐτῶν τυραννίδος ἠλευθέρωσε. Τότε δὴ τότε καὶ τὸν ἡμέτερον τῆς εὐσεβείας ἀγωνιστὴν πατέρα καὶ θεοφόρον 30 Μιχαὴλ κελεύσει τῶν ὀρθοδόξων βασιλέων σύγκελλον ἑαυτοῦ καὶ ἡγούμενον τῆς μεγάλης μονῆς τῆς Χώρας κεχειροτόνηκεν.

AG
1. Ἰωαννίκιος A: Ἰωάννης G | ἐχάρη corr. A: ἐχάρει G   5. τῶν A: om. G   7. post τὸ add. σαφέστερον καὶ G   10. ἀπέλθετε : ἀπέλθατε codd.   12. Ἐλεοβωμητῶν : Ἐλεωβωμητῶν codd.   13. εὐλαβεῖς A: εὐσεβεῖς G   15. εὐθέως post ἐκέλευσαν trsp. G   17. τοῦτο : τούτω codd.   23. αὐτοῦ post ἁγίας trsp. G   28. ἠλευθέρωσε G: -ν A

When the great man of God Ioannikios heard of these matters, he rejoiced greatly and without delay entreated the Lord God to have mercy on His flock and to reveal who was worthy to shepherd His orthodox and holy flock which He had purchased with His own blood. He closed the door of his tiny, cavelike dwelling-place to the aforesaid holy men and ordered them to assist him in prayers, that the Lord might reveal what was fitting. After the seventh day of his prayer to God, he opened the aforesaid door and issued forth, offered them a staff and addressed the following words to them: 'Depart, children, and bestow this staff on the monk and [250] presbyter Methodios,[183] who is exiled in the monastery of Elaiobomoi.'[184] After offering up a prayer, he sent them on their way.

When the aforesaid pious men, the bishops and the *spatharios*, arrived in all-fortunate Constantinople, they reported these matters to the synod and to the emperors. By means of a courier they at once commanded the aforesaid most holy man to come to the imperial city. For the staff which had been bestowed by the saint revealed this, signifying the one who was to guide the holy and apostolic Church of God. This man was the aforesaid Methodios, brethren, concerning whom we have made mention above.[185]

27. Michael is appointed *synkellos* and abbot of the monastery of Chora

When this had come to pass and the holy Methodios had arrived in all-fortunate Constantinople, in which he had suffered the trial of many tortures on behalf of Christ and His holy and venerable icon, he was ordained by the divine vote of the holy and universal synod and appointed to the apostolic throne which was revealed as his by God. After these events had taken place, he himself also condemned the heretics with countless anathemas and after a purge among all the clergy, he liberated the Church of God from their tyranny. Then by command of the orthodox emperors, he appointed our father and champion of piety, the God-inspired Michael, as his *synkellos* and as abbot of the great monastery of Chora.

---

4. 'which He had purchased with His own blood': cf. Acts 20:28

(28) Ἐπεὶ δὲ τῆς τοιαύτης βασιλικῆς καὶ ὀρθοδόξου μονῆς τῆς Χώρας μνείαν πεποίημαι, μικρόν τι λέξω καὶ τὰ περὶ αὐτῆς. Αὕτη τοίνυν ἡ προλεχθεῖσα σεβασμία μονὴ κτίζεται μὲν παρὰ τοῦ εὐσεβεστάτου καὶ ἀοιδίμου ἄνακτος Ἰουστινιανοῦ, μεγάλη λίαν καὶ φαιδρὰ καὶ
5 ὑπέρλαμπρος. Ταύτην τοιγαροῦν τὴν μονὴν εἴ τις καλέσειεν ὄρος Θεοῦ καὶ ὄρος Χωρὴβ ὄρος τε Καρμήλιον ἢ Σίναιον ὄρος εἴτε Θαβώριον εἴτε Λίβανον ἢ καὶ πόλιν ἁγίαν ὡς ἐν ὄρει τῶν ἐν Ἱεροσολύμοις κειμένην, οὐχ ἁμαρτήσει τοῦ πρέποντος. Ταύτην τοίνυν τὴν πανίερον μονὴν ὁ προλεχθεὶς ἀοίδιμος ἄναξ τοὺς ἀπὸ Ἱεροσολύμων παραγινομένους
10 ἱερεῖς τε καὶ μονάζοντας ἐκέλευσεν ἐν αὐτῇ ἀναπαύεσθαι, τὰς δὲ αὐτῶν χρείας ἐκ τῶν βασιλικῶν ταμιείων τούτοις δίδοσθαι.

Δι' ἣν δὲ αἰτίαν ἡ τοιαύτη πρόσταξις παρὰ τοῦ εὐσεβοῦς ἄνακτος γέγονεν, ἔνθεν ἐρῶ. Τοιοῦτος γὰρ μέχρις ἡμῶν κατήντηκε λόγος ἀνέκαθε πρὸς πατρὸς παιδίῳ παραδιδόμενος, ὡς ὁ ἐν ἁγίοις πατὴρ ἡμῶν καὶ
15 θεοφόρος Σάβας ἀποσταλεὶς παρὰ τοῦ τότε πατριαρχοῦντος Ἱεροσολύμων Πέτρου τοὔνομα πρὸς τὸν προλεχθέντα εὐσεβῆ ἄνακτα περὶ τῶν γεγονότων ἐφόδων καὶ αἰχμαλωσιῶν παρὰ τῶν ἀθέων Σαμαρειτῶν καὶ τῶν ὑπ' αὐτῶν ἐμπρησθέντων τοῦ Θεοῦ εὐκτηρίων οἴκων, ὅπως κελεύσῃ ἡ αὐτοῦ θεόστεπτος καὶ ἄχραντος κορυφὴ τοὺς μὲν
20 εὐκτηρίους τοῦ Θεοῦ οἴκους κτισθῆναι, τοὺς δὲ ἀθέους καὶ παμβεβήλους Σαμαρείτας ἐξεωθῆναι, καὶ ἐκ τῆς αὐτῶν τυραννίδος ἐλευθερωθῆναι τὴν τοῦ Θεοῦ ἁγίαν πόλιν, καὶ τοῖς περὶ αὐτὴν ὁρίοις· ὃ δὴ καὶ πεποίηκε κατὰ τὴν προλεχθεῖσαν παράκλησιν τοῦ σεβασμίου πατρὸς ἡμῶν Σάβα.

Παραχειμάσαντος γὰρ τοῦ προλεχθέντος σεβασμίου πατρὸς ἐν τῇ
25 πανευδαίμονι Κωνσταντινουπόλει, ἀπέστειλε τοῦτον ὁ προλεχθεὶς εὐσεβὴς ἄναξ εἰς τὴν τοιαύτην μονήν, ἤδη τέλος τῆς ἀποκαταστάσεως ἐχούσης, πρὸς τὸ κατοπτεῦσαι καὶ εὐλογῆσαι τὴν τοιαύτην παρ' αὐτοῦ κτισθεῖσαν μονήν. Ἀκήκοεν γάρ, ὅτι πλεῖστα μοναστήρια ὁ ἐν ἁγίοις Σάβας ἐν τῇ ἁγίᾳ Χριστοῦ τοῦ Θεοῦ ἡμῶν πόλει καὶ τῇ ταύτης ἐρήμῳ
30 πεποίηκεν. Εἰς ἣν εἰσελθὼν ὁ πάμμακαρ πατὴρ ἡμῶν Σάβας πάνυ ἠγάσθη τοῦ τε τόπου καὶ τῆς ποικίλης κατασκευῆς. Ἔστιν γὰρ ἡ τοιαύτη

AG
5. τοιγαροῦν A: γὰρ G   7. ἐν² G: om. A   14. παιδίῳ : παιδίον codd.   24. προλεχθέντος A: om. G   27. κατοπτεῦσαι A: καθοπτεῦσαι G   31. τόπου A: τρόπου G

LIFE OF MICHAEL THE SYNKELLOS

28. History of the monastery of Chora

Since I have made mention of that imperial and orthodox monastery of Chora,[186] I shall say something further about it. This aforesaid venerable monastery was founded by the most pious and celebrated ruler Justinian; it was exceedingly large, splendid and distinguished. If someone were to call this same monastery the mountain of God, the mountain of Horeb, the mountain of Carmel, or the mountain of Sinai, or Tabor, or Lebanon[187] or even a holy city set, so to say, upon one of the hills of Jerusalem, he would not say more than what is fitting. Indeed the aforesaid, celebrated ruler commanded that priests and monks from Jerusalem who had arrived in this all-holy monastery should take rest there, with their wants provided for them from the imperial treasury.

I shall also recount the reason for this command on the part of the pious ruler. This account came down to us after being transmitted from the beginning by father to son. Our God-inspired father Sabas of saintly memory[188] was sent by the patriarch of Jerusalem of that time, named Peter, to the aforesaid pious ruler concerning the attacks and depredations by the godless Samaritans and the burning of the houses of God's worship at their instigation, that his God-crowned, undefiled majesty might command that [251] houses for God's worship be founded, the godless and wholly profane Samaritans cast out, and the holy city of God and the surrounding territory delivered from their tyranny.[189] And indeed, the emperor acted in accordance with the aforementioned request of our pious father Sabas.

When the aforesaid venerable father had passed the winter in all-fortunate Constantinople, the aforesaid pious ruler sent him to this same monastery, <the construction of> which had reached its completion, that he might inspect and bless the monastery which the emperor had founded. For he had heard that this Sabas of saintly memory had founded a great many monasteries in the holy city of Christ our God and in the surrounding desert. On entering the monastery, our all-blessed father Sabas marvelled greatly at its setting and elaborate structure.[190] This venerable monastery is enclosed from every side

---

7. 'city set... hills': cf. Mt. 5:14

σεβασμία μονὴ οἱονεὶ τειχίῳ περιπεφραγμένη πάντοθεν καὶ ἀποκεχωρισμένη τῆς τῶν κοσμικῶν διαγωγῆς τε καὶ συναυλίας καὶ ὥσπερ πόλις ἀκράδαντος ἐπ᾽ ὄρους κειμένη, καὶ τῶν οὐρανῶν ἁπτομένη τῇ τῶν κτισμάτων ὑψότητι. Ταύτης οὖν ἕνεκα τῆς αἰτίας ἔκτοτε οἱ ἀπὸ
5 Ἱεροσολύμων παραγενόμενοι ἐν τῇ Κωνσταντινουπόλει ἐν ταύτῃ παρὰ τῶν εὐσεβῶν βασιλέων ἀπεστέλλοντο. Ὅθεν καὶ οἱ πανένδοξοι καὶ ἅγιοι τοῦ Χριστοῦ ὁμολογηταὶ καὶ μάρτυρες παρὰ τοῦ πανεχθίστου καὶ θηριωνύμου ἄνακτος ἐν τῇ αὐτῇ ἀπεστάλησαν μονῇ ἀπὸ Ἱεροσολύμων παραγενόμενοι.
10 Ταύτην τοίνυν τὴν μονὴν εὐθηνουμένην πάνυ ἔν τε χρήμασι καὶ κτήμασι καὶ ἀναλώμασιν ὁ ἀσεβὴς καὶ μετὰ τὸν διώκτην διώκτης ὁ τῆς ἁλουργίδος ἀνάξιος, Κωνσταντῖνος ὁ Κοπρώνυμος, διὰ τὸ ἐν αὐτῇ κατοικεῖν ὀρθοδόξους καὶ ἁγίους πατέρας, οὐ μὴν ἀλλὰ καὶ διὰ τὸν ἐν ἁγίοις καὶ μέγαν πατριάρχην Γερμανὸν (ὁ γὰρ τούτου θηριώνυμος καὶ
15 πρῶτος αἱρεσιάρχης πατὴρ διὰ τὸ ὑπ᾽ αὐτοῦ τοῦ θεσπεσίου πατρὸς Γερμανοῦ ἀναθέματι αἰωνίῳ παραδοθῆναι ὡς εἰκονοκαύστου καὶ ἰουδαόφρονος, καὶ ὑπ᾽ αὐτοῦ ἐξορίστου γεγονότος ἐν ταύτῃ τῇ προλεχθείσῃ λαμπρᾷ καὶ ὀρθοδόξῳ μονῇ) ἐγύμνωσέ τε καὶ ἐξηφάνισε καὶ μικροῦ δεῖν κατηδάφισεν. Ἐκτυφλώσας γὰρ τὸν τῆς αὐτοῦ ἀδελφῆς
20 Ἄννης σύζυγον, τὸν ὀρθοδοξότατον ἄνακτα Ἀρτάβασδον τοὔνομα, ἐν ὑπερορίᾳ κατεδίκασεν ἐν τῇ προλεχθείσῃ μονῇ σὺν τῇ αὐτοῦ συζύγῳ καὶ τοῖς αὐτοῦ ἐννέα παισί, καταγώγιον κοσμικῶν ἀπεργασάμενος καὶ παντελῶς γυμνώσας αὐτὴν ἐκ τῆς τῶν μοναχῶν συναυλίας. Εἰς ἣν μονὴν κατάκεινται τὰ αὐτῶν ὀρθόδοξα λείψανα.
25 (29) Ἐν ταύτῃ τοίνυν τῇ σεβασμίᾳ μονῇ, καθὼς προλέλεκται, ὁ μέγας καὶ ἅγιος πατριάρχης Γερμανὸς τέλει τοῦ βίου ἐχρήσατο. Εἰς ἣν καὶ κατάκειται τὸ καρτερικὸν καὶ ἱερὸν αὐτοῦ λείψανον. Ταύτης ἕνεκα τῆς αἰτίας τὸν ἐν ἁγίοις καὶ ὁμολογητὴν καὶ μέγαν πατέρα ἡμῶν Μιχαὴλ ὁ ἐν ἁγίοις τελετάρχης Μεθόδιος, ὡς προλέλεκται, ἡγούμενον προυβάλετο
30 τῆς τοιαύτης μονῆς. Τὸν δὲ πάνσοφον καὶ μέγαν Θεοφάνην μητροπολίτην κεχειροτόνηκεν τῆς κατὰ Νίκαιαν ἁγιωτάτης ἐκκλησίας, εἰς ἣν πόλιν ἡ

AG
3. τῶν οὐρανῶν A: τὸν οὐρανὸν G   6-7. πανένδοξοι καὶ ἅγιοι A: om. G   18. ἐξηφάνισε G: -ν A   19. κατηδάφισεν A: κατηδάφησεν G   25. καθὼς προλέλεκται A: om. G   28. μέγαν G: μέγα A   29. προυβάλετο : προβάλλετο codd.

as if with a wall and separated from worldly life and intercourse, even as a city set firmly upon a hill and touching the heavens with the height of its buildings. It was on this account that those who arrived in Constantinople from Jerusalem were sent by pious emperors to this monastery. Thus our most glorious and holy confessors and martyrs of Christ on arriving from Jerusalem were sent to the same monastery by the utterly wicked ruler who was named after a wild beast.[191]

It was this monastery, which throve on account of its money, possessions, and dispensations,[192] which the impious persecutor and persecutor's successor Constantine Kopronymos, who was unworthy of the purple,[193] stripped bare, destroyed and all but razed to the ground[194] because the orthodox and holy fathers were dwelling there, and especially because of the great patriarch Germanos of saintly memory,[195] for since the holy father Germanos had delivered his father, the first heresiarch named after a wild beast, to eternal anathema as a burner of icons and Jewish-minded, Leo exiled him to this aforementioned splendid and orthodox monastery. After blinding the husband of his sister Anna, the most orthodox ruler Artabasdos, Constantine banished him with his wife and nine children to the aforesaid monastery, after he had turned the monastery into a lodging house for laymen and removed the monastic community from it altogether.[196] Their orthodox relics lie stored in that monastery.

29. The appointment of Theophanes *Graptos* as metropolitan of Nicaea

The great, holy patriarch Germanos ended his life in this venerable monastery, as we have said. Within it lie his enduring and holy relics. On this account, as has been said before, the high priest Methodios of saintly memory appointed our great confessor and father Michael of blessed memory as abbot of this monastery. He appointed the all-wise and [252] great Theophanes metropolitan of the most holy church of Nicaea,[197] where the great emperor

---

3. cf. Mt. 5:14

ἁγία καὶ οἰκουμενικὴ πρώτη σύνοδος κατὰ Ἀρείου τοῦ δυσσεβοῦς ἐπὶ Κωνσταντίνου τοῦ ἐν ἁγίοις μεγάλου βασιλέως συνηθροίσθη, τῶν τριακοσίων λέγω δέκα καὶ ὀκτὼ ἁγίων πατέρων. Ἐν δὲ τῷ μέλλειν τοῦτον χειροτονεῖσθαι τινὲς τῶν ἀρχιερέων πρὸς τὸν ἅγιον Μεθόδιον
5 οὑτωσὶ λέλεχαν, ὡς ὅτι οὐκ ὀφείλει τῆς τοιαύτης ἐντὸς γενέσθαι ἀρχιερωσύνης, μὴ ὄντων τῶν τοιούτων μαρτύρων ἐκ τῆς αὐτῆς γῆς· "Ἡμεῖς γὰρ τὰ κατ᾽ αὐτὸν καὶ τὴν αὐτοῦ πολιτείαν καὶ ἀναστροφὴν οὐ γινώσκομεν.᾽ Ὅθεν πρὸς αὐτοὺς ὁ μέγας τῆς εὐσεβείας ἀγωνιστὴς Μεθόδιος ἀποκριθεὶς ἔφη· Πιστεύσατέ μοι, πατέρες, οὔτε ἐγὼ βουλῆς
10 εἶχον τοῦτον χειροτονίας τοιαύτης μεγίστης ἀξιῶσαι, ἀλλ᾽ ἡ τοῦ προσώπου αὐτοῦ γραμμὴ καὶ αἱ τοῦ νώτου μάστιγες καὶ ἡ ἐν τῇ ὑπερορίᾳ καὶ φρουρᾷ πολυετὴς κάθειρξις καὶ ἄκοντά με καὶ μὴ βουλόμενον ἕλκει τοῦτον χειροτονίας καὶ μεγίστου θρόνου ἄξιον κρῖναι. Ἀλλὰ Χριστὸς ὁ ἀληθινὸς ἡμῶν Θεός, ὑπὲρ ὃν πολλὰς ποινὰς καὶ μάστιγας ὑπέμεινε,
15 τοῦτό μοι προσευχομένῳ δεδήλωκε.᾽ Τότε δὴ τότε καὶ ὁ τῆς εὐσεβείας ἀγωνιστὴς καὶ μέγας Μιχαὴλ πρὸς τὸν προλεχθέντα πατριάρχην Μεθόδιον ἀποκριθεὶς ἔφη· Εἴ τι ἂν ποιῇς καὶ πράττῃς εἰς τὸ ἐμὸν πνευματικὸν τέκνον, τὸν πάνσοφον Θεοφάνην, τῷ συνεκδήμῳ καὶ συναιχμαλώτῳ ἐμοὶ ποιεῖς· ἐγὼ γὰρ ἐκεῖνος, καὶ ἐκεῖνος ἐγώ.᾽ Ὁ γὰρ
20 ἁγιώτατος πατριάρχης οὕτω προσεῖχε τοῖς παρὰ τοῦ πατρὸς ἡμῶν, τοῦ ἐν ἁγίοις φημὶ Μιχαήλ, λεγομένοις καὶ πραττομένοις, ὡς ἐκ Θεοῦ καὶ οὐκ ἐξ ἀνθρώπου ἐνεργουμένοις.

(30) Τούτων δὲ οὕτως πραχθέντων, ὁ ἐν ἁγίοις πατὴρ ἡμῶν καὶ ὁμολογητὴς Θεόδωρος, ὁ γνήσιος συναίμων τοῦ ἁγίου Θεοφάνους, τέλει
25 τοῦ βίου ἐχρήσατο τῇ εἰκάδι καὶ ἑβδόμῃ τοῦ δεκεμβρίου μηνός, ζήσας ἔτη ἑβδομήκοντα. Οὕτινος καὶ ἡ βίβλος ἡ λεγομένη 'Κυνόλυκος᾽ τῆς αὐτοῦ σοφίας τὸ ὑψηλὸν καὶ ἀκρότατον ἀναφανδὸν διαπρυσίως κηρύττει, τῶν δὲ αἱρετικῶν καὶ εἰκονοκαυστῶν ἐμφράττει τὰ ἀπύλωτα στόματα διὰ τῶν πανσόφων αὐτοῦ ἀποδείξεων, τῶν ἐκ τῶν θείων γραφῶν
30 συλλεγεισῶν. Ὁ δὲ μέγας καὶ θεοφόρος Θεοφάνης σὺν τῷ αὐτοῦ καθηγητῇ

AG
6. τοιούτων A: τούτων G | αὐτῆς : αὐτοῦ codd. | γῆς A: γαίης G 7. γὰρ A: δὲ G 10. τοιαύτης μεγίστης A: om. G 16. προλεχθέντα A: om. G 23-4. καὶ ὁμολογητὴς A: om. G 30. συλλεγεισῶν : συλλεγέντων codd.

Constantine of saintly memory assembled the first holy and universal council against the impious Arius, I mean that of the three hundred eighteen holy fathers.[198] When he was about to be appointed, some of the bishops indicated to the holy Methodios that it was not fitting that he should be placed in that office of bishop as no witnesses were present from his land, saying, 'For we know nothing about him, his way of life or his bearing.' However the great champion of piety Methodios answered them and said, 'Believe me, fathers, I did not intend to honour him with such a high appointment, but the marking of his face and scourging of his back and the confinement for many years in exile and in prison lead me, even were I unwilling and undesirous of this, to judge him worthy for the ordination and most exalted throne. Christ our true God, on Whose behalf he endured many penalties and scourgings, has revealed this to me when I was praying.' It was then that the great champion of piety Michael answered the aforesaid patriarch Methodios and said, 'Whatever you practise and do to my spiritual child, the all-wise Theophanes, you do to me, his travelling companion and fellow captive. For I am he, and he I.' The most holy patriarch attended to the words and deeds of our father, I mean Michael of saintly memory, as if they were prompted by God, rather than by man.

30. The death of Theodore *Graptos*

When these matters had been accomplished in this manner, our father and confessor of blessed memory Theodore, the true kinsman of the holy Theophanes, expired on the twenty-seventh day of the month of December, having lived to be seventy years of age.[199] His book called 'Kynolykos' proclaims openly and clearly the loftiness and elevation of his wisdom and stops the unbridled mouths of heretics and icon-burners by means of his all-wise proofs of passages gathered from the Scriptures.[200] The great and God-inspired Theophanes in company with his all-wise teacher Michael, after

---

28. 'stops the unbridled mouths': cf. Job 5:16; Ps. 62:12 (63:11); 106:42 (107:42)

τῷ πανσόφῳ Μιχαήλ, ἐγκωμίοις καταστέψαντες τὴν αὐτοῦ ἁγίαν καὶ θεοφόρον κοίμησιν, τοῦτον κατέθεντο ἐν θήκαις ὁσίαις καὶ παρέδωκαν τῇ σορῷ τῶν πρὸ αὐτοῦ τετελευτηκότων ἁγίων πατέρων.

(31) Τοῦ δὲ ὁμολογητοῦ Θεοφάνους ὀρθοδόξως ποιμάναντος τὴν αὐτοῦ
5 λογικὴν ποίμνην ἐπὶ τέτρασιν ἔτεσι καὶ καρποὺς πεπείρους τῷ Θεῷ προσκομίσαντος, τῶν δι᾽ αὐτοῦ καὶ τῆς αὐτοῦ πανσόφου διδασκαλίας διασωθέντων εἴσω τῶν λιμένων τῆς τῶν οὐρανῶν βασιλείας τὰς μακαρίας ψυχὰς αὐτῶν ἀπεθησαύρισεν. Τούτου τοίνυν τοῦ πανσόφου ἀρχιερέως Χριστοῦ τοῦ Θεοῦ ἡμῶν καταλαβόντος ποτὲ τὴν πανευδαίμονα
10 Κωνσταντινούπολιν καὶ πρὸς τὸν τῆς αὐτῆς ἀρχιερέα εἰσελθόντος καὶ τοῦτον ἀσπασαμένου, παρεγένετο καὶ πρὸς τὴν μονὴν τῆς Χώρας πρὸς τὸν αὐτοῦ καθηγητὴν καὶ κηδεμόνα, τὸν πάνσοφον Μιχαήλ. Καὶ τοῦτον ἀσπασάμενος ἦν σὺν αὐτῷ χρόνον οὐκ ὀλίγον. Καὶ δὴ ἀρρωστίᾳ περιέπεσεν, ἐν ᾗ καὶ τετελεύτηκεν. Ὅθεν προσκαλεσάμενος τὸν αὐτοῦ
15 πάνσοφον καὶ μέγαν ποιμενάρχην, Μιχαὴλ φημι τὸν πάνυ, φησὶ πρὸς αὐτόν· Εὖξαι, πάτερ, τὸ τέκνον σου· ἐκλείπω γάρ, καὶ ἀπόδος κἀμέ, τὸν καρπὸν τῶν πόνων σου, ὡς καὶ τὸν ἐμὸν ὁμαίμονα καὶ ἀδελφόν, Χριστῷ τῷ πανυψίστῳ Θεῷ· καὶ κήδευσον ταῖς σαῖς ὁσίαις χερσίν, ὃ μετὰ πολλῶν κόπων καὶ σοφῶν παραινέσεων ἐξέθρεψας σῶμα· καὶ παράδος
20 με τῷ χοῒ τῶν πατέρων μου. Ἰδοὺ γὰρ ἡ δύναμις τοῦ εὐτελοῦς καὶ δυστήνου μου σαρκίου εἰς τέλος ἐξέλιπεν. Καὶ μνείαν ποιοῦ τοῦ σοῦ ὡς ποιμὴν προβάτου ἐν ταῖς πρὸς Θεόν σου ἐντεύξεσιν. Καὶ ταῦτα εἰπὼν καὶ *Εἰς χεῖράς σου, Κύριε, παρατίθημι τὸ πνεῦμά μου* λέξας, παρέδωκε τὴν παναγίαν αὐτοῦ ψυχὴν εἰς χεῖρας τῶν ἁγίων ἀγγέλων, ὧν καὶ τὸν
25 βίον ζεζήλωκεν. Κεκοίμηται δὲ οὗτος ὁ πάνσοφος ἱεράρχης καὶ ὁμολογητὴς καὶ μάρτυς τοῦ Χριστοῦ Θεοφάνης τῇ ἑνδεκάτῃ τοῦ ὀκτωβρίου μηνὸς τῆς ἐνάτης ἰνδικτιῶνος, ἐπὶ τῆς βασιλείας τῶν φιλοχρίστων καὶ ὀρθοδόξων βασιλέων, Μιχαὴλ καὶ Θεοδώρας τῆς αὐτοῦ μητρός, ὧν ἐτῶν ἑξήκοντα καὶ ἑπτά.

AG
5. ἔτεσι G: -ν A | πεπείρους : πεπήρους codd. 8. ψυχὰς post αὐτῶν trsp. G 14-5. τὸν¹ -- φημι A: Μιχαὴλ G 17. τὸν ἐμὸν ὁμαίμονα καὶ ἀδελφόν corr. Schmitt : τῷ ἐμῷ ὁμαίμονι καὶ ἀδελφῷ codd. 21. ἐξέλιπεν A: ἐξέλιπε G 22. ἐντεύξεσιν A: ἐντεύξεσι G 24. παναγίαν A: ἁγίαν G | τῶν A: om.G 25. πάνσοφος ἱεράρχης καὶ A: om. G 26.καὶ ¯ Χριστοῦ A: om. G 27. ἐνάτης : ἐννάτης codd. 28. καὶ ὀρθοδόξων A: om. G

adorning his holy and God-inspired repose with eulogies,[201] laid him to rest in the holy coffin and delivered him to the resting place of the holy fathers who had died before him.

31. The death of Theophanes

When the confessor Theophanes had guided his spiritual flock in an orthodox manner for four years and borne ripe fruits for God, he stored up within the haven of the heavenly kingdom the blessed souls of those who had been saved by him and by his all-wise teachings.[202] Indeed, when this all-wise bishop of Christ our God had once reached all-fortunate Constantinople, and had approached and [253] embraced her high priest, he went to the monastery of Chora to see his teacher and guardian, the all-wise Michael. And after greeting <Michael>, he remained with him for a considerable length of time. Soon afterwards <Theophanes> was stricken with the illness from which he actually died. Therefore he summoned his all-wise and great chief shepherd, I mean the excellent Michael, and said to him, 'Father, pray for your child, for I am passing on. Deliver me, the fruit of your labours, to Christ God the most high, even as you did my kinsman and brother. And bury with your holy hands the body which you reared through many exertions and through wise counsels. Deliver me to the dust of my fathers. For behold, the power of my worthless and wretched body has been utterly exhausted. And be mindful of him who is yours as a shepherd is of his sheep in your prayers to God.' Having said these words and declared, 'Into thy hands, Lord, I commend my spirit,' he delivered his all-holy soul into the hands of the holy angels whose way of life he had emulated. This all-wise bishop, confessor, and martyr of Christ Theophanes was laid to rest on the eleventh day of October of the ninth indiction,[203] during the reign of the Christ-loving and orthodox emperors Michael and his mother Theodora, having reached the age of sixty-seven.

---

23. Lu. 23:46

ΒΙΟΣ ΤΟΥ ΜΙΧΑΗΛ ΤΟΥ ΣΥΝΚΕΛΛΟΥ

Τούτου τοίνυν τοῦ πανσόφου καὶ ἱερομάρτυρος Θεοφάνους ἡ τοῦ Θεοῦ καθολικὴ καὶ ἀποστολικὴ ἐκκλησία πολλὰ πονήματα καὶ διδασκαλίας κατέχει, ὡς θησαυρὸν ἄσυλον παρ' ἑαυτῇ ἀποθησαυρίσασα. Οὗτος γὰρ ὁ θεσπέσιος καὶ μέγας Θεοφάνης δεύτερος
5 Δαυὶδ μελῳδὸς ἀνεδείχθη τῇ τοῦ Θεοῦ ἐκκλησίᾳ. Τὰς γὰρ θείας πανηγύρεις τοῦ μεγάλου Θεοῦ καὶ Σωτῆρος ἡμῶν Ἰησοῦ Χριστοῦ καὶ τῆς αὐτοῦ πανάγνου μητρὸς τῆς εὐλογημένης Θεοτόκου καὶ ἀειπαρθένου Μαρίας καὶ τῶν αὐτοῦ ἐνδόξων προφητῶν, ἀποστόλων, μαρτύρων, ὁσίων τε καὶ δικαίων οὐ μὴν ἀλλὰ καὶ ἀρχαγγέλων κανόσι θείοις
10 εὐμελεστάτοις κατεκόσμησεν.

Τοῦτον τοίνυν τὸν μέγαν καὶ θεοφόρον Θεοφάνην ὁ ἐν ἁγίοις πατὴρ ἡμῶν καὶ μέγας Μιχαὴλ ἐγκωμίοις ἐπιταφίοις καταστέψας καὶ τελευταῖον ἀσπασάμενος, κατέθετο ἐν θήκαις ὁσίαις τῆς αὐτοῦ σεβασμίας μονῆς πλησίον τοῦ καρτερικοῦ καὶ ἁγίου λειψάνου τοῦ πανσόφου καὶ
15 ὁμολογητοῦ Γερμανοῦ. Καὶ ταῦτα μὲν οὕτως περὶ τῆς σεπτῆς καὶ αὐταδέλφου ξυνωρίδος Θεοδώρου καὶ Θεοφάνους τῶν ὁμολογητῶν καὶ μαρτύρων ἐπράχθη τε καὶ ἐγένετο. Οὕτως γὰρ ἀθλήσαντες καὶ τὸν δρόμον τελέσαντες καὶ τοὺς τυράννους καὶ ἀθέους αἱρετικοὺς καταισχύναντες τὸν χορὸν κατέλαβον ἐκεῖνον, ὃν ἐπόθησαν, ἐν παρρησίᾳ
20 πρεσβεύοντες ὑπὲρ τῆς αὐτῶν ὀρθοδόξου καὶ ἱερᾶς ποίμνης, ὡς ποιμένες ἄριστοι.

(32) Ἀλλά μοι δεῦρο θεοφόρον καὶ ὀρθόδοξον σύστημα, ὥσπερ ἐκ δυνάμεως εἰς δύναμιν, οὕτως ἐξ ἁγίων εἰς ἅγιον ἐπανάξωμεν τὸν λόγον, καὶ μάθωμεν τί καὶ περὶ τὸν ἐν ἁγίοις πατέρα ἡμῶν τὸν θεοφόρον καὶ
25 ὁμολογητὴν καὶ μέγαν Μιχαὴλ ὁ τῶν ὅλων Θεὸς θαυματουργεῖ· καθὼς γὰρ προείπομεν, μετὰ τὸ προβληθῆναι αὐτὸν εἰς τὴν τοιαύτην μονὴν ἡγούμενον, εὗρεν αὐτὴν πάνυ ὀλιγωθεῖσαν καὶ μικροῦ δεῖν κατεσκαμμένην. Παρὰ γὰρ τῶν ἀθέων αἱρετικῶν, καθὼς προλέλεκται,

---

AG
1. πανσόφου καὶ A: om. G   3. διδασκαλίας G: διδασκαλείας A   4. οὗτος add. post γὰρ codd. | θεσπέσιος καὶ A: om. G   7. πανάγνου A: παναγίας G | εὐλογημένης Θεοτόκου καὶ¹ A: om. G   10. κατεκόσμησεν A: κατεκόσμησε G   11. καὶ θεοφόρον A: om. G   12. καὶ μέγας A: om. G   26. προείπομεν : προείπωμεν codd. | προβληθῆναι A: γενέσθαι G   26-7. εἰς -- ἡγούμενον A: ἐν τῇ τοιαύτῃ μονῇ καθηγούμενον G   27-8. εὗρεν -- κατεσκαμμένην A: om. G   28. γὰρ A: om. G | καθὼς προλέλεκται A: om.G

The catholic and apostolic Church of God preserves many works and teachings by this all-wise holy martyr Theophanes, which she stored up within herself as an inviolate treasure. For this great and divine Theophanes was made manifest to the Church of God as a second David, singer of psalms. He adorned the divine feast-days of our great God and Saviour Jesus Christ, of His all-pure Mother, the blessed Mother of God and ever-Virgin Mary, of His glorious prophets, apostles, and martyrs, both holy and righteous, and even those of the archangels with divine and most melodious canons.[204]

After adorning this great and God-inspired Theophanes with funeral eulogies and embracing him for the last time, our great father Michael of saintly memory laid him to rest among the holy coffins of his venerable monastery near the enduring, holy relics of the venerable, all-wise confessor Germanos. And so these events concerning the revered pair of brothers, Theodore and Theophanes, the confessors and martyrs, were accomplished and came to pass. After they had thus struggled, finished their course, and put to shame the tyrants and godless heretics, they attained that choir for which they longed, and like the best shepherds they are now interceding outspokenly on behalf of their orthodox and holy flock.

32. Michael restores the monastery of Chora

[254] But come hither, orthodox and God-inspired assembly, <and> as it were from strength to strength, so from saints let us direct our account back to one saint, and let us learn what the God of all things marvellously wrought on behalf of our God-inspired father and confessor, the great Michael, of saintly memory. After he was appointed abbot of this monastery, as we have said, he found that the monastery was badly reduced and all but destroyed. After the monks had been banished from this monastery by the impious heretics, as has been said, a very small number encamped themselves in the

---

18. 'finished their course': cf. II Tim. 4:7

ἐκδιωχθέντων τῶν μοναχῶν ἐκ τῆς τοιαύτης μονῆς καὶ σκηνωσάντων πάνυ ὀλίγων ἔν τινι ἀγρῷ τῆς αὐτῆς μονῆς, Καστώρεον οὕτω λεγόμενον, ἐν τῷ ναῷ τοῦ ἁγίου μάρτυρος Τρύφωνος καὶ μετὰ πολλῆς στενοχωρίας τὸν ἑαυτῶν βίον διαγόντων, ὁ πανόσιος πατὴρ ἡμῶν Μιχαὴλ ἀποστείλας
5 καὶ τούτους πρὸς ἑαυτὸν ἀγαγὼν καὶ τῇ αὐτῶν μονῇ καθιδρύσας, ἣν σὺν αὐτοῖς ἐκτελῶν τὴν τοῦ Θεοῦ δοξολογίαν. Καὶ δὴ τῆς τοῦ Θεοῦ προνοίας τῆς πάντα καλῶς οἰκονομούσης πρὸς τὸ μεγαλῦναι τὸν αὐτῆς ὑπέρμαχον καὶ θεοφόρον Μιχαήλ, οὐ μετὰ πολὺν χρόνον ἐπληθύνθη ἡ αὐτοῦ συνοδία, καὶ ἔφθασεν μέχρι τῶν ἑκατὸν μοναχῶν.
10 Ὡς δὲ περὶ τῶν σωματικῶν χρειῶν ἐστενοῦτο πάνυ ἡ αὐτοῦ ἐνάρετος καὶ θεοφιλὴς συνοδία (λίαν γὰρ ἐν στενώσει ὑπῆρχεν ἡ τοιαύτη μονὴ περὶ τῶν τοιούτων χρειῶν) βουλῇ θεαρέστῳ χρησάμενος πρὸς τὸν ἐν ἁγίοις καὶ μέγαν πατριάρχην Μεθόδιον ἐπανῆλθεν, καὶ δῆλα ταῦτα τούτῳ ποιεῖ καὶ ζητεῖ παρ' αὐτοῦ βοήθειαν, ὥστε μὴ τὴν αὐτοῦ συνοδίαν
15 διὰ τὴν κατέχουσαν αὐτοὺς σπάνιν τῶν ἐδωδίμων σκορπισθῆναι καὶ ὑποχωρῆσαι. Ὁ δὲ μέγας Μεθόδιος τοῦτον παραλαβὼν ἀνέρχεται πρὸς τὸν μέγαν καὶ ὀρθόδοξον ἄνακτα Μιχαὴλ καὶ τὴν αὐτοῦ θεοσεβεστάτην μητέρα καὶ δῆλα ποιεῖ ταῦτα τῷ θεοστέπτῳ σκηπτούχῳ. Καὶ αἰτοῦνται παρ' αὐτοῦ συμμαχίαν, ὥστε ὅπου ἂν ἐξεδόθη παρὰ τοῦ βεβήλου καὶ
20 Κοπρωνύμου βασιλέως τῆς αὐτῆς εὐαγεστάτης μονῆς, εἴτε οἴκημα εἴτε καὶ ἀγρός, κελεύσῃ ἡ αὐτοῦ θεόστεπτος βασιλεία ἀνυπερθέτως χωρὶς πάσης ἀντιλογίας ἀποδοθῆναι πάντα πρὸς τὴν τοιαύτην αὐτοῦ βασιλικὴν μονήν. Καὶ δὴ τούτου γεγονότος καὶ τοῦ ἐν ἁγίοις πατρὸς ἡμῶν καὶ τῆς αὐτοῦ συνοδίας ἐν εὐθηνίᾳ πολλῇ καταστάντος, *ηὔξανεν ἡ τοῦ Θεοῦ*
25 *ποίμνη, καὶ προέκοπτε ταῖς κατὰ Θεὸν ἀρεταῖς καὶ ταῖς πανσόφοις αὐτοῦ διδασκαλίαις καὶ παραινέσεσιν.* Ὅθεν καὶ διέλαμπεν ἡ αὐτοῦ ἐνάρετος πολιτεία φωστῆρος δίκην, ὥστε πάντας σχεδὸν τοὺς τοῦ παλατίου καὶ τῆς καθολικῆς ἐκκλησίας φοιτᾶν πρὸς αὐτὸν εὐχῆς χάριν καὶ ἀπολαύσεως τῆς αὐτοῦ πανσόφου διδασκαλίας. Ταῦτα δὲ ἀκούων καὶ ὁ μέγας

AG
13. ἐπανῆλθεν post Μεθόδιον suppl. Schmitt | καὶ ² A: om. G   14. τούτῳ G: τοῦτο A   15. αὐτοὺς σπάνιν : αὐτοῖς σπάνην codd. | ἐδωδίμων : ἐδωδήμων codd.   18. τῷ -- σκηπτούχῳ A: om. G | αἰτοῦνται A: αἰτεῖται G   19. βεβήλου καὶ A: om. G   21. κελεύσῃ : κελεύσει codd.   21-2. ἀνυπερθέτως -- ἀντιλογίας A: om. G   22-3. πρὸς -- μονὴν A: τῇ μονῇ G   23. καὶ ³ A: μετὰ G   26. παραινέσεσιν A: παραινέσεσι G

church of the holy martyr Tryphon[205] in a certain field belonging to the same monastery, called Kastorion, and with great hardship carried on their way of life. Our all-holy father Michael sent for them and after leading them to himself and settling them in their monastery, he sang with them the praises of God. And as the providence of God was dispensing all things well in order to exalt her God-inspired champion Michael, after a short time his community multiplied, to include as many as one hundred monks.

As his virtuous and God-loving community was exceedingly constrained with respect to their bodily needs (for this monastery was in great want as regards such needs), Michael applied his God-pleasing counsel, went up to the great patriarch Methodios of saintly memory, explained these matters to him, and sought his aid, that his community might not be dispersed and be forced to move away due to the lack of provisions which confronted them. The great Methodios took him and went before the great, orthodox ruler Michael and his most pious mother and explained these matters to the God-crowned sovereign. They begged assistance from him, that his God-crowned majesty might forthwith and without any dispute return to this his imperial monastery[206] whatever had been confiscated by the impious emperor Kopronymos from the same sacred monastery, whether buildings or fields. When this had come to pass and our father of blessed memory and his community had come to prosper greatly, God's flock increased and advanced in virtues according to God and through Michael's all-wise teachings and exhortations. Thus his virtuous way of life shone like a star, so that almost all of those belonging to the palace and to the catholic church came to him for the sake of his prayer and for the benefit of his all-wise teaching. When the

---

25. Lu. 2:40   25-6. Lu. 2:52

πατριάρχης Μεθόδιος ἔχαιρε καὶ ἠγαλλιᾶτο τῷ πνεύματι, ὅτι ἡ τοῦ Θεοῦ ἐκκλησία τοιούτοις ἀνδράσι κατεκεκόσμητο. Ἀλλὰ καὶ αὐτὸς μικροῦ δεῖν ἀχώριστος ἦν πάντοτε τοῦ θεοφόρου Μιχαήλ.

(33) Ὡς δὲ ταῦτα οὕτως εἶχεν, ἔφθασε καὶ ἡ ἁγία αὐτοῦ καὶ ἔνδοξος ἐκ τοῦ βίου τούτου τοῦ ματαίου μετάστασις. Εἰς γὰρ ἔσχατον γῆρας ἦν ἐληλακώς, μέχρι που τῶν ὀγδοήκοντα καὶ πέντε ἐτῶν. Ἤσχαλλε γὰρ καὶ ἐδυσφόρει καὶ ἐσπούδαζεν δεόμενος τοῦ Θεοῦ νυκτὸς καὶ ἡμέρας, ὥστε αὐτὸν *ἀναλῦσαι καὶ σὺν Χριστῷ εἶναι*, κατὰ τὸν μακάριον Παῦλον, μετὰ τῶν αὐτοῦ φοιτητῶν καὶ ὀπαδῶν, Θεοδώρου φημὶ καὶ Θεοφάνους. Ὁ δὲ τῶν ὅλων Θεὸς προσέσχε τῇ δεήσει τοῦ οἰκείου θεράποντος καὶ διὰ νυκτερινῆς ὄψεως δήλην αὐτῷ ποιεῖται τὴν αὐτοῦ μετάστασιν. Ἡσυχάζοντι γὰρ αὐτῷ κατὰ τὸ ἔθος τῶν νηστειῶν τῆς ἁγίας Χριστοῦ τοῦ Θεοῦ ἡμῶν γεννήσεως παρίσταται αὐτῷ τοῦ Θεοῦ ἄγγελος λέγων αὐτῷ· Μιχαήλ, Μιχαήλ, ἀνάστα καὶ ἑτοίμασον σαυτόν. Ὁ γὰρ τῶν ὅλων Θεὸς κέκληκέ σε καὶ ἐκέλευσεν ἀναλῦσαί σε ἐκ τοῦδε τοῦ ματαίου βίου καὶ ἀπαλλαγῆναι τῶν πολλῶν κόπων καὶ μόχθων καὶ σὺν αὐτῷ εἶναι ἐν τῇ ἀναπαύσει τῶν δικαίων. Μετὰ γὰρ δέκα ἡμέρας ἔρχει πρὸς αὐτόν.'

Ὡς δὲ ἔξυπνος ἐγένετο ὁ τοῦ Θεοῦ ἄνθρωπος ὁ μέγας Μιχαήλ, σύνδακρυς γεγονὼς εὐθέως εἰς εὐχὴν ἔστη καὶ πρὸς τὸν Θεὸν εὐχόμενος μετὰ δακρύων καὶ πολλῆς χαρᾶς ἔλεγεν· ' Εὐχαριστῶ σοι, Χριστὲ ὁ Θεός μου, ὅτι εἰσήκουσας τῆς εὐτελοῦς μου δεήσεως καὶ ἐκέλευσάς με πρὸς σὲ ἐλθεῖν· αὐτός, Κύριε ὁ Θεός μου, τὴν ποίμνην, ἥν μοι ἀναξίῳ ὄντι πεπίστευκας, ἐκ πάσης αἱρέσεως ψυχοβλαβοῦς καὶ πάντων τῶν τοῦ πονηροῦ ἐπιτηδευμάτων, ἀβλαβῆ καὶ ἀκράδαντον διατήρησον καὶ στήτω μέχρις ἡμῶν τῶν δούλων σου ἡ τῶν αἱρετικῶν θρασύτης καὶ ὁ κατὰ τῆς ἐκκλησίας σου πόλεμος, καὶ ἡμεῖς γενώμεθα τέλος τῆς μαρτυρίας τῶν ὑπὲρ σοῦ ἀθλησάντων ἁγίων· καὶ παῦσον τὰ σκάνδαλα τῆς ἁγίας καθολικῆς καὶ ἀποστολικῆς ἐκκλησίας σου, ἣν περιποιήσω τῷ ἰδίῳ σου αἵματι. Ὅτι πρέπει σοι ἡ δόξα εἰς τοὺς αἰῶνας. Ἀμήν.'

AG
p.116, 26- p. 118, 1. Ὅθεν -- διδασκαλίας A: om. G   p.116, 29- p. 118, 1. Ταῦτα -- πατριάρχης A: Ταῦτα ἀκούων ὁ μέγας G   3. πάντοτε A: διαπαντὸς G   5. τούτου τοῦ ματαίου A: om. G   10. προσέσχε G: -v A   15. κέκληκε G: -v A   20-1. πρὸς -- χαρᾶς A: οὑτωσὶ δακρυρροῶν G   24. ψυχοβλαβοῦς A: om. G   27. γενώμεθα: γενόμεθα codd.   29. ἦν A: ἧς G

great patriarch Methodios heard of these matters, he was overjoyed and rejoiced in spirit that the Church of God should be adorned with such men. But he himself was always virtually inseparable from the God-inspired Michael.

33. Michael's approaching death foretold in a vision

[255] When these events had come to pass, the saint's holy and glorious translation from this vain life approached, for he was extremely old, having reached the age of about eighty-five. Being grieved, anxious and eager, he entreated God by night and by day that he might depart to be with Christ, according to the blessed Paul, in the company of his disciples and companions, I mean Theodore and Theophanes. The Lord of all things attended to the prayer of his own servant and revealed to him through a night-time vision his approaching translation. When he was in contemplation as is usual during the fasting preceding the holy day of the birth of Christ our God, an angel of God appeared to him and said: 'Michael, Michael, arise and prepare yourself. For the Lord of all creation has called upon you and ordered you to depart from this vain life and to be released from many sufferings and hardships, that you may be with him in the repose of the righteous. For you will rejoin Him after ten days.'[207]

When the great man of God Michael awoke, he was in tears and at once arose to pray, praying to God tearfully and with great joy, saying, 'I thank Thee, Christ my God, that Thou hast hearkened to my worthless prayer and commanded me to return to Thee. Thou, my Lord God, preserve the flock which Thou didst entrust to me although I was unworthy, unharmed and innocent from all soul-destroying heresy and from all the pursuits of the Devil; and may the arrogance of the heretics and the battle against Thy Church cease with us Thy servants, that we may be the last witnesses among the saints who have struggled on Thy behalf. And bring to an end the offences in Thy holy, catholic and apostolic Church, which Thou hast preserved with Thine own blood. For Thine is the glory unto the ages. Amen.'

---

1. cf. Lu. 10:21   8. Philipp. 1:23

(34) Ταῦτα αὐτοῦ εὐξαμένου, ἐκέλευσε κροῦσαι τὸ ξύλον. Καὶ συναχθείσης τῆς αὐτοῦ ἁγίας συνοδίας, ἤρξατο τῶν ὀρθρινῶν ὕμνων τῆς τοῦ Θεοῦ δοξολογίας. Τῆς δὲ κρούσεως τοῦ ξύλου παρὰ τὸ εἰωθὸς γενομένης, ἐπυνθάνοντο οἱ αὐτοῦ φοιτηταὶ λέγοντες ΄Τίς ἡ αἰτία,πάτερ,
5 δι' ἣν οὕτως παρὰ τὸ εἰωθὸς τοῦτο πεποίηκας;' Τότε δὲ μετὰ τὴν ἀπόλυσιν τῶν ἑωθινῶν ὕμνων λέγει αὐτοῖς ὁ θεσπέσιος Μιχαήλ· 'Μηδὲν ὑμῖν λυπηρὸν καταφανεῖ, τέκνα μου ἀγαπητά· ὁ γὰρ Κύριός μου Ἰησοῦς Χριστὸς προσεκαλέσατό με τοῦ ἀναλῦσαι καὶ σὺν αὐτῷ εἶναί με.'
   Τούτων δὲ εἰς ἐπήκοον πάντων λεχθέντων, λύπης ἐπληρώθησαν πάντες
10 καὶ δακρύων πολλῶν, τὴν ὀρφανίαν αὐτῶν μὴ φέροντες. Τοῦ δὲ ὁσίου πατρὸς ἡμῶν τούτοις ἐν τῇ καρδίᾳ λαλήσαντος καὶ παρακλητικοῖς λόγοις νουθετήσαντος, ἤρξατο λέγειν οὕτως· 'Τέκνα μου ἀγαπητά, μὴ ἐπιλάθεσθε τῶν ἐμῶν ἐντολῶν, μᾶλλον δὲ τῶν τοῦ Κυρίου ἡμῶν Ἰησοῦ Χριστοῦ, καὶ μὴ χαυνωθῇ ὑμῶν ὁ λογισμὸς μήτε ὀκνήσῃ πρὸς τὴν τοῦ
15 Θεοῦ λειτουργίαν. Ἀλλὰ πάσης ἀγαθοεργίας τὴν εἰλικρινῆ ἀγάπην διὰ παντὸς κτήσασθε, σύνδεσμον οὖσαν τῆς τελειότητος· πᾶσα γὰρ ἀρετὴ δι' ἀγάπης καὶ ταπεινοφροσύνης τελειοῦται. Καὶ ἡ μὲν ταπεινοφροσύνη ὑψοῖ, ἡ δὲ ἀγάπη τοῦ ὕψους πεσεῖν οὐκ ἐᾷ. Μείζων δὲ ἡ ἀγάπη τῆς ταπεινοφροσύνης ἐστί· διὰ γὰρ τὴν πρὸς ἡμᾶς ἀγάπην ἐταπείνωσεν
20 ἑαυτὸν ὁ τοῦ Θεοῦ Λόγος, ὁ Κύριος ἡμῶν Ἰησοῦς Χριστός, καθ' ἡμᾶς γενόμενος ἄνθρωπος. Διὸ ὀφείλομεν ἀδιαλείπτως ἐκ θελήματος αὐτῷ ἐξομολογεῖσθαι καὶ ὕμνους καὶ εὐχαριστίας ἀναπέμπειν διὰ τὰς πρὸς αὐτὸν συνθήκας, καὶ μάλιστα ἡμεῖς οἱ πραγμάτων καὶ φροντίδων ἀπηλλαγμένοι, καὶ δῶρα προσάγειν ὑπὲρ λύτρου τῶν ἡμῶν ἁμαρτιῶν
25 τὴν τῆς ψυχῆς καθαρότητα καὶ τὴν τοῦ σώματος ἁγνείαν καὶ εἰλικρινῆ ἀγάπην καὶ ὑπὲρ αὐτοῦ καὶ τῆς αὐτοῦ εἰκόνος προθύμως θεῖναι τὴν ἑαυτῶν ψυχὴν καὶ ἐκχέειν τὸ ἴδιον αἷμα καὶ μὴ προδοῦναι τὴν ἡμῶν ὀρθόδοξον καὶ ἀποστολικὴν καὶ καθολικὴν πίστιν.' Ταῦτα δὲ αὐτοῦ εἰπόντος, ἀπέλυσε πάντας.

AG
5. εἰωθὸς A: εἰωθὼς G   7. καταφανεῖ A: καταφανῇ G   8. με A: om. G   11. τούτοις A: τούτου G | add. αὐτῶν post τῇ G   19. ἐστί G: -ν A   27. ἐκχέειν : ἐκχέε codd.

34. Michael informs his disciples of his approaching translation

When he had prayed thus, he commanded that the sounding board be struck.[208] And having gathered together his holy community, he began the Mattins hymns in praise of God's glory. As the striking of the sounding board occurred contrary to custom, his disciples enquired of him, saying, 'For what reason, father, have you done this contrary to custom?'[209] After the dismissal of the morning hymns, the divine Michael said to them, 'It is nothing that will seem painful to you, my beloved children. For my Lord Jesus Christ has summoned me to depart and to be with Him.'

When he had said this in the hearing of all, they were all filled with grief and many tears, as they could not bear their state of orphanhood.[210] After our holy father had spoken with them from his heart and admonished them with consolatory words, he began to speak thus: 'My beloved children, do not forget my commands, or rather those of our Lord Jesus Christ. May your reason [256] not become weak or shrink from the service of God. Always secure the pure charity of all good works, which is the bond of perfection. For all virtue is perfected through charity and humility. While humility raises one up, charity does not suffer one to fall from that height. Charity is greater than humility.[211] For it was through charity towards us that the Word of God, our Lord Jesus Christ, humbled Himself and became a man with us. For this reason we ought incessantly out of our free will to confess unto Him and to send up hymns and thanksgivings in the form of covenants with Him, especially those of us who have been released from worldly matters and cares; and for the sake of the atonement of our sins we ought to offer as gifts purity of soul, bodily chastity, and pure charity. And we ought eagerly to lay down our souls and pour forth our own blood on behalf of Him and His icon, and not to betray our orthodox, apostolic and catholic faith.'[212] When he had said these words, he dismissed them all.

(35) Καὶ δὴ ἕωθεν ἀνέρχεται πρὸς τὸν ἁγιώτατον πατριάρχην Μεθόδιον φαιδρῷ τῷ προσώπῳ, ὥστε θεασάμενον αὐτὸν τὸν πατριάρχην εἰπεῖν πρὸς αὐτόν· Τίς ἡ φαιδρότης τοῦ προσώπου σου, τιμιώτατε πάτερ; Οὐδέποτε γάρ σε τοιοῦτον τεθέαμαι.· Ἦν γὰρ ὁ ἅγιος ὠχρὸς τῇ ὄψει ἐκ
5 τῆς ἄγαν ἐγκρατείας καὶ ταπεινώσεως. Ὁ δὲ πρὸς αὐτὸν πρὸς τὸ οὖς κατ᾽ ἰδίαν ἔφη· Καὶ γάρ, μακαριώτατε καὶ οἰκουμενικὲ διδάσκαλε, χαρῆναι καὶ εὐφρανθῆναι δεῖ, ὅτι ὁ Κύριός μου καὶ Θεὸς Ἰησοῦς ὁ Χριστὸς προσκέκληκέ με τὸν ἀνάξιον εἰς τὴν αὐτοῦ βασιλείαν.·
(36) Ὡς δὲ τούτων ἤκουσεν ὁ ἁγιώτατος ἀρχιεπίσκοπος, λύπης ἐπληρώθη·
10 πάνυ γὰρ ἠγάπα καὶ ἐσέβετο τὸν μακάριον. Καὶ λέγει αὐτῷ·· Ἀπέλθωμεν δή, μακαριώτατε, πρὸς τοὺς ὀρθοδόξους ἡμῶν βασιλεῖς, ὅπως καὶ αὐτοὶ ἐν ἀπολαύσει γένωνται τῶν ἁγίων εὐχῶν σου.· Καὶ παραλαβὼν τοῦτον ὁ ἁγιώτατος πατριάρχης καὶ πρὸς τὸν ὀρθόδοξον καὶ θεόστεπτον ἄνακτα Μιχαὴλ ἀνελθὼν καὶ τὴν αὐτοῦ θεοφιλῆ μητέρα, Θεοδώραν
15 λέγω τὴν ὀρθόδοξον καὶ μεγάλην βασίλισσαν, καὶ τούτους ἀπολαβὼν κατ᾽ ἰδίαν, ὁ ἐν ἁγίοις πατριάρχης ἀπήγγειλεν αὐτοῖς τὰ τοῦ πράγματος. Οἱ δὲ πιστότατοι καὶ ὀρθόδοξοι βασιλεῖς προσκαλεσάμενοι τὸν μακαριώτατον καὶ ἅγιον Μιχαὴλ πίπτουσιν εἰς τοὺς πόδας τοῦ σεβασμίου πατρός, εὐχὴν αἰτοῦντες καὶ πρεσβείαν ποιεῖσθαι πρὸς τὸν τῶν ὅλων
20 Θεὸν ὑπέρ τε αὐτῶν καὶ τῆς οἰκουμενικῆς καταστάσεως. Καὶ δὴ συνταξάμενος τούτοις ὁ μέγας Μιχαὴλ καὶ τελευταῖον ἀσπασάμενος λέγει πρὸς αὐτούς· Σώζεσθε, ἐπίγειοι βασιλεῖς, σώζεσθε· καὶ μὴ ἐπιλάθησθε τοῦ οὐρανίου βασιλέως Ἰησοῦ Χριστοῦ καὶ τὴν αὐτοῦ ἐκκλησίαν ἀσφαλῶς ἐκ πάσης αἱρέσεως φυλάξατε καὶ τὴν αὐτοῦ εἰκόνα
25 μηδ᾽ ὅλως ἀρνήσησθε. Ἰδοὺ τοῦτο θαρρῶν εἰς τὸν Χριστὸν καὶ Θεόν μου ὑμῖν λέγω, ὅτι τῆς ἐπουρανίου βασιλείας σὺν πᾶσι τοῖς ἁγίοις ἀξιωθήσεσθε μετὰ Κωνσταντίνου τοῦ ἐν ἁγίοις καὶ Θεοδοσίου καὶ Ἐλεσβοᾶ, τῶν χριστιανικωτάτων καὶ ὀρθοδόξων καὶ θεοστέπτων βασιλέων, ὅτι ἀπεδώκατε τὸ ἴδιον κάλλος, τὴν τῶν εἰκόνων ἀνατύπωσιν,
30 τῇ τοῦ Θεοῦ νύμφῃ, τὴν καθολικήν φημι καὶ ἀποστολικὴν ἐκκλησίαν.· Ταῦτα δὲ αὐτοῦ εἰπόντος, ἀπέστη ἀπ᾽ αὐτῶν.

AG
3. σου G: om. A 8. προσκέκληκέ G: -ν A 13. καὶ θεόστεπτον A: om. G 25. ἀρνήσησθε: ἀρνήσησθε codd. 28. καὶ θεοστέπτων A: om. G 30. τῇ -- νύμφῃ : τὴν -- νύμφην codd.

35. The patriarch Methodios is informed

At dawn he went up to the most holy patriarch Methodios with a radiant countenance, so that on perceiving him that patriarch said to him, 'What is this radiance in your countenance, most honoured father? I have never before seen you like this.' For the saint's face was usually wan from excessive abstinence and humility. He said to him privately in his ear, 'Most blessed and universal teacher, we must rejoice and be cheered that my Lord and God Jesus Christ has summoned me an unworthy one into His kingdom.'

36. Michael's final farewell to the emperor Michael and his mother Theodora

When the most holy archbishop heard these words, he was filled with grief, for he greatly loved and reverenced the blessed man. He then said to him, 'Let us go at once, most blessed one, to our orthodox emperors, in order that they may have the benefit of your holy prayers.' Taking him, the most holy patriarch went to the orthodox and God-crowned ruler, Michael and his God-loving mother, I mean the great orthodox empress Theodora.[213] After taking them aside, the patriarch of saintly memory reported this matter to them. The most faithful and orthodox emperors, after summoning the most blessed and holy Michael, fell down at the feet of the venerable father, begging him to pray and to intercede with the Lord of all creation on behalf both of themselves and of the universal state. After bidding them farewell and embracing them for the last time, Michael said to them, 'Farewell, earthly emperors, farewell; and do not forget the heavenly Emperor, Jesus Christ. Guard His Church safely from all heresy, and do not deny in any way His icon. For behold, I say this to you with confidence in Christ my God, that you shall be deemed worthy of the heavenly kingdom with all the saints, along with Constantine of blessed memory[214] and Theodosius [215] and Elesboas,[216] the most Christian, orthodox, [257] and God-crowned emperors, since you have given back the peculiar beauty, namely that of the representation of icons, to the bride of God, I mean the catholic and apostolic Church.' When he had said these words, he departed from them.

ΒΙΟΣ ΤΟΥ ΜΙΧΑΗΛ ΤΟΥ ΣΥΝΚΕΛΛΟΥ

Κατελθόντων δὲ ἀμφοτέρων τοῦ τε πατριάρχου καὶ τοῦ μεγάλου Μιχαὴλ ἐκ τῶν βασιλείων αὐλῶν, ὁ ἁγιώτατος πατριάρχης παρέλαβεν αὐτὸν μετ᾽ αὐτοῦ καὶ ἀνῆλθον εἰς τὸ αὐτοῦ κελλίον. Καὶ δὴ παρακαλεῖ αὐτὸν μεῖναι σὺν αὐτῷ μέχρι τῆς ὡρισμένης αὐτῷ παρὰ Θεοῦ τελευταίας
5 ἡμέρας. Ὁ δὲ ὅσιος πατὴρ ἡμῶν, μὴ γινώσκων παρακούειν, εἶξεν τῇ αὐτοῦ παρακλήσει καὶ ἦν σὺν αὐτῷ εὐφραινόμενος καὶ σχολάζων τῇ τε εὐχῇ καὶ νηστείᾳ καὶ ταῖς παννύχοις στάσεσί τε καὶ ἀγρυπνίαις. Μετὰ δὲ πέντε ἡμέρας πρὸ τῆς αὐτοῦ τελευτῆς παρακαλεῖ τὸν ἁγιώτατον καὶ οἰκουμενικὸν πατριάρχην Μεθόδιον ἀπολῦσαι αὐτὸν εἰς τὴν αὐτοῦ
10 μονὴν πρὸς τὸ τελειωθῆναι αὐτὸν ἐν τῷ αὐτοῦ κελλίῳ. Ὁ δὲ οὐκ ἐβούλετο τούτου χωρισθῆναι, ἀλλ᾽ ἐδέετο αὐτοῦ τελειωθῆναι ἐν τῷ αὐτοῦ κελλίῳ ἐν τῷ πατριαρχείῳ. Ὁρῶν δὲ τὸν ἅγιον σφόδρα λυπούμενον καὶ ἀδημονοῦντα διὰ τὸ μὴ ἀπολύεσθαι αὐτὸν παρ᾽ αὐτοῦ εἰς τὴν αὐτοῦ μονὴν καὶ μὴ θέλων λυπῆσαι αὐτόν, ἀπέστειλεν αὐτὸν μετὰ πάσης
15 δορυφορίας τοῦ αὐτοῦ εὐαγοῦς κλήρου.

(37) Εἰσελθόντος δὲ αὐτοῦ εἰς τὴν αὐτοῦ μονήν, εἰσέρχεται ἐν τῷ ναῷ τοῦ ἁγίου ἱερομάρτυρος Ἀνθίμου. Καὶ οἱονεὶ συνταξάμενος αὐτῷ τῷ τοῦ Χριστοῦ μάρτυρι, ὁ τοῦ Χριστοῦ ὁμολογητὴς καὶ μάρτυς κατέρχεται ἐν τῇ ἐκεῖσε λεγομένῃ καταφυγῇ, ἐν ᾗ ἐναπόκεινται τὰ καλλίνικα καὶ ἅγια
20 λείψανα τῶν ἁγίων μαρτύρων Βαβύλα καὶ τῶν σὺν αὐτῷ ὀγδοήκοντα τεσσάρων νηπίων. Καὶ πεσὼν εἰς τὰς αὐτῶν ἁγίας θήκας ἱκέτευε τοὺς ἁγίους μάρτυρας συνοδεῦσαι αὐτῷ ἐν τῇ ὁδῷ, ᾗ ἔμελλεν πορεύεσθαι, τηρῆσαι δὲ τὴν αὐτοῦ καὶ αὐτῶν σεβασμίαν μονὴν ἄτρωτον ἐκ τῶν τοῦ πονηροῦ σκανδάλων ταῖς πρὸς Θεὸν αὐτῶν πρεσβείαις. Συνταξάμενος
25 δὲ τοὺς μάρτυρας ἐξῆλθε τοῦ ναοῦ καὶ ἀπέλυσε πάντας τοὺς μετ᾽ αὐτοῦ ἐλθόντας κληρικοὺς τῆς τοῦ Θεοῦ μεγάλης ἐκκλησίας, ἀσπασάμενος τούτους ἐν φιλήματι ἁγίῳ καὶ ἐπευξάμενος αὐτούς.

Αὐτῶν δὲ ἐξελθόντων, ἰδοὺ οἱ αὐτοῦ φοιτηταὶ ὑπήντησαν αὐτῷ μετὰ κηρῶν καὶ θυμιαμάτων, ψάλλοντες τὸ ˊΔόξα σοι, Χριστὲ ὁ Θεός,
30 ἀποστόλων καύχημα, μαρτύρων ἀγαλλίαμα᾽ καὶ τὰ ἑξῆς. Καὶ ἀσπασάμενος τούτους ἔρχεται μετ᾽ αὐτῶν ἐν τῷ ναῷ τῶν ἁγίων τεσσαράκοντα μαρτύρων. Καὶ δὴ συνταξάμενος καὶ αὐτοὺς εἰσέρχεται

AG
3. αὐτοῦ² A: om. G   12. πατριαρχείῳ : πατριαρχίῳ codd.   18. κατέρχεται A: om. G
21. αὐτῶν post ἁγίας trsp.G   22. ἔμελλεν A: ἤμελλε G

When both the patriarch and the great Michael had left the imperial court, the most holy patriarch took him and they both went up to his cell. There he entreated Michael to remain in his company until the final day which was ordained for him by God. Our holy father, who did not know how to disobey, yielded to his entreaty and rejoiced with him and devoted himself to prayer, fasting, standing all night and vigils. Five days later, just before his death, he besought the most holy and universal patriarch Methodios to grant him leave to return to his monastery that he might die in his cell. But Methodios did not wish to be separated from him and begged him to die in his cell in the patriarchal residence. However, when he perceived that the saint was greatly grieved and distressed that he did not grant him leave to go to his monastery, not wishing to grieve him, he sent him forth with all the escort of his holy clergy.

37. Michael's final prayers at the monastery of Chora

When he arrived in his monastery, he entered the church of the holy martyr Anthimos.[217] Having so to speak said farewell to this martyr of Christ, the confessor and martyr of Christ entered the place which was called 'the refuge' there, in which were stored up the gloriously triumphant and holy relics of the holy martyrs Babylas and the eighty-four infants who were with him.[218] He fell down on their holy coffins and besought the holy martyrs to accompany him on the road which he was about to travel and to preserve inviolate his and likewise their venerable monastery from the snares of the evil one through their intercessions with God. After bidding the martyrs farewell,[219] he left the church and dismissed all the clergy of the great Church of God who had accompanied him, after dismissing them with a holy embrace and praying for them.

When they had departed, behold, his disciples came to meet him with candles and incense, singing, 'Glory to Thee, Christ our God, boast of apostles, exultation of martyrs,' and the rest of the prayer.[220] When he had embraced them, he went in their company into the church of the forty holy martyrs.[221] Taking leave also of them, he entered the tombs of our fathers,

ΒΙΟΣ ΤΟΥ ΜΙΧΑΗΛ ΤΟΥ ΣΥΝΚΕΛΛΟΥ

ἐν τοῖς σοροῖς τῶν ἁγίων καὶ ὁμολογητῶν πατέρων ἡμῶν Γερμανοῦ καὶ Θεοφάνους καὶ πίπτει ἐπάνω τῶν αὐτῶν ἁγίων τύμβων εὐχόμενος μετὰ δακρύων καὶ λέγων ˙ ' Ἰδού, ἅγιοι καὶ ὁμολογηταὶ τοῦ Χριστοῦ καὶ θεοφόροι πατέρες, ἔρχομαι πρὸς ὑμᾶς κελεύσει Θεοῦ, σύγκοιτος ὑμῶν
5 σωματικῶς γενησόμενος. Δέομαι δὲ ὑμῶν, ἵνα καὶ συγχορευτὴς ὑμῶν γένωμαι ἐν τῇ ἄνω Ἰερουσαλὴμ εὐχαῖς ὑμῶν.' Συνταξάμενος δὲ καὶ αὐτοὺς ὑποδείκνυσι τὸν τόπον, ἐν ᾧ ἔμελλε κατατίθεσθαι τὸ αὐτοῦ καρτερικὸν καὶ ἀθλητικώτατον ἅγιον σῶμα. Καὶ ἀνέρχεται ἐν τῷ αὐτοῦ κελλίῳ.
10 (39) Τῷ δὲ σαββάτῳ ἤγουν τῇ ἐννεακαιδεκάτῃ τοῦ δεκεμβρίου μηνός, τῇ παραμονῇ τοῦ ἁγίου ἱερομάρτυρος Ἰγνατίου, ἐκέλευσε παννύχιον ἀγρυπνίαν γενέσθαι ἐν τῷ αὐτοῦ εὐκτηρίῳ οἴκῳ τῷ ὄντι ἐν τῷ ναῷ τοῦ ἁγίου ἱερομάρτυρος Ἀνθίμου. Τούτου δὲ γενομένου μετὰ τὰς ἑωθινὰς ὑμνῳδίας ἀνέρχεται ἐν τῷ αὐτοῦ κελλίῳ καὶ προσκαλεῖται τοὺς αὐτοῦ
15 φοιτητὰς πολλοὺς ὄντας καὶ λέγει αὐτοῖς ˙ ' Ἀπὸ τοῦ νῦν ἄλλην ἀγρυπνίαν οὐ ποιῶ μεθ᾽ ὑμῶν ἐν τῷδε τῷ σαρκίῳ ˙ ὡς γὰρ προεῖπον ὑμῖν, ὅτι προσκέκληκέ με ὁ Θεός.' Τούτου λεχθέντος παρὰ τοῦ ἁγίου, ἤρξαντο θρηνεῖν καὶ ὀλοφύρεσθαι πάντες, τὴν στέρησιν μὴ φέροντες τοῦ σεβασμίου πατρός. Ὁ δὲ μέγας τοῦ Θεοῦ ἄνθρωπος σύνδακρυς γεγονὼς
20 λέγει πρὸς αὐτούς ˙ ' Ὑπομείνατε, ὦ πατέρες καὶ ἀδελφοί, ὑπομείνατε ἐν τῷ τόπῳ τούτῳ, εὐχαρίστως τοὺς ἐπερχομένους ὑμῖν πειρασμοὺς φέροντες ἄχρι τῆς ἀπὸ τοῦ βίου τούτου ἐξόδου, καὶ ὑπήκοοι τὸ κατὰ δύναμιν τοῖς μετ᾽ ἐμὲ γινομένοις ἡγουμένοις ὑμῖν γενήθητε. Κἀγὼ δώσω λόγον τῷ Θεῷ ὑπὲρ ὑμῶν ἐν τῇ φοβερᾷ τῆς κρίσεως ἡμέρᾳ, ἐν ᾗ ἔρχεται ἀποδοῦναι
25 ἑκάστῳ κατὰ τὰ ἔργα αὐτοῦ.' Καὶ ταῦτα εἰπὼν καὶ τὸ τελευταῖον ἅπαντας ἀσπασάμενος οὕτω τυποῖ τὰς χεῖρας εἰς προσευχήν, κείμενος ἐν τῇ κλίνῃ. Καὶ τὸ τελευταῖον ' Εἰς χεῖράς σου,' λέξας, ' Παρατίθημι τὸ πνεῦμά μου,' τετελείωται τῇ τετάρτῃ τοῦ ἰανουαρίου μηνός.
(39) Εὔκαιρον δὲ καὶ ἐπὶ τοῦτο τὸ γραφικὸν ἐκεῖνο λόγιον φθέγξασθαι ˙
30 ' τίμιος ἐναντίον Κυρίου ὁ θάνατος τῶν ὁσίων αὐτοῦ.' τιμᾷ δὲ θαύματι

AG
2. ἐπάνω -- τύμβων A: τῶν ἁγίων ἐπάνω τάφων G   7. ἔμελλε A: ἤμελλε G   16. ποιῶ μεθ᾽ ὑμῶν A: ποιούμεθα ὁμοῦ G | ἐν -- σαρκίῳ A: om. G   17. προσκέκληκέ G: -ν A   25-6. τὸ -- ἀσπασάμενος A: τὸν τελευταῖον ἀσπασμὸν ἅπαντας G   27. τὸ τελευταῖον A: φησί G | λέξας A: om. G   28. τετελείωται A: καὶ κεκοίμηται G | ἰανουαρίου : ἰαννουαρίου codd.

the saints and confessors, Germanos and Theophanes.[222] He fell down upon their holy coffins and prayed tearfully, saying, 'Behold, saints and confessors of Christ and God-inspired fathers, I come to you by the command of God since I shall lie beside you in the flesh. I entreat you that I may become your fellow celebrant in Jerusalem on high through your prayers.' He bade them farewell and pointed out the place in which he was about to [258] lay down his steadfast and holy body, <the body> of a great contestant. Then he went up to his cell.

38. The death of Michael

On Saturday, that is to say on the nineteenth of December on the eve of the feast of the holy martyr Ignatios,[223] he commanded that an all-night watch be held in his oratory, which was actually in the church of the holy martyr Anthimos. After this had taken place and after the morning hymns, he went up to his cell and summoned his many disciples and said to them, 'From this time forth I shall pass no more vigils with you in this flesh. For as I have foretold to you, God has summoned me.' When the saint had said this they all began to lament and mourn, unable to bear the loss of the venerable father. But the great man of God, weeping with them, said, 'Abide, O fathers and brethren, abide in this place, gratefully bearing the trials which will beset you until your departure from this life and remain obedient as far as it lies in your power to those who shall be your abbots who follow after me. And I shall render account to God on your behalf on the fearful day of judgment, on which He comes "to reward every man according to his works."'[224]

After saying these words, he embraced them all for the last time and folded his hands in prayer thus, lying in his bed. Saying as his last words, 'Into Thy hands I commend my spirit,'[225] he died on the fourth day of the month of January.[226]

39. A final miracle

It is timely here to quote that word of scripture: 'Precious in the sight of the Lord is the death of His saints.' For the Lord of all creation honoured his death

---

25. cf. II Tim. 4:14   27-8. Lu. 23:46   30. Ps. 115:6

τὴν αὐτοῦ τελευτὴν ὁ τῶν ὅλων Θεός. Μοναχὸς γάρ τις ἐκ τῆς αὐτοῦ ποίμνης ἔχων πνεῦμα ἀκάθαρτον ἔτη πολλά (τίνος δὲ ἕνεκεν κρίματος, οὐκ οἶδα· ὁ Θεὸς οἶδεν, κατὰ τὸν θεῖον ἀπόστολον), ἀπαλλαγῆναι τοῦ τοιούτου δαίμονος ἄχρι τῆς τοῦ δικαίου τελευτῆς οὐ συνεχωρήθη, τοῦ
5 Θεοῦ τάχα κρεῖττόν τι προβλεψαμένου, ὅπως τῇ τοῦ δικαίου τελευτῇ καὶ οὗτος καθαρισθῇ, κἀκεῖνος μεγαλυνθῇ διὰ τῆς τοῦ θαύματος ἐκπλήξεως. Μετὰ γὰρ τὸ παραδοῦναι τὸν ὅσιον εἰς χεῖρας Θεοῦ τὴν αὐτοῦ ἁγίαν ψυχὴν ἀνακρᾶξαν τὸ ἀκάθαρτον πνεῦμα καὶ πολλὰ σπαράξαν αὐτὸν ἐξῆλθεν ἀπ᾽ αὐτοῦ ἀφανὲς γενόμενον τῇ τοῦ Θεοῦ ἀοράτῳ δυνάμει.
10 Ταῦτά μοι τοῦ ἐλαχίστου τοῦδε πονήματος τὰ ἐκλεχθέντα παρὰ τῶν τοῦ ὁσίου ἀγχιστέων, γνωρίμων, συσσίτων, ὁμορόφων καὶ φοιτητῶν, οὐ μὴν ἀλλὰ καὶ παρὰ τῶν τοῦ τυράννου συμμυστῶν τῶν ἀκμὴν τῷδε τῷ βίῳ συστάντων. Τί δὲ πρὸς σὲ φθέγξομαι, ὦ πάτερ ὁσιώτατε καὶ ἅγιε Μιχαήλ; Ὑπὲρ γὰρ ἄνθρωπον ὑπάρχει σου τὸ τῆς ὁμολογίας καὶ τοῦ βίου διήγημα,
15 ὧν καὶ τὸ ἔργον ἐξαίρετον καὶ ὁ ἔπαινος ὑπὲρ ἄνθρωπον. Ἀλλ᾽ ὦ Θεοῦ μάρτυς, ὁ μόνος τὸν δεσπότην Χριστὸν τῷ ὑπὲρ αὐτοῦ τῆς εἰκόνος πάθει καὶ τῇ τῆς ὁμολογίας παρρησίᾳ μιμησάμενος, ὦ κοινὲ φύλαξ τοῦ γένους ἡμῶν, δαιμόνων ὀλοθρευτὰ καὶ ἁγίων εἰκόνων προσκυνητά, ὦ νοσούντων ἰατρὲ καὶ χειμαζομένων ἀκύμαντον ὁρμητήριον, ὦ πεπλανημένων ὁδηγὲ
20 καὶ ὀρθοδόξων στήριγμα, φωστὴρ παγκόσμιε φωτίζων τὰς ψυχὰς τῇ αἱρέσει ἐσκοτισμένας, ὦ ἀγγέλων συνόμιλε καὶ ἀρχαγγέλων συγχορευτὰ καὶ συνώνυμε, ὦ τῆς ἁγίας τριάδος θεράπον καὶ ψυχῶν ἀνθρωπίνων ἱερουργὲ τῶν ἐν ἀληθινῇ πίστει δεχομένων καὶ δοξαζόντων σου τὴν ἄθλησιν, καί, ἵνα συντόμως εἴπω, ὦ παντὸς ὀνόματος ἀγαθοῦ καὶ πάσης
25 πράξεως ὑπερεκτεινόμενε δίκαιε, ἀσκητῶν ἐγκαλλώπισμα, ὁσίων ἐκλόγιον, μοναστῶν σύστημα, καθηγητῶν λαμπτήρ, ὑποτακτητῶν ἅμιλλα καὶ μαρτύρων ὁμόστεφε πανάγιε Μιχαήλ, δέχου παρ᾽ ἐμοῦ τὸν λόγον ὡς Θεοῦ Λόγου θεράπων, ἵνα ψυχῇ καὶ σώματι εὐεκτῶν καὶ ὑγιαίνων εὐχαριστίαν καὶ δόξαν ἀναπέμπω Χριστῷ τῷ Θεῷ ἡμῶν, τῷ σὲ ἐπαξίως
30 δοξάσαντι, ᾧ πρέπει τιμὴ καὶ προσκύνησις νῦν καὶ ἀεὶ καὶ εἰς τοὺς αἰῶνας τῶν αἰώνων. Ἀμήν.

AG
2. ἔτη G: ἔτι A   6. μεγαλυνθῇ G: μεγαλυνθεῖ A   12. ἀλλὰ A: om. G   12-31. τοῦ - - Ἀμήν G: deest in A

with a miracle. A certain monk of his flock, possessed for many years with an unclean spirit (on account of what judgment I do not know; 'God knoweth,' according to the divine apostle), was not permitted to be released from this demon until the death of our righteous man took place. It seems that 'God provided some better thing' in order that the monk might be purified by the death of the righteous man, and that Michael might be exalted because of the general amazement at the miracle. For after the saint had committed his holy soul into the hands of God, the unclean spirit, having cried out and greatly torn the monk, came out of him and vanished by the unseen power of God.[227]

These events were collected by me for this modest work from the saint's kinsmen, acquaintances, eating and living companions, and disciples and in addition to these from those associates of the tyrant who are still alive.[228] What shall I declare in addressing thee, O most holy and saintly father, Michael? For the narrative of thy confession and life is above man's power since the matter is extraordinary [259] and its praise beyond man. O martyr of God, who alone imitated the Lord Christ in suffering on behalf of His icon and in the outspokenness of confession; O common guardian of our race, destroyer of demons, and worshipper of holy icons; O healer of the sick and calm harbour of those tossed in the tempest; O guide for those led astray and support of the orthodox; O universal light illuminating the souls which have been darkened by heresy; O companion of the angels and fellow celebrant and namesake of the archangels; O servant of the Holy Trinity and sanctifier of human souls which have accepted and glorified thy contest in true faith and, to speak concisely, O righteous one, thou who art beyond every good name and deed, ornament of those engaged in spiritual training, elect member of the saints, upholder of monks, shining light of teachers, goal for those who follow a rule and sharer of the crown with the martyrs, all-holy Michael, accept as a servant of God the Word these words from me, in order that I may stay sound and healthy in body and soul and send up thanksgiving and glory to Christ our God, Who has glorified thee as is meet and to Whom be honour and worship now and forever and unto the ages of the ages. Amen.

---

3. II Cor. 11:11   4-5. Heb. 11:40   8-9. cf. Mk. 1:26

Commentary

1. Although Michael died on 4 January according to his hagiographer, the *Synaxaria* of Constantinople mistakenly celebrate his memory on 18 or 20 December, which in fact represent the possible dates of the beginning of his illness. See *Synax. Eccl. CP*, cols. 324-6, 329-32.

2. *Synkellos*: associate or assistant of a patriarch or other ecclesiastical official. Literally, 'cell-sharer'. See J. Darrouzès, *Recherches sur les ὀφφίκια de l'église byzantine* (*Archives de l'orient chrétien*, 11, Paris, 1970), 17-9.

3. This introductory paragraph corresponds almost word for word with that found in Symeon the Metaphrast's re-working of the Life of St John the Merciful. Cf. *PG*, 114, col. 896. The Life of John the Merciful by Sophronios and John Moschos does not survive, but it is possible that both our author and the Metaphrast copied this passage from it. On the likelihood that the first six chapters of Symeon's version are based on Sophronios' Life, see H. Delehaye, 'Une vie inédite de saint Jean l'Aumônier', *AnalBoll*, 45 (1927), 6-7. Two epitomes of the Life survive, one edited by Delehaye, *ibid.*, 19-74, and the other by E. Lappa-Zizicas, 'Un épitomé inédit de la Vie de s. Jean l'Aumonier par Jean et Sophronios', *AnalBoll*, 88 (1970), 265-78.

4. The monastery of Chora: this monastery occupied the site of the church known today as the Kariye Djami, located by the Theodosian walls near the Adrianople gate in Istanbul. Two traditions exist concerning its foundation. According to the anonymous ninth-century Life of St Theodore, the monastery was begun after 536 and finished in 554 by this saint, who is said to have been the maternal uncle of the empress Theodora. Only three years after its completion, the monastery was destroyed by an earthquake and was rebuilt on a grander scale by Justinian. Schmitt, 'Kahrie-Džame', 11-8, 27-9; Ch. Loparev, *De s.Theodoro (504-595) monacho hegumenoque Chorensi* (St.Petersburg,

1903), 1-16; Gédéon, Βυζαντινὸν Ἑορτολόγιον, 227-31. A second tradition, found in the *Patria* of Constantinople, states that the Chora was founded in the early seventh century by the son-in-law of the emperor Phocas, named Crispus (*recte* Priscus). Th. Preger, *Scriptores originum Constantinopolitanarum*, III (Leipzig, 1901-7), 273. Against the first tradition, no evidence of the legendary uncle of Theodora survives in the literary sources of the sixth century. Nevertheless, substructures dating from that period have been found under part of the existing building, which suggest that it was founded then. See R. Janin, *La géographie écclésiastique de l'empire byzantin, III: Les églises et les monastères de Constantinople* (2nd ed., Paris, 1969), 531-9; P. Underwood, *The Kariye Djami*, I (New York, 1966), 6. Little is known of the history of the monastery from the seventh to the ninth century. During the period of iconoclasm the Chora appears to have suffered, especially at the hands of Constantine V. Although the monastery was deconsecrated during his reign, an abbot Symeon participated at the seventh ecumenical council at Nicaea in 787. According to Theodore of Stoudios, the monastery became iconoclast during the second period of iconoclasm. See Mansi XII, col. llllD, XIII, col. 152A; Theodore of Stoudios, *Epistolae* in Mai, *Nova patrum bibliotheca*, VIII, 34. After the triumph of orthodoxy in 843, the Chora began to flourish once more when Michael the *Synkellos* was appointed as its abbot. See Theophanes, *Chronographia*, ed. De Boor, 648; above, pp.114-9.

5. No other references to Michael's 'Persian' ancestry exist, either in the *synaxaria* or in other *vitae* dealing with the saint.

6. None of Michael's letters survives. See Beck, *Kirche und Theologische Literatur*, 504.

7. If Michael died in 846 at the age of 85, his birth date would be circa 761. See below, note 226.

8. The *topos* of comparison with Anna, who promised to dedicate a son to God's service if He should grant her one, appears in the writings of

the Cappadocian fathers, as well as in later saints' lives. The story of Anna and Samuel prefigured the miraculous birth of Christ in the Byzantine Church. In Mattins on Christmas Day, the canticle of Anna (I Kings 3:1) is sung, followed by *troparia* on the nativity of Christ. J.Mateos, *Le typicon de la grande église*, I, 154-5. The *topos* of Anna in hagiography can thus be seen as another reminder of the saints' similarity to Christ. See also Gregory the Presbyter, *Vita s.Gregorii Theologi, PG*, 35, col. 248; Gregory of Nazianzus, *De vita sua, PG*, 37, cols. 1001-2; Gregory of Nyssa, *In laudem fratris Basilii, PG* 46, col. 808; Eustratios' Life of St Eutychios, *PG*, 86, cols. 2280-1. (I am indebted to Dr. A. M. Wilson for furnishing me with these references.)

9. τῷ τῆς παλιγγενεσίας λουτρῷ: baptism (Tit. 3:5). See also Origen, *Hom. 16.5 in Jeremiam, GCS* (1901), 137; ed. Nautin (1983), 137 (*PG*, 13, col. 445B); *In Ioannem* 6.33, *GCS* ed. Preuschen (1903), 143 (*PG*, 14, col. 257B).

10. The epithet 'general of God' for the name Michael appears in Jerome's book of the interpretation of Hebrew names (*Onomastika*). The epithet refers to the archangel Michael and his military attributes. See F. Wutz, *Onomastika Sacra; Liber Interpretationis Nominum Hebraicorum des H. Hieronymus* (Leipzig, 1914-5), 184, 185, 233, 236-701, 704n, 716, 726, 732. The idea that names can foretell the character or actions of the individuals who bear them occurs frequently in hagiography. See for example the *martyrion* of saints Agape, Eirene and Chione in J. Musurillo, *The Acts of the Christian Martyrs* (Oxford, 1972), 283; Gregory of Nazianzus, *In Laudem s. Basilii, PG*, 36, col. 505 (Emmelia); Eustratios, *Vita s. Eutychii, PG*, 86, col. 2280, C-D (Synesia). On Michael's role in combatting 'the serpent of the sea and beast who bore the name of lion' and its parallel with Revelation 12: 7, ff., see below, note 98.

11. The church which forms part of the complex known as the Holy Sepulchre. The original church was built by Constantine on the site where Christ's Passion and Resurrection were believed to have taken place. The whole sanctuary consisted of three parts: the Anastasis, the

Calvary and the Martyrium. The Anastasis, or church of the Resurrection, commemorated the site of Christ's tomb. See L.H. Vincent and F.M. Abel, *Jérusalem: Recherches de topographie, d'archéologie et d'histoire II: Jérusalem nouvelle* (Paris, 1914), 181-5.

12. The patriarch of Jerusalem in 764 was Theodore I. See M. Lequien, *Oriens christianus in quatuor patriarchatus digestus*, III (Paris, 1740), col. 291; V. Grumel, *La chronologie* (*Traité de textes byzantines*, I, Paris, 1958), 451.

13. It is surprising that Michael should be appointed to this clerical order at such a young age. In the *Novels* of Justinian the minimum age for a reader is stated to be eighteen. See Justinian, *Novellae constitutiones*, ed. R. Schoell and W. Kroll, *Corpus iuris civilis*, III (Berlin, 1895), 604. On the abuse of this rule, see *Concilium Nicaenum* (787), canon 14, F. Lauchert, ed., *Die Kanones der wichtigsten altkirchlichen Concilien* (Freiburg and Leipzig, 1896), 147.

14. κεκαρπωμένον: 'offered'. See Leviticus 2:11 for this meaning. The use of the word here recalls the phrase καρπὸν κοιλίας, describing Michael, above, p.44, line 26.

15. On the elementary education attested in other lives of roughly the same period, see P. Lemerle, *Le premier humanisme byzantin*, 99-100; A. Moffatt, 'Schooling in the Iconoclast centuries', *Iconoclasm*, eds. Bryer and Herrin, 85-92.

16. This phrase recalls the parable of the sower (Matthew 13: 18-23).

17. This course of middle education, which normally lasted from the age of about ten or eleven years to seventeen or eighteen, is also typical of the period. The three literary subjects, grammar, rhetoric and philosophy, are recognizable as the first three liberal arts, but the four scientific subjects which would complete the cycle (arithmetic, geometry, music and astronomy) are replaced here by poetry and astronomy. See Lemerle, *Premier humanisme byzantin*, 100-4.

COMMENTARY

18. ἐξ ἁπαλῶν ὀνύχων: *Anthologia Graeca*, V, 128. This phrase may be proverbial. In Latin, it is found in Horace, *Carmina*, 3.6.24 (*de tenero ungui*); Cicero, *Epistulae ad familiares*, 1.6.2 (*a teneris unguiculis*).

19. ὅσον ἐστὶ δυνατὸν ἀνθρώπῳ: a Platonic phrase. See Plato, *Phaedrus*, 277a; *Cratylus* 422d, etc.

20. The holy Sion: this sanctuary, which was located on one of the western hills of Jerusalem and which commemorated the place where Christ celebrated the Last Supper, consisted originally of a small church, sometimes called 'the mother of all churches' since it represented one of the earliest Christian places of worship in Jerusalem. This church was replaced by a large basilica between 336 and 348 and it is mentioned in the late fourth-century journal of the pilgrim Egeria. Also commemorated in this church were the first appearances of Christ to the apostles after the Resurrection and Pentecost. Later, the Dormition of the Mother of God was connected with the site as well. Vincent and Abel, *Jérusalem nouvelle*, 421-72; H. Pétré, *Éthérie, journal de voyage*, (*SC*, 21, Paris, 1971), 60-1, 201, note 2; J. Wilkinson, *Egeria's Travels to the Holy Land* (Jerusalem-Warminster, 1981), 38-9, 158, 191.

21. This action is reminiscent of St Anthony's call to the ascetic life after he had placed his sister in the care of nuns. See *Vita s. Antonii*, *PG*, 26, cols. 841-4. In his case it is inspired by Jesus' commands to His disciples (Mt 10: 5-42 and 16:24).

22. The term *laura* refers to a form of monasticism which is half-way between the life of a solitary anchorite and the communal life of a coenobitic monastery. The *laura* originated in Palestine and it comprised a central complex containing a church, a refectory, storehouses, a bakery and other necessary buildings, as well as individual cells or caves for the monks. The members of this community would remain in their own cells throughout the week,

coming together on Saturdays and Sundays to celebrate the evening office and the Divine Liturgy. The saints Euthymios and Sabas, who both founded *lauras* in Palestine, would not receive novices unless they had first spent some time in a *koinobion*. See Cyril of Skythopolis, *Vitae s. Euthymii et s. Sabae*, ed. Schwartz, 50, 53, 166, 206; Chitty, *The Desert a City*, 15-16.

23. The *laura* of St Sabas, founded in the late fifth century, still stands in the Judaean desert east of Jerusalem. It underwent many vicissitudes between the sixth and the ninth centuries, including disputes with monophysites and origenists and devastation at the hands of both Persians and Arabs. According to the Passion of the twenty martyrs written by St Stephen the Melodist, a tribe of Arabs sacked the monastery on March 13, 796 or 797 and a week later massacred many of the monks. See *Passio sanctorum XX Martyrum, AASS*, March, III, 166-79. By the ninth century, the *laura* of St Sabas seems to have been operating as a coenobitic monastery. See Papachryssanthou, 'La vie monastique', 166-73, 179. For a history of the monastery, see S. Vailhé, 'Le monastère de Saint Sabas', *EO*, 3 (1899-1900), 18-28, 168-77; J. Phocylides, *History of the Laura of St. Sabas* (Alexandria, 1927) (in Greek).

24. προεστῶτα: abbot or superior of a monastery. See also a fourth-century Egyptian papyrus collected in H.I. Bell, *Jews and Christians in Egypt* (London, 1924), 49; Basil of Caesarea, *Regulae fusius tractatae*, 35, 3, *PG* 31, col. 1005C.

25. μαννουθίων: faggots or shrubs. St Sabas is said to have exerted himself in a similar manner, bringing three loads of faggots to his monastery while the other monks brought only one. See Cyril of Skythopolis, *Vita s. Sabae*, ed. Schwartz, *TU* 49, 92, line 8.

26. πρὸς ἓν φορτίον: The meaning of πρὸς in this phrase is unclear. If it modifies ἓν φορτίον, it might mean 'almost', in the sense that they carried something approaching one burden.

COMMENTARY

27. If Michael entered the monastery of St Sabas at the age of twenty-five in 786, his ordination to the priesthood would have taken place in 798. In his study of the saints Michael, Theodore and Theophanes, S. Vailhé suggests that this date is problematic since it is unlikely that Thomas was yet patriarch in 798. In 796 or 797, at the time of the sacking of St Sabas, Elias was patriarch, and it is known that his *synkellos* George succeeded him. Whether the patriarchate of Thomas immediately followed that of George is unknown; it nevertheless seems unlikely that within a year or two he should have been transferred from his monastic role to the office of patriarch. See Vailhé, 'Saint Michel le Syncelle', 317-8. By 807 Thomas was patriarch, since in that office he was corresponding with the emperor Charlemagne. See Le Quien, *Oriens christianus*, III, cols. 321ff.; Grumel, *La chronologie*, 452.

28. The imperial and ecclesiastical terminology applied to God is striking here. On the concept of earthly kingship as a reflection of kingship in Heaven, see S. MacCormack, *Art and Ceremony in Late Antiquity* (Berkeley, 1981), especially 206-7.

29. ἡσυχάσαι: In the early Byzantine period, ἡσυχάζειν meant to live in solitude and contemplation. See Evagrius Ponticus, *Oratio* III, *PG*, 79, col. 1168C; *Rerum monachalium rationes*, 5, *PG*, 40, col. 1257A; *Apophthegmata patrum*, *PG*, 65, col. 201C, etc.

30. πληροφορεῖν: in the *Shepherd of Hermas*, this word is used to mean a request that is fulfilled. See J.B. Lightfoot, *Apostolic Fathers*, V (London, 1926), 330.

31. ψιάθιον: a rush mat for sleeping on. See Athanasius' Life of St. Anthony, *PG*, 26, col. 853A, *Apophthegmata patrum*, *PG*, 65, col. 185C.

32. βαυκάλιον: Dim. of βαυκάλη, βαύκαλις, ἡ. The Alexandrian name for a fat, narrow-necked, earthenware vessel. See Palladius, *Historia lausiaca*, *PG*, 34, col. 1057A (καυκάλιον); *Apophthegmata patrum*, *PG*, 65, col. 276C, etc. Prof. Ševčenko suggests that the noun

is related to the verb βαυκαλάω, meaning 'to lull to sleep'. The βαυκάλιον emitted a 'lulling' sound when water was poured out of it.

33. Two years after Michael's ordination in 798 gives us the year 800. Thus Theodore would have been born in 775 and Theophanes in 778. These dates correspond with chronological details given later in the Life. The hagiographer tells us that Theophanes died in October 845 at the age of sixty-seven, and Theodore in December 844 at the age of seventy years. See above, pp. 16-7 and 110-3.

34. The active role assigned to Michael in training the brothers Theodore and Theophanes suggests that he had achieved a position of some importance in the monastery. On the existence of anchorites such as Michael within monasteries and *lauras* in this period, see Papachryssanthou, 'La vie monastique', 165-6. Also see introduction above, pp. 30-5.

35. τὸ ἀγγελικὸν... σχῆμα: although a distinction is sometimes made between the μέγα (also called ἀγγελικὸν) and μικρὸν σχῆμα, this passage seems to refer simply to the monastic habit which is bestowed on novices. See Lampe, 1359.

36. παιδοτρίβης: trainer (of athletes). Also used to mean teacher or instructor. See John Chrysostom, *Hom. in Rom. 5.3*, *PG*, 51, col. 158.

37. σκέμματα: works of poetry, from the verb, σκέπτομαι. In this context, the word means compositions or works.

38. It is noticeable that Michael did not teach the brothers rhetoric in addition to these subjects. According to the metaphrastic Life of Theodore, the latter temporarily left St Sabas and went to a learned and pious man for further education in rhetoric, after finishing his studies with Michael. See *Vita s. Theodori*, *PG*, 116, col. 657; Moffatt, 'Schooling in the Iconoclast Centuries', 91. This is somewhat surprising in view of Michael's demonstrated competence in rhetoric later in life. See introduction above, pp. 36-8.

39. The comparison of divine learning with flowing water is commonly made in the writings of the Fathers. To take one example, Sophronios of Jerusalem, in his commentary on the Divine Liturgy, uses the image of a spring flowing with life-giving waters with reference to the teachings of the Holy Spirit. Cf. *PG*, 87, col. 3981. The source of this imagery may be John 4:14. The tenth-century manuscript of John Chrysostom's homilies, Athen. gr. 211, contains miniatures depicting water, which represents wisdom, flowing directly from a roll placed on a lectern or from the lectern itself. See C. Walter, *Art and Ritual of the Byzantine Church* (*Birmingham Byzantine Series*, 1, London, 1982), 114.

40. If Michael was born in 761, this would be 811. See note 7.

41. See above, note 2.

42. This monastery, founded in 494-5 by the patriarch Elias, was situated near the Holy Sepulchre and the Patriarchate. It housed the clergy attached to the Holy Sepulchre. See Vincent and Abel, *Jérusalem nouvelle*, 516, 911, 923; P. Petrides, 'Le Monastère des Spoudaei à Jérusalem et les Spoudaei de Constantinople', *EO*, 4 (1901), 225-31.

43. Patriarch of Jerusalem, 494-516. An Arab by birth, Elias was educated in one of the Nitrian monasteries in Egypt. In 457 he and his friend Martyrios were driven from Egypt by Timothy Aelurus and took refuge at the *laura* of St Euthymios in Palestine. After 473 he joined the clergy of the church of the Resurrection in Jerusalem and in 494 was made patriarch. At the time of his succession, the Christian world was divided between those churches which accepted the *Henotikon* and those which did not. Elias remained in the centre, both subscribing to the *Henotikon* and at the same time upholding the council of Chalcedon. During the reign of Anastasius I, Elias was deposed and banished to Aila on the shores of the Red Sea. He lived on until 518. See Cyril of Skythopolis, *Vita s. Euthymii*, ed. Schwartz, 51, 56-7, 60, 62; *Vita s. Sabae*, *ibid*., 121, 130, 139-41, 161-2, 175; John Moschos, *Pratum*

spirituale, chap. 35, *PG*, 87, col. 2884; Evagrius, *Historia ecclesiae*, IV, 37, eds. J. Bidez and L. Parmentier, *The Ecclesiastical History of Evagrius* (London, 1898), 186; Theophanes, *Chronographia*, I, ed. De Boor, 151-3, 156.

44. The relics of the apostles Peter and Paul are first mentioned circa 200 by the Roman priest Gaius in a disputation with the Montanist Proclus, which is recorded by Eusebius. Calling the relics τὰ τρόπαια, he records their deposition on the Vatican and the Via Ostia respectively. See Eusebius, *Historia ecclesiae*, II, 25, 7, ed. G. Schwartz, (*GCS*, Leipzig, 1903), 176-8. A later pilgrim to describe the tombs of the two apostles was Prudentius in his *Peristephanon*, 12, 30. See M. Schantz, *Geschichte der römischen Literatur*, IV, I (Munich, 1914), 239; H. Chadwick, 'St. Peter and St. Paul in Rome: The Problem of the Memoria Apostolorum ad Catacumbas', *JTS*, n.s., 8 (1957), 31-52.

45. Nero: emperor of Rome, AD 54-68.

46. Theodosius I: 379-95. Although popular tradition from the middle of the fifth century onward held that the Constantinopolitan Creed was formulated at the second general council in 381, it is in fact first attested at the council of Chalcedon in 451. The Acts of the later council represent the primary source for the Creed. See *Acta conciliorum oecumenicorum II,* ed. E.Schwartz, (Berlin and Leipzig, 1914--) I, ii, 79, 128 and 141; Kelly, *Early Christian Creeds*, 296-331.

47. Macedonius, patriarch of Constantinople, 342-6, 351-60, was not in fact the founder of the group named after him. These were the Pneumatomachians or Macedonians, who did not believe that the Holy Spirit was consubstantial with the Father and the Son. One of the objects of the council of Constantinople in 381 was to reaffirm the divinity of the Holy Spirit and to anathematise the Pneumatomachians. Kelly, *Early Christian Creeds*, 339-44.

48. From the fifth and sixth centuries the *filioque* clause was added to the Constantinopolitan Creed in certain parts of the West, beginning in Spain. Originating in the writings of St Augustine, the doctrine was seen as clinching the case against arianism, since in stating that the Holy Spirit proceeds from the Father *and the Son* it upholds the unity of the Trinity. Although the formula was not adopted by the papacy until much later, it appears in the councils of Toledo in 589 and Hatfield in 690. Conflict between Latins and Greeks over the matter first flared up at the council of Gentilly in 767, when the ambassadors of the emperor Constantine V accused the Latin delegates of inserting the *filioque* into the Creed. In 794 Frankish theologians objected to the absence of the *filioque* in the Acts of the seventh ecumenical council at Nicaea (787), but they were overruled by pope Hadrian. In 796 or 797 at the synod of Cividale the symbol contained the *filioque*. After 798 it is likely that the clause was included in the royal chapel at Aachen and throughout the Frankish dominions. In 807 two Benedictine monks from the Mount of Olives were sent to Charlemagne's court and on returning to Jerusalem revised the Creed in accordance with the Frankish practice. It was this addition of the *filioque* in Jerusalem which caused the monks of St Sabas anxiety and which on Christmas day 808 erupted into open conflict. The Benedictine monks immediately sent a letter to pope Leo III, who responded with a *Symbolum orthodoxae fidei*. The surviving version of this text may not be authentic, since it vigorously supports the *filioque* clause on doctrinal grounds and thus does not seem consistent with the pope's conservative response throughout the rest of the affair. In the next two years, despite pressure from Charlemagne and his Frankish theologians, pope Leo III remained firm in his opposition to the *filioque* clause. He even caused two silver shields to be erected in St Peter's, bearing inscriptions of the Creed in Greek and Latin, neither of which contained the *filioque*. For bibliography, see introduction, notes 13 and 34.

49. These letters, if they ever existed, no longer survive. There is no question that the pope was opposed to the insertion of the *filioque*, but that he would appeal to the patriarch of Jerusalem for help is unlikely. Vailhé, 'Saint Michel le Syncelle', 324-5.

COMMENTARY

50. These letters do not survive.

51. See note 48.

52. Hagarenes: 'children of Hagar' or Muslims. Hagar was the mother of Ishmael, the supposed progenitor of the Arabs (Genesis 16:1 ff.).

53. τῇ ἁγίᾳ Ἰερουσαλήμ: it is unusual for our author to describe Jerusalem in this way. Usually the city is called ἡ ἁγία πόλις Χριστοῦ τοῦ Θεοῦ ἡμῶν as at p.44, line 10.

54. This fine could refer either to the djizya (poll-tax) or to the kharaj (property tax) which were both levied on non-Muslims in Muslim states. I have found no reference in the Arab chronicles (in translation) to an extra fine being imposed on the churches of Jerusalem at this time, although such a policy had been pursued in Egypt in the previous century. D.C. Dennett, *Conversion and the Poll Tax in Early Islam* (Cambridge, Mass., 1950), 78. The Greek chronographer Theophanes tells us only of devastation which occurred in Jerusalem and in the outlying monasteries in 809 and again in 812 without mentioning any fine. Theophanes, *Chronographia*, ed. De Boor, I, 484, 499. The disruption was caused by the civil war then being waged between the two sons of the Abbasid caliph Harun al-Rashid.

55. Leo V: 813-20. According to some sources, Leo was of Syrian as well as of Armenian descent: γένος δὲ τὸ μὲν ἐξ Ἀσσυρίων τὸ δὲ καὶ αὐτῶν Ἀρμενίων. Theophanes Continuatus, *Chronographia*, I, 1, ed. I. Bekker (*CSHB*, Bonn, 1838), 6; Genesios, *Historia de rebus constantinopolitanis*, I, ed. C. Lachmann (*CSHB*, Bonn, 1834), 10.

56. The real motives for Michael's and his disciples' journey to Constantinople and Rome are probably the dispute over the *filioque* and the fine or perhaps more broadly speaking, the Arab threat. Michael's hagiographer, preoccupied above all with the saints' role in defending icons, understandably wished to make this the prime motive for the

journey. As Vailhé points out, the decisive clue for the actual date of the saints' departure can be found in the letter of Theophanes Graptos to John of Kyzikos, which is preserved in the metaphrastic Life of Theodore. In the course of a conversation with Theophilos' logothete of the course, the saints are asked whether they did not in fact arrive in Constantinople during the reign of Leo V. The saints reply, Οὔκουν...ἀλλ᾽ ἐπὶ τοῦ πρὸ αὐτοῦ βασιλεύσαντος. If this is indeed the case, iconoclasm cannot have been the cause of the saints' journey. See *Vita s. Theodori, PG*, 116, col. 676; Vailhé, 'Saint Michel le Syncelle', 329-31. On the probable authenticity of the letter, See Ševčenko, 'Hagiography', 119, note 44. Also see introduction, pp. 11-12.

57. Nikephoros I: 802-11.

58. ἀρχιτελετάρχην: perhaps coined by the author, this means literally: 'chief priest of the mysteries'.

59. The hagiographer is mistaken in stating that Theodore was exiled ἐν τῇ ἀνατολῇ during the reign of Nikephoros I. In 809 he was in fact banished to the island of Chalke. Theophanes, *Chronographia*, ed. De Boor, I, 484; Michael, *Vita s. Theodori, PG*, 99, col. 269; Anon., *Vita s. Theodori, ibid.*, col. 160. Also see four epigrams by Theodore on his prison in Chalke, *ibid.*, cols. 1804-5. In 817 or 818 Theodore did send a letter to the patriarch of Jerusalem from Boneta in the Anatolic theme, seeking his aid in combatting the iconoclasts. The letter from the patriarch to Leo V and Theodotos was probably sent in response to this rather than at the time of Michael's arrival in Constantinople. Theodore, *Ep.* 15, Lib.II, *PG*, 99, col. 1160; Michael,*Vita s. Theod., ibid.*, col. 288; Anon., *Vita s.Theod., ibid.*, col. 192.

60. πατριάρχην...φατριάρχην: notice the play on words. This pun is also used in the *Vita s. Stephani iunioris, PG*, 100, col. 1113C.

61. Theodotos: patriarch of Constantinople, 815-21. Theodotos belonged to the important family of Melissenos. His father Michael,

COMMENTARY

patrician and general of the Anatolic theme, had been a leading iconoclast under Constantine V. Theophanes, *Chronographia*, I, 440, 445. On the family, see C. Du Cange, *Historia byzantina duplici commentario illustrata* I (Venice, 1729), 145a.

62. ἐπιστομίζαντες: refuting. Gregory Thaumatourgos, *In Origenem*, *PG*, 10, col. 1052A; Eusebius, *Demonstratio evangelica*, ed. I.A. Heikel (*GCS*, Leipzig, 1913), 6, lines 7-8 (*PG*, 22, col. 20D).

63. πρόθεσιν: It is unclear from the context whether this means 'counsel' or 'the Eucharist'. The word has both meanings. Lampe, 1148-9.

64. ἐν ἁγίοις: 'among the saints'. Usually used of saintly figures who are no longer alive.

65. Located to the west of Jerusalem, Lydda-Diospolis would have been *en route* to the port of Joppe if, as is likely, the saints sailed from Palestine to Asia Minor. F.-M. Abel, *Géographie de la Palestine*, II (Paris, 1938), 173, 225.

66. Seleukeia, on the south-east coast of Anatolia. From here a Roman road led to Ikonion, which would have represented the first stage in the saints' journey if they travelled overland to Constantinople. See W. M. Ramsay, *The Historical Geography of Asia Minor* (London, 1890), 358.

67. The council of 787, which restored the icons and condemned the *horos* of the iconoclast council of Hiereia of 754. J. D. Mansi, *Sacrorum conciliorum nova et amplissima collectio*, XII-XIII (Florence, 1766-7).

68. Constantine VI reigned with his mother Eirene as regent from 780 until 797. In that year, Eirene caused him to be deposed after being blinded and thus assumed sole power until her deposition in 802.

69. As patriarch of Constantinople (784-806), Tarasios presided over the council of Nicaea in 787.

70. Diptychs: tablets which folded in two, containing the names of bishops or other saintly figures who were to be remembered during the Divine Liturgy. When there were too many names to be contained within tablets, books were substituted. In the Byzantine rite, these prayers took place after the invocation and before the Lord's prayer in the Liturgy of the Faithful. F.E. Brightman, *Liturgies Eastern and Western*, I (Oxford, 1896), 331-7; 388-9. On the possible place of the reading of the diptychs in the early eastern liturgy, see E. Bishop, 'Liturgical Comments and Memoranda', *JTS*, 12 (1911), 384-413; R.J. Connolly, *The Liturgical Homilies of Narsai Translated into English*, (*Texts and Studies*, 8, Cambridge, 1909), 97-114.

71. πᾶσιν: Grammatically it would make more sense if πᾶσιν (line 22) were in the accusative case (πάντας), thus linking the first clause with the second. Since this error occurs in both manuscripts, it was probably committed by the author himself.

72. Leo V: 813-20. On the hagiographer's mistake in chronology, see note 56.

73. This is an example of punning on the name of a bad character, which parallels the emphasis on the names of good ones in hagiography. Cf. for example, *Martyrium ss. XL martyrum Sebast.*, ed. O. von Gebhardt, *Acta martyrum selecta* (Berlin, 1902), 173: καλῶς ἀπεκλήθη τὸ ὄνομά σου Ἀγρικόλαος· ἄγριος γὰρ εἶ κολακευτής. The suggestion that Leo resembled a wild beast draws on a long tradition of comparing tyrannical emperors to beasts in Hebrew and Christian apocalyptic literature. Cf. for example, Daniel 7-8, Revelation 12-13, etc. The idea continued to be used by Christian writers to describe their pagan persecutors. See Lactantius, *De mortibus persecutorum*, ed. J.L. Creed (Oxford, 1984), 2, 7, p. 7 etc; Eusebius, *Vita Constantini*, II, ed. F. Winkelmann (*GCS*, Berlin, 1975),

47; Alexander, *The Oracle of Baalbek*, 17, line 136; 18, lines 151-2 etc. Also see below, note 98.

74. ἱεράρχῃ... αἱρεσιάρχῃ: This pun parallels the one cited above, note 60.

75. See note 61.

76. ἀγωνιστής: The use of this word, with its background in the early accounts of martyrs, suggests that the hagiographer is beginning to set the scene for Michael's role as a champion of the faith. This is the first occasion when the saint experiences any sort of set-back and faces the devil in the form of the persecuting ruler.

77. Notice the unusual use of ἐν with the dative following the main verb 'entered'.

78. πανευδαίμονι: 'all-fortunate.' See also John of Damascus, *Artem.* 67, *PG*, 96, col. 1316A.

79. Vailhé has shown that Michael's biographer was mistaken in assigning May 814 as the date of the saints' arrival. In fact they arrived during the reign of Michael I Rhangabe (811-3). See above, note 53 and introduction, p. 12.

80. δόλον: 'deceit'. This word appears frequently in the scriptures. Perhaps the closest parallel to the meaning here is Proverbs 26:26.

81. See note 4. On the likelihood that the monastery of Chora, and perhaps its environs as well, represented a refuge for Palestinian travellers in Constantinople, see J. Gouillard, 'Un "quartier" d'émigrés palestiniens à Constantinople au IXe siècle?', *RESEE*, 7 (1969), 73-6.

82. ἐν... ἐν: Note again the incorrect use of the preposition ἐν with the dative.

COMMENTARY

83. The Chrysotriklinos, built by Justin II (565-78), was a large octagonal throne room, topped by a cupola with sixteen windows. Theophilos (829-42) connected the Chrysotriklinos with the older palace of Daphne for the first time by constructing two more buildings, the Sigma and the Triconchos. See R. Cormack, *Writing in Gold*, 182; R. Janin, *Constantinople byzantine* (Paris, 1964), 108, 115-6.

84. θεοφόροι: 'God-bearing'. Used to describe saints, who bear God in themselves through the grace of the Holy Spirit. John Moschos, *Pratum spirituale*, 148, *PG*, 87, col. 3012C; John of Damascus, *De fide orthodoxa*, III, 12, *PG*, 94, col. 1032B, etc.

85. See introduction, pp. 13-4.

86. Exodus 25: 18-20. This was a standard argument in defence of images, showing that God overruled His own prohibition against their veneration. See John of Damascus, *De imaginibus*, I, 15; II, 9; III, 9, *PG*, 94, cols. 1244, 1292, 1329; Theodore of Stoudios, *Antirrheticus*, I, 5, 11, *PG*, 99, cols, 333, 341.

87. III Kings 8: 1-4 (I Kings 8: 1-4). The prefiguration of the Virgin Mary in the ark of the covenant appears in liturgical texts and was continually developed by the Church fathers. The typology is also illustrated in Byzantine art. See J. Ledit, *Marie dans la liturgie de Byzance* (Paris, 1971), 71-2; Underwood, *The Kariye Djami*, I, 228 ff.

88. Cf. John of Damascus, *De imaginibus*, II, 20; III, 26, *PG* , 94, cols. 1308, 1345.

89. *Ibid.* I, 9; III, 18, cols. 1240, 1340.

90. λογικὰ πρόβατα: Christ's spiritual flock. Eusebius, *Historia ecclesiae*, VIII, xiii, 3, ed. Schwartz (*GCS*, 1908), 772 (*PG*, 20, col. 773C); *idem.*, *De martyribus Palestinae*, 12, (*GCS*,1908), 946 (*PG*, 20, col. 1512B, etc.)

COMMENTARY

91. Cf. John 21: 15-17.

92. According to the seventh- or eighth-century *Vita* of St Pankratios, which purports to have been written in the time of the apostle Peter, the saint was instructed by St Peter to establish a church and to decorate it with scenes from the life of Christ. Excerpts of the *Vita* are published by A.N. Veselovskij in *Sbornik Otdelenija Russkogo Jazyka i Slovesnoski Imp. Akad. Nauk.* 40, 2 (1886), 73-110, and it has been edited critically by Cynthia Stallman (DPhil thesis, Oxford, 1986). See also Theodore of Stoudios, *Ep.* II, 42, 72, 199, *PG*, 99, cols. 1244, 1304, 1605; C. Mango, *The Art of the Byzantine Empire, 312-1453* (Englewood Cliffs, N.J., 1972), 137-8.

93. Various legends concerning the icon of the Virgin and Child painted by St Luke seem to have existed in the Byzantine period. The icon is first recorded by Theodore Anagnostes (c. 530), who tells how the empress Eudokia on her pilgrimage to Jerusalem sent it back to Constantinople. See Theodorus Anagnostes, *Kirchengeschichte*, ed. G.C. Hansen, (Berlin, 1971), 100. Another legend states that after painting the icon Luke sent it to Theophilos in Rome. See Ps.-John of Damascus, *Adv. Constantinum Cabalinum*, 6, *PG*, 95, col. 321; Andreas of Crete (died ca. 740) mentions two icons, one of Christ and one of the Theotokos, in his fragment on the veneration of icons, stating that they can both be found both in Rome *and* in Jerusalem (*PG*, 97, col. 1304). It is clear that our hagiographer knows this tradition as well, since the passage states clearly that the icon exists in both places (note however that he implies that there is only one icon, depicting both Christ and his mother). On the legend of the image and other witnesses to its cult, see E. von Dobschütz, *Christusbilder: Untersuchungen zur christlichen Legende* (*TU*, XVIII. iii, Leipzig, 1899), 267**-80**.

94. Toparch: governor of a district (Lampe). This is the title used for Abgar in the *Epistula Abgari ad Christum*, ed. R.A. Lipsius and M. Bonnet, *Acta apostolorum apocrypha*, I (Leipzig, 1891-1903), 279, 3.

COMMENTARY

95. The story of the portrait of Christ 'made without hands' is first given in literary sources in the sixth century. See Bidez and Parmentier, eds., *The Ecclesiastical History of Evagrius*, 174-6, etc. Other references to this icon include John of Damascus, *De fide orthodoxa* IV, 16, *PG*, 94, col. 1173; *Ep. ad Theophilum*, *PG*, 95, col. 352; Theodore of Stoudios, *Epp*. I, 33; II, 12, 65, *PG*, 99, cols. 1020, 1153 and 1288. See Dobschütz, *Christusbilder*, 102-96. A. Cameron argues that the icon must have appeared after the Persian siege of Edessa in 544 since it is not mentioned by Procopius. A. Cameron, 'The Sceptic and the Shroud', *Inaugural Lecture at King's College* (London, 1980) and 'The History of the Image of Edessa: the Telling of a Story', *Harvard Ukrainian Studies*, 7 (1983), 80-94.

96. The Greek switches from the singular to the plural in this address to the emperor. Since this inconsistency exists for no apparent reason it has not been rendered in the translation.

97. As Vailhé demonstrates, this letter from the patriarch Thomas could not have been sent in August 814, when iconoclasm had not yet been declared the state policy. It was most likely sent in response to the letter sent by the exiled Theodore the Stoudite in 817. The audience of the Jerusalem monks with Leo would thus have taken place several years after their arrival in Constantinople. Vailhé, 'Saint Michel le Syncelle', 613-4.

98. ὁ βύθιος δράκων καὶ λεοντώνυμος θύρ: the imagery here is strongly influenced by both Old and New Testament apocalyptic texts. The dragon, mentioned also in Psalms 73: 13-14 (74: 13-14) and 148:7, appears in Revelation 12: 3, ff. Another beast 'with its mouth like a lion's' (Rev. 13: 2) may parallel this emperor 'who bore the name of lion,' since they both intend 'to make war on the saints and to conquer them' (Rev. 13:7). What is most significant in this parallel is the fact that the champion who stands on the right hand of Israel or the Church and destroys the dragon is the archangel Michael in Rev. 12:7-12 and to a lesser extent, Dan. 10: 13-20. Our author must have perceived this parallel and was exploiting it here. The connection between Michael the

Synkellos and his patron saint the archangel has already been established. (See above, note 10).

99. The exact location of this prison is unknown, but it was situated inside the Great Palace. Many iconophile monks were imprisoned here during the iconoclast period, especially during the reigns of Constantine V and Theophilos. Janin, *Constantinople byzantine*, 409.

100. It is common for saints to pray in prison in the passions of the early martyrs. See Delehaye, *Les passions des martyres*, 270-3; *Martyrium ss. XL mart.*, 172.

101. Iconophiles, including Theodore of Stoudios, considered it permissible to speak or drink with iconoclasts, but not to partake of food with them. See Alexander, 'Religious Persecution and Resistance', 240, 249.

102. This is the same psalm cited by Theodore in his letters enjoining iconophiles not to eat with iconoclasts. Theodore of Stoudios, *Epp.*, I, 49; II, 119; II, 32; *PG*, 99, cols. 1089B, 1393A, 1205A.

103. This probably refers to John the Grammarian (patriarch of Constantinople, 837-43), who played an active role in collecting iconoclast arguments for the synod of 815. He is portrayed as the arch-enemy in many iconophile saints' lives. I. Ševčenko suggests that the author's deliberate omission of John's name here may mean that the latter was still alive at the time the Life was written. Ševčenko, 'Hagiography', 116, note 19. For the dates of John's patriarchate, see V. Grumel, 'Chronologie des patriarches iconoclastes du IXème siècle', *EO*, 34 (1935), 162-6.

104. It is significant that the hagiographer puts the words of the pharaoh into the persecutors' mouths at this point (Genesis 41: 40). In view of the tyrannical role played by pharaohs in the Old Testament, this passage subtly condemns the emperor by means of his own speech. Leo V's attempts to reconcile iconophiles with his decree and to persuade

them to accept communion from iconoclasts at Easter 816 are well attested in other sources. Peter of Nicaea and Niketas of Medikion both yielded to such persuasion. Theosteriktos, *Vita s. Nicetae, AASS*, April, I, nos. 40-1, XXX-I. Also see Theodore Stoudites, *Epp.*, II, 9, 31, *PG*, 99, cols. 1140 and 1204; Mai, *Nova patrum bibliotheca*, VIII, nos. 145, 127.

105. ὑπολακήσαντες: perhaps 'they wrung their hands', from the otherwise unattested verb ὑπολακίζω. λακίζω means 'to break or rend'.

106. εἰς τοσοῦτον: the expression is ambiguous. It is possible either that it refers back to the declaration of faith in the previous sentence or that it looks forward to the punishments which the saints are prepared to undergo. The translation 'to this extent' accords with the second possibility.

107. Aphousia, one of the Proconnesian islands now known as Avşa Adasi, is located to the west of the Kyzikos peninsula. Among those exiled there during the iconoclastic period were the saints Makarios, abbot of Pelekete, John of Kathara, Hilarion of Dalmatos, and the brothers *Graptoi*. See R. Janin, *Les églises et les monastères des grands centres byzantins* (Paris, 1975), 200-1. In fact it is likely that Michael's biographer has once again got his facts wrong. According to the metaphrastic Life of Theodore, the brothers were exiled to a fortress near the meeting of the Bosphoros with the Black Sea. After the assassination of Leo V in 820 and the elevation of Michael II (820-9), Theodore and Theophanes were allowed to move to the monastery of Sosthenios, on the European side of the Bosphoros. *Vita s. Theodori*, *PG*, 116, cols. 665, 668. On the monastery of Sosthenios, see J. Pargoire, 'Anaple et Sosthène', *IRAIK*, 3 (1898), 61-5. After the accession of the emperor Theophilos (829-42), Theodore and Theophanes were interrogated once more and exiled to Aphousia. This took place before their audience with the emperor in 836. See *PG*, 116, col. 669.

COMMENTARY

108. August 814. Since iconoclastic persecution did not begin before May 815, this date must be wrong. See above, notes 97 and 107.

109. None of these letters survives.

110. ἀνέστη: 'there arose.' This way of decribing the beginning of a new emperor's reign is common in apocalyptic texts. See, for example, Alexander, *The Oracle of Baalbek*, 13, lines 76 and 81, etc.

111. Michael II: 820-9. Although Michael was himself an iconoclast, he allowed a more lenient policy towards iconophiles than had existed under Leo V. He permitted iconophiles to live freely and to worship images as long as they remained outside the capital. See C. Mango, 'Historical Introduction', eds. Bryer and Herrin, *Iconoclasm*, 5; J.B. Bury, *A History of the Eastern Roman Empire* (London, 1912), 110-9.

112. According to Janin, the hagiographer meant Prousias or Kios, which would have been well situated for imperial supervision of iconophile monks. Janin, *Grands centres*, 176-7.

113. ἄνακτος: 'ruler'. It is possible that the hagiographer uses this word rather than βασιλεύς in a derogatory sense. Later he also applies it to the orthodox emperor, Michael III, perhaps in this case with reference to his youth at the time of his accession (see above, p. 102, line 4, etc).

114. Theophilos: 829-42.

115. Of the two prisons in Constantinople called Praetorium, the first was located in the eastern part of the city and dated from the time of Constantine, or perhaps even that of Septimius Severus. A second prison, dating from before the time of Justinian, was located further to the north-west, between the Augusteon and the forum of Constantine. It was in one of these that many victims of the iconoclastic persecution were imprisoned, including, besides Michael and his disciples, St Stephen the Younger. See Janin, *Constantinople byzantine*, 165-9; R.

COMMENTARY

Guilland, *Études de topographie de Constantinople byzantine*, II (Berlin-Amsterdam, 1969), 36-9.

116. κυφότητι: being bent or hump-backed. Heliodorus, VI, 11, ed. W.A. Hirschig, *Erotici scriptores* (Paris, 1856), 327.

117. W. Treadgold believes that this might have been the dowager empress Euphrosyne, daughter of Constantine VI and second wife of Michael II, who retired to a monastery soon after Theophilos came to power. See W. Treadgold, 'The Chronological Accuracy of the *Chronicle* of Symeon the Logothete for the Years 813 to 845', *DOP*, 33 (1979), 188 and note 139. On Euphrosyne, see B. Melioranski, *VizVrem*, 8 (1901), 32-3; Bury, *History of the Eastern Roman Empire*, 125-6, note 1. This possibility is intriguing but if as some sources state, she retired to a cloister on the island of Prinkipo, it would have been difficult for her to attend to Michael's needs in the Praetorium prison. See Theophanes Continuatus, III, 1, ed. Becker, 86. The devotion of pious women to Christians in captivity is in fact a *topos* in the passions of martyrs. See for example the pre-metaphrastic Passion of St Blasios, *PG*, 116, cols. 821-4; Ehrhard, *Überlieferung*, II, 613, note 4 and 612.

118. ἀσηκρῆτις: (Lat. *a secretis*) an imperial secretary.

119. The wording of this sentence is somewhat confused. The author means that although Stephen was swayed by Michael's persuasion, he submitted again owing to the emperor's threats and finally returned to orthodoxy under Michael's influence. εἰ καὶ μικρόν τι could mean either 'to a slight extent' or 'for a short time'. The latter meaning has been chosen because it leads up to ἔσχατον δὲ in the next sentence.

120. σπαθάριον: by this period the title of *spatharios* was purely honorary. See J.B. Bury, *The Imperial Administrative System in the Ninth Century (British Academy. Supplemental Papers*, I, Oxford-London, 1911), 20-2, 112-3; N. Oikonomides, *Les listes de préséance byzantines des IXe et Xe siècles* (Paris, 1972).

121. This image of an angry persecutor 'boiling over with anger' occurs frequently in encomia and passions. Cf. for example Basil of Caesarea, *Homilia in quadraginta martyres, PG*, 31, col. 513D.

122. ὑπασπιστῶν: (plural) bodyguards. Eusebius, *Vita Constantini*, II, 5, ed. Winkelmann, 49 (*PG*, 20, col. 984A); Philostratus, *Historia ecclesiae*, XI, 1, *PG*, 65, col. 593B, etc. Cf. the similar term used by Theophanes for the iconoclast emperors' comrades-in-arms, *Chronographia*, I, 408, 21.

123. This passage is reminiscent of Christ's words to His disciples in Matthew 10: 17-18, when He tells them that they will be delivered up to councils and scourged in synagogues for preaching the gospel.

124. On the comparison of a persecuting emperor to a wild beast, see above, note 98. In the passions of the early martyrs the persecutors are often described in a similar manner, e.g. ἔβρυξεν ὡς λέων καὶ κροτήσας τὰς χεῖρας αὐτοῦ, *Passio s. Irenarchi*, ed. G. Garitte, *AnalBoll*, 73 (1955), 44; also *Martyrium ss. XL mart. Sebast.*, 173, etc. The source for this image is in fact scriptural. See Psalm 34: 16 (35:16), Acts 7: 54, etc.

125. ὡς ἄτε: 'since they were.' A.M. Wilson has suggested that this might mean 'despite the fact that', since the punishments which follow seem too severe to have been imposed *on account of* the saints' advanced age. Since I have found no parallel examples of the phrase being used in this sense, I have rendered it literally; it is possible that the hagiographer wishes to contrast the mere imprisonment of Michael and Job with the more severe punishments meted out to Theodore and Theophanes.

126. This phrase represents an adaptation of both scriptural and patristic texts: ἀχαρίστους καὶ πονηροὺς, Luke 6: 35; πλάσμα Θεοῦ, Gregory of Nazianzus, *Oratio* XXXI, 11, *PG*, 36, col. 144D.

127. The image of the saints as bright stars of the Church has many biblical overtones. Perhaps the closest parallel is the passage in Philippians 2: 15: ... ἐν οἷς φαίνεσθε ὡς φωστῆρες ἐν κόσμῳ. As in that passage, the saints shine out in the midst of a crooked and perverse generation. A.M. Wilson has pointed out to me a number of parallels for light imagery in the *Vita s. Eutychii*, e.g. with regard to Eutychios' parents: γεννήτορες φωστήρων ὑπέρλαμπροι (*PG*, 86, col. 2280B), his grandfather: ...τὸν ἐν ἱερεῦσι διαλάμποντα (col. 2280B) and himself: ὁ ἐξ αὐτῆς (his mother) ἀνατέλλων φωσφόρος ἀστήρ, ἢ μᾶλλον εἰπεῖν, δικαῖος ἐκλάμπων ὑπὲρ τὸν ἥλιον ἑπταπλάσιον, φωτίσειεν πολλοὺς καθεζομένους ἐν ἀγνοίᾳ... (col. 2281B). Our hagiographer uses the image elsewhere in the Life, e.g. p. 54, line 5, and p. 128, lines 20-1.

128. In this section of the Life, the hagiographer closely follows the account found in the letter sent by Theodore *Graptos* to John of Kyzikos. This passage is copied almost verbatim from the beginning of the letter. Cf. *PG*, 116, col. 672 B-C. The author continues to rely on the document through chapter 23.

129. 8 July 836.

130. According to Theodore's account, there was a lapse of six days before the saints were summoned to the presence of the emperor, on 14 July. Cf. *PG*, 116, col. 672 C.

131. Modern Greek meaning of διαμαρτύρομαι.

132. Τῆς δὲ ἀφίξεως...ἤκουον: cf. *PG*, 116, col. 672, C-D.

133. Καὶ τῆς πύλης...ὀφθαλμῶν: cf. *ibid.*, cols. 672-3.

134. A hagiographical *topos*. Ignatios, in his Life of Nikephoros, ed. C. de Boor, *Nicephori archiepiscopi Constantinopolitani opuscula historica* (Leipzig, 1880), 142, describes how Nikephoros' father, Theodore, went to an imperial summons as if he were attending a banquet and not a

trial. The biblical sources of this *topos* are Matthew 22: 2-14 and Revelation 19: 7-9. Both passages suggest the reward which awaits the martyrs of Christ and hence explain the confidence with which they enter into their ἄθλησις.

135. ποίας χώρας...Μωαβίτιδος: cf. *PG*, 116, col. 673A. The land of the Moabites, now called Kenak, is on the eastern side of the Dead Sea.

136. πάλιν...ἐνταῦθα: cf. *PG*, 116, col. 673A. This dialogue suggests the emperor's hostility towards Theodore and Theophanes as Palestinians. The harshness of the punishment which follows also suggests that he felt a particular grudge towards monks hailing from the east.

137. IV Maccabees 6:8. The influence of this book on the passions of martyrs is discussed by H. Delehaye in his *Les passions des martyres*, 314-5.

138. καὶ πρὶν...ἐκέλευσεν: cf. *PG*, 116, col. 673 A-B.

139. This is reminiscent of the *imitatio Christi* found in the early Acts of the martyrs. Delehaye, *Les passions des martyrs*, 153-4; A. von Harnack, 'Das ursprüngliche Motiv der Abfassung von Märtyrer und Heilungsacten in der Kirche', *Sitzungsberichte der königlich preussischen Akademie der Wissenschaften* (Berlin, 1910), 106-25. On the hagiographer's explicit comparison between the saints and Christ in this passage, see introduction, p. 19.

140. Mk 15: 15-9; Mt 27: 26-30; Jn 19: 1-3.

141. γράψον: it is not clear exactly how the iambics were to be inscribed, but it seems more likely that a form of tattooing was used than one of branding, as some scholars have implied. If the saints had been branded, a special iron would have had to be made and the process would have been swift, instead of being long and drawn out, involving much pricking (see chap. 23).

142. This final command, which in fact was not carried out, is an interesting one. It was perhaps intended as a further humiliation, on the grounds that the saints were not worthy to have intercourse with other Christians or in the knowledge that Muslims would be particularly harsh towards iconophiles. It may also have been intended to suggest the brothers' alien status as Palestinians and thus their affinity with the Arabs.

143. Τῶν δὲ ἁγίων...ἐνθήσωμεν: cf. *PG*, 116, col. 673C.

144. θρυλλολέκται: see also Ps. John of Damascus, *Adv.Constantinum*, 18, *PG*, 95, col. 336B; *Vita s. Stephani iunioris*, *PG*, 100, col. 1145A.

145. I am most grateful to Dr A.M. Wilson for providing this translation of the iambic poem. The verses are also recorded in Theodora Raoulaina's *Vita* of Theophanes, 206; Georgios Monachos, *De Theophilo*, ed. Becker (*CSHB*, Bonn, 1838), 807; Theophanes Continuatus, *Chronographia*, ed. Bekker, 105; Symeon Magister, *Annales*, ed. Becker, 641-2; Zonaras, *Epitomae historiarum*, III, ed. Büttner-Wobst (*CSHB*, Bonn, 1897), 366. A few textual variations occur in these texts; to my knowledge no one has yet attempted a critical edition of the poem.

146. The hagiographer contradicts his own account in this sentence, having previously stated that the saints arrived in Constantinople with the letter during the reign of Leo V. On the probable date of the letter of the patriarch, see note 97.

147. This passage must be inspired by Revelation 7:3 ff., in which the servants of God who are sealed on their foreheads by the angels are granted entrance to paradise. Dressed in white garments and bearing palms in their hands, these are surely the martyrs, and it is with them that the hagiographer compares Theodore and Theophanes.

148. This image could be inspired by the parable of the treasure hidden in the field, which represents the kingdom of heaven (Matthew 13:44), or by the advice to store up treasures in heaven rather than on earth (Matthew 6:19-20). The idea is taken up again at the time of Theophanes' death with reference to the Christian souls whom he has saved. See below, chap. 31.

149. Thermastra: the Thermastra, which means a hypocaust or furnace for heating baths, probably acquired its name through its proximity to the Great Palace. The room to which our text refers here served as a passageway between the palace and the hippodrome. Constantine Porphyrogennetos' *De ceremoniis* speaks of patricians entering and departing from the Great Palace through the Thermastra. See *Constantini Porphyrogeniti imperatoris de ceremoniis*, ed. J.J. Reiske (*CSHB*, Bonn, 1829), II, 18, 600-2. Also see J. Ebersolt, *Le grand palais de Constantinople et le livre de cérémonies* (Paris, 1910), 154-7; S. Miranda, *Étude de topographie du palais sacré de Byzance* (Mexico, 1971), 103-4; Guilland, *Étude de topographie*, I, 120-9. I am most grateful to Professor J. Herrin for pointing out the importance of our text as a hitherto unnoticed source of information about the Thermastra and to Eugenia Bolognesi for supplying these references.

150. εἰκὸς ὑμᾶς...ἀπολύσω: cf. *PG*, 116, col. 676A.

151. Theodore describes his own and his brother's cries in more detail in his letter. cf. *PG*, 116, col. 676 A-B.

152. ὡς ἔχεις ἐμέ, δὸς καλά: cf. *ibid.*, col. 676A.

153. The head of administrative bureaux and foreign minister. This would have been Theoktistos, who had also served under Michael II and who after Theophilos' death assisted Theodora in the restoration of images. Theophanes, *Chronographia*, ed. De Boor, 492, 500; Genesios, IV, ed. C. Lachmann (*CSHB*, Bonn, 1834), 77-8; Theophanes Continuatus, IV, 1, ed. Bekker, 148; Georgios Monachos, ed. Bekker, 811; F. Dvornik, *Les légendes de Constantin et de Méthode vues de*

COMMENTARY

Byzance (Prague, 1933), 35-7, 41-5. On the office itself, see Bury, *The Imperial Administrative System*, 91-3; D.A. Miller, 'The Logothete of the Drome in the Middle Byzantine Period', *B*, 36 (1966), 438-70.

154. The hagiographer does not include in this exchange the messenger's question to the brothers concerning the actual date of their arrival in Constantinople, which appears in Theodore's letter: Τέως γοῦν οὐκ ἐπὶ τοῦ Λέοντος ἤλθετε; and the saints' reply: Οὔκουν, (ἔφημεν), ἀλλ᾽ ἐπὶ τοῦ πρὸ αὐτοῦ βασιλεύσαντος, *PG*, 116, col. 676.

155. Μετὰ δὲ τεσσάρων...παραδίδειν: cf. *ibid.*, col. 676 C.

156. καὶ τῶν ἁγίων...διαβεβαιοῖ: cf.*ibid.*, col. 676-7.

157. ὁ ἔπαρχος...πίστεως: cf. *ibid.*, col. 677, B-C.

158. This curious image could possibly be a reference to Muhammed's night-time journey to Jerusalem and from there up to paradise. Muhammed is said to have been mounted on a mysterious animal which was like a white horse, but with a human face, named Burraq. The prophet did not of course ride Burraq to Heaven, but left him tethered to a rock down below. In view of the *Graptoi* brothers' near eastern origins, it is quite possible that they knew this legend. Cf. *The Koran*, Sura XVII, 1; B. Lewis, Ch. Pellat and J. Schacht, *The Encyclopedia of Islam*, I (Leiden-London, 1960), 1310-1, s.v. 'Al-Burak'.

159. Τότε κελεύει...πρόσωπα αὐτῶν: cf. *PG*, 116, col. 677 B.

160. See above, note 147. It is clear that our hagiographer was inspired by this passage in Theodore's letter in his reference to the cherubim and fiery sword above, as well as in his apostrophe comparing the saints to Christ.

161. μέλλοντες δὲ...ἔγραψα ἂν οὕτως: ibid., col. 677 C-D. Theodore's letter concludes several lines later, after asserting his direct experience of the events which he has just described.

COMMENTARY

162. 18 July 836. On the accuracy of this date, see introduction above, note 50. The hagiographer confuses the number of days which elapsed between the saints' arrival in Constantinople and their punishment. If they were summoned to the emperor on 8 July and tattooed four days later, the date should be 12 July. In Theodore's letter the first audience with the emperor takes place on 14 July and the brothers are tattooed four days later on the 18th. This is probably the correct sequence of events. See *PG*, 116, col. 680 A and above, note 130.

163. The play on the words χαρακτῆρα...χαράγμασιν here subtly reinforces the identification of the saints with Christ. Just as the icons of Christ are in His image, so are the saints, especially as they are marked with His sign.

164. Taking this image further, the comparison of the saints to icons suggests the holiness of their bodies themselves. Like an icon, a saint represents in his material substance a reflection of divine power and grace. See also *Vita s. Danielis*, ed. H. Delehaye in *Les saints stylites*, (*SubsHag*, 14, Brussels, 1923), 92, lines 2-3.

165. Daniel 3: 23-7.

166. II Maccabees 7: 1-48.

167. Patriarch of Constantinople, March 843-June 847. Born in Syracuse, Sicily, in the second half of the eighth century, Methodios became abbot of the monastery of Chenolakkos, on the south side of the Propontis, probably to the west of Prousa. Janin, *Grands centres*, III, 189-90. After 815 he went to Rome, returning in 821 with letters from pope Pascal I to Michael II upholding the worship of icons. Concerning his subsequent persecution under Michael II and Theophilos, several traditions exist. According to the anonymous Life of Methodios, the saint was beaten severely and exiled to the island of St Andrew near the peninsula of Akritas, where he was imprisoned in an underground tomb in company with a criminal. When Michael II died and Theophilos

COMMENTARY

came to the throne, Methodios was released and after undergoing one more interrogation and beating, he was pardoned by the emperor and admitted to the imperial court. *Vita s. Methodii, PG*, 100, cols. 1244-61. A second tradition, found first in the *Chronicle* of Symeon Magister and copied by many later authors, states that Methodios suffered no ill treatment during the reign of Michael II, but that it was during the reign of Theophilos that he was imprisoned in a tomb, this time on the island of Antigone near Constantinople, along with two robbers. According to this account, it was while Methodios was still imprisoned here that Theodore and Theophanes *Graptoi*, exiled to Karta Limen after the tattooing of their faces, were able to send some iambic verses as a greeting to the imprisoned saint:

Τῷ ζῶντι νεκρῷ καὶ νεκρῷ ζωηφόρῳ,
Οἰκοῦντι τὴν γῆν καὶ πολοῦντι τὸν πόλον,
γραπτοὶ γράφουσι δέσμιοι τῷ δεσμίῳ.

Methodios replied with the lines:

Τοῖς ταῖς βίβλοισιν οὐρανῶν κλησιγράφοις
καὶ πρὸς μέτωπα σωφρόνως ἐστιγμένοις
προσεῖπεν ὁ ζώθαπτος ὡς συνδεσμίοις.

See Symeon Magister, *Annales*, ed. Bekker, 642-3. J. Pargoire discusses the various traditions concerning Methodios' life and outlines arguments in favour of each. J. Pargoire, 'Saint Méthode de Constantinople et la persécution', *EO*, 6 (1903), 183-91.

168. In the light of the various accounts of Methodios' whereabouts during the reign of Theophilos, this passage is interesting. It is not clear whether he was in the Praetorium prison at the time of these events or whether he had spent time there in the past and was now exiled somewhere else. It is also significant that Michael's biographer does not mention the exchange of iambic verses between the brothers *Graptoi* and Methodios which is described in the *Chronicle* of Symeon Magister. See above, note 167.

169. This conflicts with Symeon the Metaphrast's Life of Theodore, in which the saints are exiled to Apameia after their tattooing. *PG*, 116, col. 680 A.

170. Michael III, 842-67. His mother, Theodora, acted as regent until 856 when she was forced to retire and enter a monastery. On the precise chronology of the events of 842-3, see A. Markopoulos, 'Βίος τῆς αὐτοκρατείρας Θεοδώρας (*BHG* 1731)', *Symmeikta of the Centre of Byzantine Research*, 5 (1983), 249-85.

171. It is common to find praiseworthy women described in this way in Byzantine texts. It is their 'manly' qualities which allow them to overcome their feminine weakness. See, for example, Gregory of Nyssa on Makrina, *Grégoire de Nysse, vie de sainte Macrine*, ed. P. Maraval (*SC*, 178, Paris, 1971), 140. In Gerontios' Life of Melania, the author states, 'It is true to say that she had surpassed the measure of her femininity and acquired a masculine, or rather heavenly, mentality,' ed. D. Gorce, *Vie de Sainte Mélanie*, (*SC*, 90, Paris, 1962), 203. Also cf. Gregory of Nazianzus, *In laudem Basilii Magni*, *PG*, 36, col. 569B: αἳ οὐδὲ γυναῖκες ἔμενον ἔτι, τῷ ζήλῳ ῥωσθεῖσαι, καὶ εἰς ἀνδρῶν θάρσος μεταλλαττόμεναι.

172. Theodora's devotion to icons, even during her husband Theophilos' persecution of iconophiles, is attested by the chroniclers. See Symeon Magister, *Annales*, ed. Bekker, 629-30; Theophanes Continuatus, ed. Bekker, 91-2. For a discussion of Theodora's iconophilism and for the importance of icons to women in particular, see J. Herrin, 'Women and Faith in Icons in Early Christianity', *Culture, Ideology and Politics*, eds. R. Samuel and G.S. Jones, (London, 1982), 68-75.

173. ἔμπνοοι στῆλαι: 'living monuments', meaning holy men. See also Theodoret, *Historia religiosa*, *PG*, 82, col. 1356A.

174. ὡς ἐκ λειμώνων ἐαρινῶν πάντερπνα ἄνθη: The comparison of holy men to flowers in meadows is a common *topos*. Perhaps the best

example is the title of John Moschos' collection of stories concerning ascetics: 'The Spiritual Meadow' (Λειμωνάριον), *PG*, 87, cols. 2852-3112.

175. This 'quotation' is interesting because it combines and adapts several different scriptural passages, with an added iconophile emphasis in the final phrase.

176. John the Grammarian: patriarch of Constantinople, 837-43. According to one source, John was forced to retire to the monastery at Kleidion on the European side of the Bosphoros. Cf. Georgios Monachos, ed. Bekker, 811. Theophanes Continuatus states that he was banished to his surburban house called τὰ ψιχά, which was probably at Kleidion. Theophanes Continuatus, ed. Bekker, 151; Bury, *History of the Eastern Roman Empire*, 151, note 1.

177. Ὁ δὲ πατὴρ...ἀνασχόμενος: nominative absolute.

178. Mt Olympos: this mountainous area was situated to the south of Prousa, on the Asian side of the Sea of Marmara, in Bithynia. Solitary ascetics sought refuge here from an early period. A monastery was founded in the fifth century, but the number of religious houses did not increase significantly until the eighth century. See Janin, *Grands centres*, 127-31.

179. Born in 762 of humble origins, St Ioannikios served in the imperial army before entering the Bithynian monastery of Antidion in 792. Between 794 and 815, he lived as a hermit on Mt Agaurinon, near the monastery of Agauroi. After 815 he went into hiding and appears to have moved from place to place in eastern Asia Minor. He returned to Antidion sometime before the death of Theophilos, where the patriarch Methodios visited him in 846. These facts are based on the Life written by Peter and conflict with the account given in the less trustworthy Life by the monk Sabas. The two *vitae* are published in *AASS*, Nov, II/1 (1894), 332-435. For an evaluation of their relative historical value, see C. Mango, 'The Two Lives of St Ioannikios and the

Bulgarians', *Okeanos: A Tribute to I. Ševčenko (Harvard Ukrainian Studies*, 7, 1983), 393-404.

180. Eustratios, who began his career as a monk in the monastery of Agauroi, became the close friend and companion of St Ioannikios. He became abbot of Agauroi under Theophilos, only to be expelled and replaced by an iconoclast abbot. With the restoration of orthodoxy in 843, Eustratios was reinstated in his former position. For his *vita*, see Papadopoulos-Kerameus, Ἀνάλεκτα, IV, 367-400; *Vita s. Ioannicii*, 332-83.

181. This monastery was situated slightly to the west of Prousa in Bithynia. The first mention of the monastery occurs in the *Acta* of the council of Nicaeà (787), which was signed by the abbot Gregory, who was St Eustratios' uncle. Agauroi had five dependencies, probably including the monastery of Elaiobomoi or Elegmoi. See Janin, *Grand centres*, 132-4.

182. Two monasteries of St Elias are recorded in the Acts of 787. One of these was a dependency of the monastery of Agauroi and was the scene of a conference in 824, which St Ioannikios and St Theodore of Stoudios both attended. Most likely the monastery was located not far from either Prousa or the monastery of Agauroi. If Michael's biographer is to be believed, St Ioannikios must have been staying at this *metochion* when the imperial envoys arrived, since he is known to have spent the last years of his life as a hermit near the monastery of Antidion. See above, note 179; Janin, *Grands centres*, 151-2.

183. See above, note 167. Perhaps St Ioannikios' choice was due to Methodios' important role in the restoration of images after the death of Theophilos. See Th. Uspenskij, *Ocerki po Istorii Vizantiiskoi Obrazovannosti* (St Petersburg, 1892), 33.

184. The monastery τῶν Ἡλίου βωμῶν, τῶν βωμῶν, τῶν Ἐλαιοβωμῶν, etc., is first documented in the ninth century. It was located a short distance east of the modern village of Kurşunlu, on the

southern shore of the gulf of Gemlik, about twelve km. east of Mudanya. The association of St Methodios with the monastery is attested in only two sources. The *Menologium basilianum* suggests that Methodios founded the monastery in the lines ἐν τῇ τοποθεσίᾳ τοῦ ὄρους τῆς ἐπισκοπῆς Χίου (corr. Κίου) μοναστήριον κτίσας ἐκεῖσε προσεκαθέζετο. Cf. *PG*, 117, col. 500A. The other source, namely our Life of Michael, is alone in stating that Methodios was exiled here. As we have seen, the saint's movements during the reign of Theophilos are difficult to verify, so that this must remain an open question. See above, note 167; C. Mango, 'The monastery of St Abercius at Kurşunlu', *DOP*, 22 (1968), 169-76; Janin, *Grands centres*, 142-8.

185. See above, note 167.

186. See above, note 4. The words, 'that imperial ...monastery' have a technical meaning here. Constantine Porphyrogennetos' *De administrando*, written in the tenth century, mentions five different types of monasteries: imperial, patriarchal, archiepiscopal, metropolitan and episcopal. See Constantine Porphyrogennetos, *De administrando imperio*, I, ed. tr. G. Moravcsik and R.J.H. Jenkins (2nd ed., Dumbarton Oaks, 1963), chap. 52, 257. Theophanes also mentions 'imperial monasteries' in his *Chronographia*, I, ed. De Boor, 486-7. Dr Rosemary Morris believes on the basis of these texts that these different types of houses evolved in the ninth century. See R. Morris, *The Byzantine Church and the Land in the Tenth and Eleventh Centuries* (Oxford, DPhil thesis, 1978), 160-1; E. Herman, 'Recerche sulle instituzioni monastiche bizantini', *OCP*, 6 (1940), 293-375; P. de Meester, *De monachico statu iuxta disciplinam byzantinam* (Vatican, 1942). I am very grateful to Dr Morris for providing me with these references. Also see the more recent J.P. Thomas, *Private Religious Foundations in the Byzantine Empire* (*DOS*, 24, Washington, D.C., 1987).

187. The comparison of a monastery to a mountain is common in patristic texts. See for example Athanasius' Life of St Anthony, chaps. 50, 71, 84, *PG*, 26, cols. 917A, 944B, 961A; John Chrysostom, *Hom.7.7*

in Mt., PG, 57, col. 81; *Vita s. Eutychii, PG*, 86, col.2288B and 2297C-D. It is possible that our author is quoting here the *Vita s. Stephani iunioris, PG*, 100, col. 1088.

188. Born near Caesarea in Cappadocia in 439, St Sabas went to Jerusalem at the age of eighteen, where he entered the monastery of St Passarion. In 469 he retreated into the desert, where he founded his Great *Laura*. In 511 the saint was sent by the patriarch Elias to Constantinople in an effort to undermine the influence of the monophysites at the court of the emperor Anastasius. His second visit in 531 was prompted by recent uprisings by the Samaritans. According to St Sabas' biographer, Cyril of Skythopolis, the saint presented the emperor with five requests: to remit the taxes owed by Palestine, to reconstruct the sacred buildings which had been destroyed by Samaritans, to take charge of the Palestinian Christians who had been impoverished by the pillaging, to found a hospital for the care of pilgrims, and to construct a fort near the monasteries which the saint had founded in the desert. Cyril of Skythopolis, *Vita s. Sabae*, ed. Schwartz, 85-200.

189. Note the author's use of the dative case here in the word 'territory'. An accusative would be more appropriate, matching 'holy city' in the preceding clause. Justinian's policy towards the Samaritans was as strict as it was towards other minorities, including heretics and pagans. After the destruction of Samaritan synagogues by imperial command, a revolt broke out in 529 which led to the massacre of Christians and the destruction of their churches in Palestine. Procopius, *Anekdota*, XI, 24-30, ed. tr. H.B. Dewing (Cambridge, 1935), 136-9; John Malalas, *Chronographia*, ed. L. Dindorf (*CSHB*, Bonn, 1831), 446-7.

190. That St Sabas actually visited the monastery of Chora in the course of his stay in Constantinople in 531 is unlikely since this took place well before the possible dates of the monastery's foundation (see note 4). Nevertheless, it was perhaps in deference to this tradition that monks from Palestine were customarily sent to the Chora.

COMMENTARY

191. Leo V: 813-20.

192. ἀναλώμασιν: this may refer to money or food. See Lampe, 111.

193. Constantine V: 741-75.

194. It is unknown how complete this devastation was or for how long the monastery remained out of use. An abbot Symeon signed the Acts of the second council of Nicaea (787). Mansi, XII, 1111D; XIII, 152A; Janin, *Églises et monastères*, (repr. 1969), 533.

195. Patriarch of Constantinople, 715-30, Germanos I opposed the iconoclast policy of Leo III and in 730 resigned and retired to his paternal monastery the Chora, or perhaps a neighbouring monastery. See*Vitae ss. martyrum CPolitanorum, AASS*, Aug.II, 441B; Mansi, XII, 269. Theophanes states: καὶ ἀπελθὼν ἐν τῷ λεγομένῳ Πλατανίῳ εἰς τὸν γονικὸν αὐτοῦ οἶκον ἡσύχασεν... Theophanes, *Chronographia*, ed. De Boor, I, 409. The *Synaxarion* simply states that Germanos was buried in the monastery of Chora. *Synax.Eccl.CP*, 677, line 55; 680, line 3. See also L. Lamza, *Patriarch Germanos I von Konstantinopel* (Wurzburg, 1975).

196. Initially an ally of the usurper Leo III, Artabasdos, as *strategos* of the Armeniakon theme, married his daughter and after Leo's coronation was appointed commander in the Opsikion theme. One year after Leo's death in 741, Artabasdos usurped the throne for several months. According to the chroniclers, Artabasdos declared himself an opponent of the iconoclast doctrine, but this has recently been questioned by S. Gero. On 2 November 743, Constantine V re-entered Constantinople and after blinding Artabasdos and his two sons, he imprisoned them in the monastery of Chora from which he had expelled the monks. Theophanes, *Chronographia*, I, 648; S. Gero, *Byzantine Iconoclasm during the Reign of Constantine V* (Louvain, 1977), 14-20; Underwood, *The Kariye Djami*, I, 7. Most recently see P. Speck, *Artabasdos, der rechtgläubige Vorkämpfer des göttlichen Lehrens* (*Poikila Byzantina*, 2, Bonn, 1981).

197. Le Quien states mistakenly that Theophanes was appointed bishop of Nicaea after the death of Peter II in 845. If Michael's biographer is correct, however, Theophanes occupied this office for four years before expiring on 11 October, 845. Thus he would have been ordained early in 842, soon after the death of the emperor Theophilos. Concerning the succession of bishops of Nicaea in the early ninth century, Vailhé offers an alternative to the sequence proposed by Le Quien, *Oriens christianus*, I, 646; Vailhé, 'Saint Michel le syncelle', 633-4. According to C. Mango, Peter was deposed c. 812 and died in 826. Theophanes was probably the successor of Ignatios (the deacon).

198. The first council of Nicaea (325).

199. The tradition that Theodore lived to see the restoration of orthodoxy, dying in 844 at the age of seventy, is supported by other Byzantine authors, including Theophanes Continuatus, IV, 11, ed. Bekker, 160-1, Cedrenus, *PG*, 121, col. 1033 and the author of the *De Theophili imperatoris absolutione*. Cf. W. Regel, ed. *Analecta Byzantina-russica* (St Petersburg, 1891), 32. According to a second tradition, Theodore and Theophanes were exiled soon after the tattooing of their faces to Apameia in Bithynia, where Theodore died in prison on December 27, 841. After the triumph of orthodoxy in 843, the coffin containing Theodore's relics was taken to Chalcedon by a certain Michael, who constructed a monastery in memory of the saint. *Vita s. Theodori*, *PG*, 116, cols. 680-4; Symeon Magister, ed. Bekker, 643; Vailhé, 'Saint Michel le syncelle', 625-6.

200. This book, which most likely did exist, is also mentioned in the Encomium of Theodore *Graptos* by Theophanes of Caesarea. The author creates an etymology for the title, which means 'the Wolfhound', chasing down 'the wolf of that time....the destroyer of Christ's flock'. J.-M. Featherstone, 'The Praise', 125.

201. Theophanes' canon in honour of Theodore begins:

COMMENTARY

Τὸν τίτλον σῆς τιμίας ὄψεως ἰδόντα παραχωρεῖ
τὰ χερουβὶμ τοῦ ξύλου τῆς ζωῆς· ἡ φλογίνη ῥομφαία
δὲ, πανευλαβῶς, τὰ νῶτα σοι δίδωσι, πάνσοφε Θεόδωρε...

Menaia, II (Rome, 1889), 698.

202. The image of Theophanes storing up the souls of his flock within the haven of the heavenly kingdom is a vivid one, although the hagiographer combines agricultural and mercantile imagery in a somewhat confused manner. The need to store up treasures in heaven is inspired by Matthew 13: 44 and 6: 19-20 (see above, note 148).

203. 11 October 845.

204. See introduction, p. 38 and note 143.

205. This church, a dependency of the monastery of Chora, is mentioned only in the Life of Michael. Janin suggests that it was located outside the walls of Constantinople, but can provide no proof, R. Janin, *Les églises et les monastères de Constantinople* (Paris, 2nd ed., 1969), 490.

206. See above, note 186.

207. It is common for saints to foretell their own deaths in hagiography. See for example Athanasius, *Vita s. Antonii*, *PG*, 26, cols. 968-9; Gregory of Nazianzus, *In laudem Basilii*, 36, col. 600. Similar visions given to saints on their deathbeds or in prison before their martyrdoms appear in a number of early encomia. See for example Gregory of Nyssa, *Laudatio s. Theodori*, *PG*, 46, col. 745C.

208. The sounding-board, sometimes called a *semantron*, was a wooden gong used for summoning monks to prayer.

209. The meaning of this passage is not entirely clear. If Michael caused the *semantron* to be struck for Mattins at the usual time there seems no

reason for the monks' surprise, unless it was not Michael's normal custom to join in celebrating this service. Alternatively, it is possible that he summoned the monks for Mattins at a different hour than the usual one, and it is this which caused them concern. On the possibility that Michael did not in fact appear at the monastic services as a general rule, see introduction, p. 33.

210. Orphanhood: this is another hagiographical *topos*. In his Life of St Eutychios, Eustratios misquotes Gregory of Nazianzus' account of St Basil's death, saying that the whole city mourned its orphanhood (ὠδύρετο τὴν ὀρφανίαν). See *PG*, 86, col. 2384A.

211. This passage is reminiscent of I Corinthians 13: 8-13.

212. The short homily preached by a dying saint is a common *topos* in hagiography. See for example, Athanasius, *Vita s. Antonii*, *PG*, 26, cols. 968-72. It is usual for a spiritual father to exhort his disciples to practise piety and to avoid falling into heretical beliefs. Here Michael's homily is monastic in character, as he stresses the importance of charity, humility, chastity and constant prayer.

213. ἄνακτα...μεγάλην βασίλισσαν: This choice of words suggests the actual state of affairs in which Theodora wielded imperial authority, as regent for the child-emperor Michael.

214. Constantine I: 324-37.

215. Theodosius I : 379-95.

216. Elesboas or Elesbaas, known in some sources as Caleb, was the monophysite king of Abyssinia during the reign of Justin I. In 523 Dhu-Nuwas, the Jewish king of Yemen, massacred many of the Christian inhabitants of the city of Nagran, including the emir of their tribe, Harith ibn-Kilab, also known as Arethas. On learning of this, the Ethiopian king Elesboas sent to Justin I through Timothy, patriarch of Alexandria, for military reinforcements in order to defend the Christian

COMMENTARY

faith in South Arabia. On being sent ships, Elesboas waged two campaigns against Dhu-Nuwas which ended in the Jewish king's defeat. Although Elesboas was a monophysite, he ranked as a defender of the faith and was numbered with Arethas among the saints of the universal church. *Synax.Eccl.CP*, 159, line 14. The main source for these events is the *Acta martyrii Arethae*, *AASS*, Oct X, 721-59. Also see A.A. Vasiliev, *Justin I* (Cambridge, Mass., 1950), 283-302; I. Shahid, *The Martyrs of Najran: New Documents* (Brussels, 1971).

217. Anthimos, bishop of Nicomedia, was martyred shortly after the first edict of persecution was issued by Diocletian in 303. *Synax.Eccl.CP*, 9; *AASS*, Apr.,III, 482-6. According to the anonymous ninth-century Life of St Theodore, the church dedicated to St Anthimos, along with those dedicated to the forty martyrs, St Michael and the Mother of God, was added to the Chora when Justinian rebuilt the monastery after its destruction by an earthquake. Schmitt, 'Kahrie Džame', 11-8; 27-9; Underwood, *The Kariye Djami*, I, 6.

218. According to legend, after St Babylas, bishop of Nicomedia, and his eighty-four disciples were martyred in 298, their bodies were taken to Constantinople and buried in three tombs in the northern part of the city on the site where the monastery of Chora was later constructed. The early *Synaxaria* of Constantinople state, however, that it was the feast of St Babylas, bishop of Antioch, which was annually celebrated at the Chora. It is thus possible that the two saints were confused at some early date in the history of the monastery. See Underwood, *The Kariye Djami*, I, 4; Janin, *Églises et monastères* (1969), 532-6; *Synax.Eccl.CP*, 12, lines 15-16.

219. συνταξάμενος δὲ τοὺς μάρτυρας: συντάσσομαι with accusative is an unusual construction.

220. The complete prayer is: Δόξα σοι, Χριστὲ ὁ Θεός, ἀποστόλων καύχημα, μαρτύρων ἀγαλλίαμα, ὧν τὸ κήρυγμα· Τριὰς ἡ ὁμοούσιος. *Euchologion to Mega* (Venice, 1869), 251, 306.

221. The forty martyrs of Sebasteia, who according to legend were martyred during the reign of Licinius (c.323) by being exposed naked one night near a frozen lake in Sebasteia (modern Sivas). Their cult grew rapidly during the fourth century, partly due to the attention paid to them by the Cappadocian fathers, Basil of Caesarea and Gregory of Nyssa. Gebhardt, *Acta martyrum selecta*, 166-81; Basil of Caesarea, *Hom. in quadraginta martyres*, *PG*, 31, cols. 508-25; Gregory of Nyssa, *Encomium in XL martyres*, *PG*, 46, cols. 749-72 and the papers of the first *Belfast Byzantine Colloquium* (*BBTT*, 2, Belfast, forthcoming). According to the anonymous Life of Theodore, this church was built by Justinian, along with that of St Anthimos. See above, note 217 and M.E. Mullett, 'Romanos's Hymns on the XL Martyrs: Date and Significance', *BBTT*, 2.

222. On the burial of the patriarch Germanos at the Chora monastery, see above, note 195. It is Theophanes *Graptos* who is buried near him. See above, p. 114, lines 14-15.

223. Ignatius, bishop of Antioch, who was martyred in Rome in about AD 110, during the reign of Trajan (98-117). He is chiefly known for the seven epistles which he wrote on the course of his journey from Antioch to Rome, as a prisoner condemned to die in the arena. K. Lake, *The Apostolic Fathers*, I-II (Cambridge, Mass., 1912-13); V. Corwin, *St Ignatius and Christianity in Antioch* (New Haven, 1960); *Synax.Eccl.CP*, 329-30.

224. The idea that a spiritual father was ultimately responsible for the souls of his disciples appears frequently in monastic texts from the fourth century onwards. See introduction, note 115.

225. It is common for saints to use these words, attributed by Luke to Christ on the cross. Cf. also Gregory of Nazianzus, *In laudem Basilii*, *PG*, 36, col. 601A.

226. The nineteenth of December fell on a Saturday in 845. Thus Michael died on 4 January 846. See Vailhé, 'Saint Michel le syncelle', 638.

227. Miracles like this one occur frequently after the deaths of saints. Cf. for example the Life of St John of Psicha (755-c.825), ed. P. van den Ven, *Le Muséon*, n.s., 3 (1902), 122-3 and the Life of St John the Merciful by Leontios of Neapolis, ed. H. Gelzer, *Leontios von Neapolis, Leben des heiligen Johannes des barmherzigen Erzbischofs von Alexandrien (Sammlungen ausgewählter kirchen- und dogmengeschichtlicher Quellenschriften*, 5, Freiburg-Leipzig, 1893), 99-103.

228. If this is true, it suggests that the Life was written no more than a generation after Michael's death. See also note 103. John the Grammarian is one of the 'associates' of the tyrant who was probably alive at the time our author was writing.

Bibliography

1. Primary Sources

Acta martyrii Arethae, AASS, Oct. X, 721-59

The Acts of the Christian Martyrs, ed. H. Musurillo (Oxford, 1972)

Anthologia graeca, ed. W.R. Paton (Loeb ed., London-New York, 1916-8)

The Apocrypha and Pseudepigraphica of the Old Testament, ed. R.H. Charles (Oxford, 1913)

Apophthegmata patrum, PG, 65, cols. 71-440

Basil of Caesarea, *Homilia in quadraginta martyres, PG*, 31, cols. 508-25

Constantine Porphyrogennetos, *De administrando imperio*, I-II, ed. and trans. G. Moravcsik and R.J.H. Jenkins (2nd ed., Dumbarton Oaks, 1963)

Constantine Porphyrogennetos, *De ceremoniis*, ed. J.J. Reiske (*CSHB*, Bonn, 1829)

Epistola Abgari ad Christum, ed. R.A. Lipsius and M. Bonnet, I (Leipzig, 1891-1903)

Epistola synodica orientalium ad Theophilum imperatorem de cultu ss. imaginum, ed. and trans. L. Duchesne, 'L'iconographie byzantine dans un document grec du IXe siècle', *Roma e l'Oriente*, 5 (1912-13), 222-39, 273-85, 349-66

Euchologion to Mega, ed. Hieromonk S. Zerbou (Venice, 1869)

Eusebius, *Historia ecclesiae*, ed. E. Schwartz, (*GCS*, Leipzig, 1903-9)

Eusebius, *Vita Constantini*, ed. F. Winkelmann, (*GCS*, Berlin, 1975)

Evagrius, *Historia ecclesiae*, ed. J. Bidez and L. Parmentier, *The Ecclesiastical History of Evagrius* (London, 1898)

Genesios, *Historia de rebus constantinopolitanis*, ed. C. Lachmann (Bonn, 1834)

BIBLIOGRAPHY

Georgios Monachos (Hamartolos), *Chronicon*, ed. C. de Boor (Leipzig, 1904)

Georgios Monachos, *Vitae imperatorum recentiorum*, ed. I. Bekker (*CSHB*, Bonn, 1838)

Gregory of Nazianzus, *In laudem s. Basilii*, *PG*, 36, cols. 493-606

Gregory of Nazianzus, *De vita sua*, *PG*, 37, cols. 1029-1166

Gregory of Nyssa, *Homiliae in quadraginta martyres*, *PG*, 46, cols. 749-88

Gregory of Nyssa, *In laudem fratris Basilii*, *PG*, 46, cols. 787-818. Also see J.A. Stein, *Encomium of St Gregory Bishop of Nyssa on his Brother St Basil* (*Patristic Studies*, 17, Washington, D.C., 1928), 2-60

Gregory of Nyssa, *Vita s. Macrinae*, ed. P. Maraval, *Grégoire de Nysse, Vie de Sainte Macrine* (*SC*, 178, Paris, 1971)

Itinerarium Aetheriae, ed. H. Pétré, *Éthérie, Journal de voyage* (*SC*, 21, Paris, 1971); J. Wilkinson, *Egeria's Travels to the Holy Land* (Jerusalem-Warminster, 1981)

John of Damascus, *De fide orthodoxa*, *PG*, 94, cols. 781-1228

Ps.-John of Damascus, *De sacris imaginibus adversus Constantinum Cabalinum*, *PG*, 95, cols. 310-44

John of Damascus(?), *Epistola ad imperatorem Theophilum de sanctis et venerandis imaginibus*, *PG*, 95, cols. 345-86

John of Damascus, *Orationes de sacris imaginibus*, *PG*, 94, cols. 1227-1420

John Klimakos, *Scala paradisi*, *PG*, 88, cols. 631-1164

John Malalas, *Chronographia*, ed. L. Dindorf (*CSHB*, Bonn, 1831)

John Moschos, *Pratum spirituale*, *PG*, 87, cols. 2851-3112

Justinian, *Novellae constitutiones*, ed. R. Schoell and W. Kroll, *Corpus iuris civilis*, III (Berlin, 1895)

Lactantius, *De mortibus persecutorum*, ed. and trans. J.L. Creed (Oxford, 1984)

Laudatio s. Theodori Grapti, ed. J.-M. Featherstone, 'The Praise of Theodore Graptos by Theophanes of Caesarea', *AnalBoll*, 98 (1980)

Liber pontificalis ecclesiae romanae, ed. L. Duchesne, I-II (Paris, 1886-92)

Martyrium ss. XL martyrum Sebast., ed. O. von Gebhardt, *Acta martyrum selecta* (Berlin, 1902), 171-81

Menaia, I-VI (Rome, 1888-1901)

Menander Rhetor, ed. D.A. Russell and N.G. Wilson (Oxford, 1981)

Menologium basilianum, *PG*, 117, cols. 13-614

Michael the Syrian, *Chronicon*, ed. and trans. J.B. Chabot, I-IV (Paris, 1899-1910)

Nikephoros, *Breviarium*. C. de Boor, ed., *Nicephori archiepiscopi constantinopolitani opuscula historica* (Leipzig, 1880), 3-77

The Old Testament Pseudepigrapha, I, ed. J.H. Charlesworth (London, 1983)

The Oracle of Baalbek, The Tiburtine Sibyl in Greek Dress, ed. P.J. Alexander, (*DOS*, 10, Washington, D.C., 1967)

Palladius, *Historia lausiaca*, *PG*, 34, cols. 1007-1260

Passio sanctorum XX martyrum, *AASS*, March III (1668), 2*-14*; 3rd ed. 2*-12*

Passio s. Irenarchi, ed. G. Garitte, 'La passion de s. Irénarque de Sébastée et la passion de s. Blaise', *AnalBoll*, 73 (1955), 41-54

Peter Damian, *Opusculum XXXVIII contra errorem Graecorum de processione Spiritus Sancti*, *PL*, 145, cols. 633-42

Procopius, *Anekdota*, ed. H.B. Dewing (Loeb ed., Cambridge, Mass., 1935)

Scriptor incertus de Leone Armeno, ed. I. Bekker (*CSHB*, Bonn, 1842)

Scriptores originum constantinopolitanarum, ed.Th. Preger (Leipzig, 1901-7)

Symeon Magister, *Annales*, ed. I. Bekker (*CSHB*, Bonn, 1838)

The Synodicon Vetus, ed. J. Duffy and J. Parker (*Corpus Fontium Historiae Byzantinae*, 15, Washington, D.C., 1979)

Theodore Anagnostes, *Historia ecclesiastica*, ed. G.C. Hansen, (*GCS*, 54, Berlin, 1971)

Theodore of Stoudios, *Antirrhetici adversus iconomachos*, *PG*, 99, cols. 327-436

Theodore of Stoudios, *Epistolae*, *PG*, 99, cols. 903-1680. Also A. Mai, ed., *Nova patrum bibliotheca*, VIII (Rome, 1871)

Theodoret, *Historia religiosa*, ed. L. Parmentier, (*GCS*, 19, Berlin, 1954)

Theophanes, *Chronographia*, I-II, ed. C. de Boor (Leipzig, 1883-5)

Theophanes Continuatus, *Chronographia*, ed. I. Bekker (Bonn, 1838)

De Theophili imperatoris absolutione, ed. W. Regel, *Analecta byzantino-russica* (St. Petersburg, 1891)

Translatio s. Theodori et Iosephi, ed. C. Van de Vorst, *AnalBoll*, 32 (1913), 50-62

Le typicon de la grande église, ed. and trans. J. Mateos, S.I. (*OCA*, 165-6, I-II, Rome, 1962-3)

Vita s. Antonii, by Athanasius, *PG*, 26, cols. 837-978

Vita s. Danielis stylitae, ed. H. Delehaye, *Les saints stylites* (*SubsHag*, 14, Brussels, 1923)

Vitae s. Eustratii Abgari, ed. A. Papadopoulos-Kerameus, Ἀνάλεκτα Ἱεροσολυμιτικῆς Σταχυολογίας, IV (St.Petersburg, 1897), 367-400

Vitae s. Euthymii et s. Sabae, by Cyril of Skythopolis, ed. E. Schwartz, *TU*, 49, 2 (Leipzig, 1939), 5-200. French translation by A.-J. Festugière, *Les moines de l'Orient*, III, 1-3 (Paris, 1961-3)

Vita s. Eutychii, by Eustratios, *PG*, 86, cols. 2273-2390

Vita s. Gregorii theologi, by Gregory the Presbyter, *PG*, 35, cols. 243-304

Vitae s. Ioannicii, *AASS*, Nov. II/I (1894), 332-435

Vita s. Ioannis eleemosynarii, by Leontios of Neapolis, ed. H. Gelzer, *Leontios von Neapolis Leben des heiligen Johannes des barmherzigen Erzbishofs von Alexandrien*, (*Sammlung ausgewählter kirchen-und dogmengeschichtlicher Quellenschriften*, 5, Freiburg - Leipzig, 1893), 1-103

Vita s. Ioannis eleemosynarii, by John Moschos and Sophronios. Two epitomes survive: H. Delehaye, 'Une vie inédite de saint Jean l'Aumonier', *AnalBoll*, 45 (1927), 19-74; E. Lappa-Zizicas, 'Un épitome inédit de la Vie de s. Jean l'Aumonier par Jean et Sophronios', *AnalBoll*, 88 (1970), 274-8

Vita s. Ioannis eleemosynarii, by Symeon the Metaphrast, *PG*, 114, cols. 895-966

Vita s. Ioannis Gotthiae, *AASS*, June V, 190-4; 3rd ed., VII, 167-71

Vita s. Ioannis Psichaitae, ed. P. Van den Ven, *Le Muséon, n.s.*, 3 (1902), 103-25

Vitae ss. martyrum X constantinopolitanorum, *AASS*, Aug. II, 434-47

Vita s. Melaniae, by Gerontios, ed. D. Gorce, *Vie de sainte Mélanie*, *SC*, 90 (Paris, 1962)

Vita s. Methodii, *PG*, 100, cols. 1243-62

Vita s. Michaelis Syncelli, ed.Th. Schmitt, 'Kachrié-Džami', *IRAIK*, 11 (1906), 227-59. Russian: S.V. Poljakova, *Vizantijskie Legendy* (Moscow, 1972), 114-39

Vita s. Michaelis Syncelli, by Nicephoros Gregoras (?), ed. Schmitt, 'Kachrié-Džami', *IRAIK*, 11 (1906), 260-79

Vita s. Nicephori, by Ignatios the Deacon, ed. C. de Boor, *Nicephori archiepiscopi constantinopolitani opuscula historica* (Leipzig, 1880), 139-217

Vita s. Nicetae Mediciensis, by Theosteriktos, *AASS*, April I, xxii-xxxii; 3rd ed., xviii-xxvii

Vita s. Nicolai Studitae, *PG*, 105, cols. 863-925

Vita et passio s. Pancratii. Excerpts in A.N.Veselovskij, *Sbornik Otdelenija Russkogo Jazyka i Slovesnoski Imp. Akad. Nauk.*, 40/2 (St.Petersburg, 1886), 73-110. Newly edited by C. Stallman (Oxford, DPhil thesis, 1986)

Vita s. Stephani iunioris, by Stephen the Deacon, *PG*, 100, cols. 1067-1186

Vita s. Tarasii, by Ignatios the Deacon, ed. I.A.Heikel, *Acta societatis scientiarum fennicae*, 17 (1891), 391-439

Vita s. Theodori Grapti, by Symeon the Metaphrast, *PG*, 116, cols. 653-84

Vita et conversatio s. Theodori praepositi studitarum, by Theodore Daphnopates (?), *PG*, 99, cols. 113-232

Vita et conversatio s. Theodori abbatis monasterii Studii, by Michael, *PG*, 99, cols. 233-328

Vita s. Theodori Sykeotae, ed. A.-J. Festugière, *Vie de Théodore de Sykéon*, I-II, *SubsHag*, 48 (1970)

Vita s. Theophanis Grapti, by Theodora Raoulaina Palaeologina, ed. Papadopoulos- Kerameus, Ἀνάλεκτα, IV, 185-223

Zonaras, *Epitomae historiarum*, III, ed. T. Büttner-Wobst (*CSHB*, Bonn, 1897)

2. Secondary Sources

P.J. Alexander, 'The Iconoclastic Council of St. Sophia (815) and its Definition (*Horos*)', *DOP*, 7 (1953), 35-66

P.J. Alexander, *The Patriarch Nicephorus of Constantinople. Ecclesiastical Policy and Image Worship in the Byzantine Empire* (Oxford, 1958)

P.J. Alexander, 'Religious Persecution and Resistance in the 8th and 9th Centuries: Methods and Justification', *Speculum*, 52 (1977), 238-64

M.V. Anastos, 'The Ethical Theory of Images Formulated by the Iconoclasts in 754 and 815', *DOP*, 8 (1954), 151-60

L.W. Barnard, *The Graeco-Roman and Oriental Background of the Iconoclastic Controversy* (*Byzantina Neerlandica*, 5, Leiden, 1974)

H.-G. Beck, *Kirche und theologische Literatur im byzantinischen Reich* (Munich, 1959)

L.Bréhier, 'L'hagiographie byzantine des 8e et 9e siècles à Constantinople et dans les provinces', *Journal des Savants, n.s.,* 14 (1916), 358-67, 450-65

L.Bréhier, 'Normal Relations between Rome and the Churches of the East before the Schism of the Eleventh Century', *The Constructive Quarterly*, 4 (1916), 645-72

L. Bréhier, 'La situation des chrétiens de Palestine à la fin du VIIIe siècle et l'établissement de Charlemagne', *Le Moyen Age*, 21 (1919), 67-75

P.R.L. Brown, 'A Dark-Age Crisis: Aspects of the Iconoclastic Controversy', *EHR*, 346 (1973), 1-34

A.A.M. Bryer and J. Herrin, *Iconoclasm* (Birmingham, 1977)

J.B. Bury, *A History of the Eastern Roman Empire from the Fall of Irene to the Accession of Basil I (A.D. 802-67)* (London, 1912)

J.B. Bury, *The Imperial Administrative System in the Ninth Century* (*British Academy, Supplemental Papers*, 1, Oxford-London, 1911)

Dom B. Capelle, 'Le Pape Léon et le Filioque', in *L'église et les églises*, I, ed. L. Beauduin (Paris, 1954), 309-22

D. Chitty, *The Desert a City* (Oxford, 1966)

BIBLIOGRAPHY

W. Christ and M. Paranikas, *Anthologia graeca carminum christianorum* (Leipzig, 1871)

G. Da Costa Louillet, 'Saints de Constantinople aux 8e, 9e et 10e siècles', *B*, 24 (1954), 179-263; 25(1958), 783-852

H. Delehaye, *Les passions des martyrs et les genres littéraires* (Brussels, 1921)

E. von Dobschütz, *Christusbilder: untersuchungen zur christlichen Legende, TU*, 18, 3 (Leipzig, 1899)

E. von Dobschütz, 'Methodius und die Studiten', *BZ*, 18 (1909), 41-105

D. Donnet, 'Le traité de grammaire de Michel le Syncelle, inventaire préalable à l'histoire du texte', *Bulletin de l'Institut belge de Rome*, 40 (1969), 33-67

D. Donnet, 'La tradition imprimée du traité de grammaire de Michel, le Syncelle de Jérusalem', *B*, 42 (1972), 441-508

D. Donnet, 'Le traité de la construction de la phrase de Michel le Syncelle de Jérusalem', *Études de philologie, d'archéologie et d'histoire anciennes*, 22 (Brussels-Rome, 1982)

D. Donnet, 'Un travail inédit de l'humaniste Nicaise van Ellebode: Notes sur le traité de grammaire de Michel le Syncelle', *Bull.Inst.Belge Rome*, 43 (1973), 401-57

D. Donnet, 'Transmission et revision: à propos du traité de grammaire de Michel le Syncelle', *Revue de l'histoire des textes*, 5 (1975), 73-86

C. Du Cange, *Familiae byzantinae, historia byzantina duplici commentario illustrata*, I (Venice, 1729)

F. Dvornik, *Les légendes de Constantin et de Méthode vues de Byzance, Byzantinoslavica*, Suppl. I (Prague, 1933)

S. Eustratiades, 'Μιχαὴλ ὁ Σύγκελλος', *Nea Sion*, 31 (1936), 329-38

A. Fliche and V. Martin, *Histoire de l'église depuis les origines jusqu'à nos jours*, IV-V (Paris, 1937)

G. Florovsky, 'Origen, Eusebius and the Iconoclastic Controversy', *CH*, 19 (1950), 77-96

M.M. Gédeon, ''Εκλογαὶ ἀπὸ τῆς βιογραφίας Μιχαὴλ τοῦ Συγκέλλου', *Βυζαντινὸν Ἑορτολόγιον* (Constantinople, 1899), 231-42

S. Gero, *Byzantine Iconoclasm during the Reign of Leo III, with Particular Attention to the Oriental Sources*, (*CSCO*, 346, Subs. 41, Louvain, 1973)

S. Gero, *Byzantine Iconoclasm during the Reign of Constantine V*, (*CSCO*, 384, Subs. 52, Louvain, 1977)

S. Gero, 'The Eucharistic Doctrine of the Byzantine Iconoclasts and its Sources', *BZ*, 68 (1975), 4-22

J. Gouillard, 'Art et littérature théologique à Byzance au lendemain de la querelle des images', *Cahiers de civilisation mediévale*, XII (1969), 1-13

J. Gouillard, 'Deux figures mals connus du second iconoclasme du IXe siècle', *B* 31 (1961), 371-401

J. Gouillard, 'Un quartier d'émigrés palestiniens à Constantinople au IXe siècle?', *RESEE*, 7 (1969), 73-6

H. Grégoire, 'Études sur le neuvième siècle', *B*, 7 (1933), 515-550

V. Grumel, 'Chronologie des patriarches iconoclastes du IXe siècle', *EO*, 34 (1935), 162-6

V. Grumel, *La chronologie, traité de textes byzantines*, I (Paris, 1958)

V. Grumel, 'Jean Grammatikos et s.Théodore Studite', EO, 36 (1937), 181-9

V. Grumel, 'La politique religieuse du patriarche Saint Méthode', *EO*, 34 (1935), 389-401

R. Guilland, *Études de topographie de Constantinople byzantine* (*Berliner Byzantinische Arbeiten*, 37, Berlin, 1969)

J. Haldon, 'Some Remarks on the Background to the Iconoclast Controversy', *BS*, 38 (1977), 161-84

A. Hergès, 'Le monastère des Agaures', *EO*, 11 (1898-99)

R. Janin, *Constantinople byzantine* (Archives de l'Orient Chrétien, 4, Paris, 1964)

R. Janin, *Les églises et les monastères des grands centres byzantins, I: Le siège de Constantinople et le patriarcat oecuménique* (Paris, 1975)

R. Janin, *La géographie écclésiastique de l'empire byzantin*, III, *Les églises et les monastères* (Paris, 2nd ed., 1969)

R. Janin, 'Les monastères nationaux et provinciaux à Byzance', *EO*, 33 (1933), 429-38

J.N.D. Kelly, *Early Christian Creeds* (London, 1960)

E. Kitzinger, 'The Cult of Images in the Age before Iconoclasm', *DOP*, 8 (1954), 83-150

G. Ladner, 'The Concept of Image in the Greek Fathers and the Byzantine Iconoclastic controversy', *DOP*, 7 (1953), 1-34

G. Ladner, 'Origin and Significance of the Byzantine Iconoclastic controversy', *Medieval Studies*, 2 (1940), 127-49

P. Lemerle, *Le premier humanisme byzantin* (Paris, 1971)

M. Lequien, *Oriens christianus in quatuor patriarchatus digestus*, I-III (Paris, 1740)

J. Leroy, 'La reforme Studite', *OCA*, 153 (Rome, 1958), 181-214

J. Leroy, 'La vie quotidienne du moine Studite', *Irénikon*, 27 (1954), 21-50

R. Loenertz, 'Le panégyrique de l'Aréopagite par Saint Michel le Syncelle', *AnalBoll*, 68 (1950), 94-107

S. MacCormack, *Art and Ceremony in Late Antiquity* (Berkeley-Los Angeles-London, 1981)

E.J. Martin, *A History of the Iconoclastic Controversy* (London, 1930)

B. Menthon, *Une terre de légendes. L'Olympe de Bithynie. Ses saints, ses couvents, ses sites* (Paris, 1935)

A. Moffatt, 'Schooling in the Iconoclast Centuries', eds. Bryer and Herrin, *Iconoclasm*, 85-92

J.W. Nesbitt, 'A Geographical and Chronological Guide to Greek Saints' Lives', *OCP*, 25, fasc. 2 (Rome, 1969), 443-89

D. Papachryssanthou, 'La vie monastique dans les campagnes byzantines', *B*, 43 (1973), 158-80

J. Pargoire, 'Saint Méthode de Constantinople et la persécution', *EO*, 6 (1903), 183-91

E. Patlagean, 'Ancienne hagiographie byzantine et histoire sociale', *Annales: Économies, Sociétés, Civilisations*, 23 (Paris, 1968), 106-26

V. Peri, 'Leone III e "il filioque". Echi del caso nell' agiografia greca', *Rivista di Storia della Chiesa in Italia* , 25 (1971), 3-58

K.M. Ringrose, *Saints, Holy Men and Byzantine Society, 726 to 843* (Rutgers University, N.J., PhD, 1976)

E. Schwartz, *Acta conciliorum oecumenicorum* (Berlin and Leipzig, 1914, ff.)

I. Ševčenko, 'Hagiography of the Iconoclast Period', in Bryer and Herrin, eds., *Iconoclasm*, 113-31

W. Treadgold, *The Byzantine Revival, 780-842* (California: Stanford University Press, 1988)

P. Underwood, *The Kariye Djami*, I-IV (London, 1967-75)

S. Vailhé, 'Le monastère de Saint Sabas', *EO*, 3 (1899-1900), 1-11, 33-47

S. Vailhé, 'Saint Michel le Syncelle et les deux frères Grapti', *ROChr*, 6 (1901), 313-32, 610-42

General Index

Abgar, king of Edessa 18, 67, 149
acheiropoietai: see icons
Agauroi, monastery of 103, 164
all-night vigils 30, 49, 51, 53, 127
anacreontic verses 38
Anastasius I 139, 166
Anna, canticle of 24-5, 45, 132-3
Anthimos, church of holy martyr 125, 171
Antidion, monastery of 163
Antigoni 17, note 57, 161
Antiochus 99
Apameia (Mudanya) 16-17, 162
Aphousia, island of 14, 15, 71, 79, 151
apocalyptic 19-21, 133, 145-6, 149-50, 152
apostles, as makers and venerators of icons 65
Arabs 1, 2, 13, 57, 59, 85, 142, 157
    raids in 796 or 797 9, 136, 137
    raids in 809 and 812 1, 11, 142
    tax imposed by 9, 11, 57, 59, 142
Arius 111, 141
Artabasdos 109, 167
asceticism 7, 26, 30-5, 49, 51, 53
Athanasius, *Life* of St Anthony 23-4, 135, 137, 165, 169, 170
authorship 5-6
Babylon, three children of 97, 160
baptism 47, 133
beatings 91
Bithynia 15, 16, 73, 163-4
Blachernai, monastery of 3
Black Sea 14, 151
Bosphoros 14, 151, 163
Charlemagne 10, 137, 141
Chenolakkos, monastery of 160
cherubim 21, 65, 89, 95, 147
Chora, monastery of 2, 4, 5, 32-4, 45, 131-2, 167
    as haven for Palestinian monks 13, 63, 109, 146
    as 'imperial' monastery 107, 165
    destruction during second iconoclasm 109, 115, 117, 132, 167
    endorsement of iconoclasm 4
    origins 107, 109, 131-2, 166, 171

restoration after 843   28, 117
Christ
    as image and likeness of God   65
    imitation of   19, 22, 24, 25, 35, 85, 133, 156, 160
Christodoulos, composer of the iambics   85, 93
Chrysotriklinos: see 'Golden Triclinium'
church of the Resurrection   47, 51, 55, 59, 133-4, 139
Constantine I   111, 123, 133, 170
Constantine V Kopronymos   3-4, 27, 132, 144, 150, 167
Constantine VI   61, 144, 153
Constantinople, iconoclasm in second period (815-43)   4, 152
Council at Aix-la-Chapelle, 809   10
Council of Chalcedon, 451   139, 140
Council of Constantinople, 381   140
Council of Gentilly, 767   141
Council of Hatfield, 690   141
Council of Hiereia, 754   144
Council of Nicaea, 325   168
Council of Nicaea (7th ecumenical), 787   3, 61, 132, 141, 144, 145, 164, 167
Council of Toledo, 589   141
Crispus (recte Priscus)   132
Cyprus   11
Daniel, Book of   20, 145, 149
Daphne, palace of   147
date of composition   6, 173
Desert fathers   30
Devil, comparison of iconoclast emperors to   20, 146
Dialogues   16, 27, 156
Diospolis, also called Lydda   61, 144
diptychs   61, 145
education   25, 134, 138
Egeria   135
Ehrhard   39-40
Eirene, empress   3, 61, 144
Elaiobomoi or Elegmoi, monastery of   105, 164-5
Eleazar   85, 97, 156
Elesboas or Elesbaas   123, 170-1
Elias, laura of prophet   103, 164
Elias, patriarch of Jerusalem, 494-516   55, 139-40, 165
Elias, patriarch of Jerusalem in 796-7   137
encomium   6, 23-4
'epic' passions   26-8, 150, 154

influenced by IV Maccabees   26, note 93, 156
'ethical' theory of images   21-3
Eudokia, empress   148
Euphrosyne   75, 153
fasting   30, 51, 53
    as method of resistance against Iconoclasts   69, 150
Filioque   1, 5, 9-13, 55, 57, 141, 142
    origins of   141
    papacy's attitude towards   141
forty martyrs of Sebasteia, church of   125, 172
forty-two martyrs of Amorion   37
Frankish Benedictine monks in Palestine   10-11, 141
George, patriarch of Jerusalem   137
Germanos, patriarch of Constantinople   109, 115, 127, 167, 172
'Golden Triclinium'   63, 83, 147
Gospels, influence of   19-20
Graptoi: see Theodore, Theophanes
Gregory of Nazianzus   24, 40, 169, 172
Hagarenes or 'sons of Hagar'   85, 93, 142
Harun Al-Rashid, caliph   11, 142
Henotikon   139
hesychia   26, 30, 34, 53, 137
Holy Sepulchre   133-4, 139
iambic verses   15, 85, 87, 95, 156, 161
iconoclasm, political background   2, note 3, 4
icons
    acheiropoietai   18, 149
    compared to idols   19, 81
    of Christ by the evangelist Luke   18-9, 67, 148
idolatry, as iconoclast accusation   77
Ignatios, bishop of Antioch, martyred in Rome circa AD 110,
    during the reign of Trajan (98-117)   127, 172
Ignatios, the deacon   168
Jerusalem   1, 9, 11, 13, 45, 57, 59, 107, 109, 134-7, 139, 141-2, 144,
    148, 159, 166
Job, disciple and companion of Michael   10, 15, 61, 71, 79, 99
John the Grammarian, patriarch, 837-43   6, 15, note 51, 103, 163, 173
    avoidance of name   6, note 16, 69, 150
Julian, emperor   3, 27, note 94
Justin I   170
Justin II   147
Justinian I   107, 131-2, 134, 152, 172
Kallonas, the *spatharios*   77, 79

GENERAL INDEX

Kariye Djami   131-2
Kleidion   163
'Kynolykos'   38, 111, 168
laura   31, note 111, 135-6
Leo III, emperor   2, 7,109, 167
Leo III, pope   10-1, 57, 59, 141
Leo V   1, 3-4, 6, 10, 12-4, 20, 27, 59, 63, 65, 69, 71, 73 143, 145, 149-51, 157, 167
    methods of persuasion   14, 71
    of Armenian descent   59, 142
letter of Theodore *Graptos* to John of Kyzikos   4, 8, 12, 15-6, 27-8, 38, 143, 155, 159
letter from patriarch of Jerusalem to Leo V   13-4, 18-9, 65, 67, 149
liberal arts   25-6, 134
literary form   6, 23-30
Divine Liturgy   31-2, 136, 144, 145, 147
logothete of the course: see Theoktistos
Maccabees, seven children of   97, 160
Macedonius, patriarch of Constantinople   57, 140
manuscripts   39-40
martyrs, early Christian   18, 20, 26-8, 146
Menaia   8
Methodios   16, 99, 105
    background of   160-1
    movements during the period of second iconoclasm   17, note 57, 99, 160-1, 165
    as patriarch of Constantinople   32, 117, 123, 125, 163
Michael I   11-3, 146
Michael II   6, 15, 73, 152, 160
Michael III   6, 28, 33, 101, 103, 123, 152, 162, 170
Michael, also monk and *synkellos* of Constantinople, 9th C   35-6
Michael the *Synkellos*
    abbot of Chora monastery   17, 28, 30, 105, 109
    birth   9, 24, 47, 132
    compared to the archangel   20, 133, 149-50
    death   29, 127, 131, 132, 173
    education   25, 47-9, 134
    'General of God'   47, 134
    letters   38, 57, 142
    mother   45, 47
    Persian ancestry   45, 132
    parents   45
    synkellos to patriarch of Jerusalem   32, 55

GENERAL INDEX

synkellos to patriarch Methodios of CP   17, 32, 105
    vision of approaching death   119, 169
    writings of   35-8
miracle, on Michael's death   127, 129, 173
Moabites, land of   85, 156
monastery, compared to a mountain   107, 165-6
monasticism   30-5
    coenobitic   31, 34, 135-6
monophysites   136, 166, 170-1
Mt Olympos   15, 34, 163
Nero, emperor of Rome   55, 140
Nikephoros I, emperor   143
Nikephoros, patriarch of Constantinople   12, 59, 61, 155-6
Nikephoros Gregoras, *Life* of Michael   8
origenists   136
Pascal I, pope   160
Paul, the apostle   55, 140
Peter, the apostle   55, 65, 67, 148
Peter, bishop of Nicaea   151, 168
Peter, patriarch of Jerusalem   107
Phiale, prison   13, 14, 69
Phocas   132
Pneumatomachians   140
Praetorium, prison   15-7, 73, 89, 91, 93, 99, 150, 152-3, 161
prefect   93, 95, 97
Priscus: see Crispus
prophets, testimony of   65
Prousias or Prousa   14-5, 73, 152, 160, 163, 164
relics, of Peter and Paul   55, 140
Revelation, Book of   20-1, 133, 145, 149, 156, 157, 160
Rome   1, 9-13, 55, 57, 59, 140, 142, 148, 160, 172
St Andreas Kalybites   3, 27, note 94
St Anthony   24-5, 134
St Babylas and his eighty-four disciples   125, 171
St Babylas of Antioch   171
St Basil of Caesarea   40, 133, 136, 154, 162, 169, 172
St Dalmatos   37
St Dionysios the Areopagite   36
St Elias, monastery of, dependency of monastery of Agauroi   103, 164
St Eustratios of Agauroi, miracle-worker and abbot   103, 164
St Eustratios and companions, Passion of   27
St Euthymios   26, 30, 136
    laura of   136, 139

GENERAL INDEX

St Hilarion of Dalmatos   151
St Ioannikios   34, 103, 163-4
St Isaakios   37
St John Chrysostom   40, 139, 165
St John of Damascus   3, 18, 22, 37, 146, 147, 148, 157
    Oration on the holy icons   18-9, 22-3, 24, note 83
St John of Kathara   151
St John the Merciful   131, 173
St Kosmas the Melodist   37
St Makarios, abbot of Pelekete   151
St Mamas, hippodrome of   3
St Maximos the Confessor   27, note 96
St Mokios   37
St Niketas of Medikion   151
St Pankratios   67, 148
St Passarion, monastery of   166
St Sabas   26, 30, 107, 136, 137, 166
    laura of   7, 9, 25, 34, 49, 136, 166
    as *coenobium* rather than *laura*   31, 136
St Stephen the Younger   3, 152
    Life of by Stephen the Deacon   3, 27
St Theodore, maternal uncle of empress Theodora and founder of Chora monastery   131-2
St Theodore of Stoudios   3, 10, 11-2, 23, 59, 132, 143, 149, 150, 164
    exile in Boneta   14, note 43
St Theodore of Sykeon   29, note 101
St Zacharias   36
saint's *life*
    its resemblance to an icon   24
    genre   7, 28-9
    iconophile   18
saints, the iconic qualities of   24, 97, 160
Samaritans   107, 166
Samuel, the prophet   24, 45, 133
Schmitt   1, note 1, 8, note 25, 39, note 144, 41, 131, 171
Seleukeia, iconoclast monks in   61, 144
senate   63, 83
Ševčenko   3, note 7, 6, note 16, 8, note 28, 18, note 60, 137, 143, 150
Sicilian monks   57, 141
Sion   49, 135
Sosthenios, monastery of   14-5, 151
sounding board (*semantron*)   33, 121, 169
spatharios   77, 105, 153

spiritual father   26, 34, note 115, 113, 169, 170, 172
Spoudaei, monastery of   9, 55, 61, 139
Stephen, the *asekretis*   75, 79
Stoudios, monastery of   34
stylite saints   29
Symeon the Metaphrast, *Life* of Theodore *Graptos*   4, 8, 13, 15, 162
Symeon, abbot of Chora monastery who participated at seventh
    ecumenical council at Nicaea, 787   132, 167
Synaxaria   8, 131, 167, 171
synkellos   1, 2, 17, 32, 79, 131
Synod of Cividale, 796 or 797   141
Tarasios   61, 145
tattooing   15, 95, 156
    date at which it took place   15, note 51, 97, 160
Theodora   2, 5, 28, 33, 101, 123, 158, 162, 170
Theodora Raoulaina Kantekouzena Palaiologina, *Life* of Theophanes
    Graptos   8
Theodore Abu Qurra   37
Theodore Anagnostes   148
Theodore I, patriarch of Jerusalem in 764   134
Theodore *Graptos*
    birth   138
    death   16-7, 111, 113, 168
    education   53, 55
    exile to Aphousia   14-5, 71, 73, 79, 151
    interrogations of   4, 27-8, 83-91, 156
    relics   168
    writings of   38-9, 168
Theodosius I   123, 140, 170
Theodotos, patriarch of Constantinople   10, 12, 59, 63, 65, 143-4
Theoktistos, logothete of the course   28, 91, 93, 143, 158-9
theology of images   23
Theophanes, chronicler   3, 11, 142
Theophanes of Caesarea, *Encomium* of Theodore   8, 13, 168
Theophanes Continuatus   153, 168
Theophanes *Graptos*
    birth   138
    bishop of Nicaea   2, 17, 28, 109, 111, 168
    death   113, 169
    interrogations of: see Theodore
    tomb   127, 172
    writings of   39, 115

GENERAL INDEX

Theophilos, emperor (829-842) 4, 6, 8, 12, 20, 27, 28, 73-93, 145, 149, 152
Theotokos 39, 135, 147, 148
Thermastra 91, 158
Thomas, patriarch of Jerusalem in 807 9, 51, 55, 57, 137, 149
Timothy Aelurus 139
topos 5, note 15, 24, 27, 28, 132, 155-6, 162-3, 170
Triconchos 147
triumph of orthodoxy 17, 23, 32, 101-3, 132, 168
Tryphon, church of 117, 169
Vailhé 7, note 21, 11-3, 137, 141, 143, 149
Virgin Mary: see *Theotokos*
water imagery 55, 139
women
    caring for imprisoned martyrs as *topos* 153
    iconophilism of 162
    'manly' qualities of holy women 101, 162

Index of Greek Words

ἀγαλλιάζομαι 54,3; 66,29, 118,1
ἀγγελικόν (σχῆμα) 50,10; 52,23
ἀγρυπνία 50,18; 124,7; 126,11,14
ἀγχιστής 128,11
ἀγωνιστής 62,4; 72,14; 146
ἀειπάρθενος (of the Theotokos) 64,20; 66,3
ἄθεος 72,17,23; 78,15; 98,3; 106,17,20; 114,18,28
ἄθεσμος 76,4
ἄθλησις 76,16
ἀθλητικός 100,30
ἀθλοφόρος 84,28
αἱρεσιάρχης 62,2; 108,15; 146
αἵρεσις 76,2,5; 88,3
ἀλιτήριος 76,19
ἀλουργίς 68,3; 88,6,22; 108,12
ἀμβλυωπία 74,7; 78,29
ἀμείλικτος 48,6
ἀναγνώστης 46,20
ἀνάθεμα 66,26; 68,4; 102,6,11; 104,27; 108,16
ἀνάληψις 66,6
ἀναλύω (to depart) 118,8,15; 120,8
ἀνάλωμα 108,11; 167
ἄναξ (of iconoclast emperors) 58,27; 62,2; 72,18,24; 74,22; 76,17,20; 80,23; 82,14; 98,5;100,4 (of Michael III) 102,4; 116,17; 122,14 (of Justinian I) 106,4,9,12;16,26 (of Artabasdos) 108,20 (general comments) 152; 170
ἀνάπαυσις 72,31; 118,18
ἀναστηλόω (of an icon) 96,24
ἀναστροφή 110,7
ἀνατύπωσις 62,26; 66,26; 122,29
ἀναχωρητικός 52,7; 54,15
ἀνεξικακία 80,2
ἀνίστημι (as in 'the tyrant arose') 54,30; 72,8,19; 152 ('to recover') 74,11
ἀνόσιος 84,17; 86,19
ἀντιπαρατάσσω 56,13
ἀοίδιμος 106,4,9
ἀπογαλακτίζω 46,1

ἀποθησαυρίζω   112,8; 114,4
ἀποκάλυψις   ('revelation')   54,13
ἀποκείρω   ('to tonsure') 46,20   ('to dedicate to monastic life') 52,21
ἀπόλαυσις   58,18
ἀπολύω   ('to dismiss; bid farewell')   104,12; 120,29; 124,9,13,25
ἀποστάτης   86,13
ἀποστολικ ός   (δόγμα) 78,20;   100,14   (ἐκκλησία) 104,19;   114,2; 118,29; 122,30   (θρόνος) 46,14; 102,12; 104,25
ἀπύλωτος   56,23; 110,28
ἀρτοκοπεῖον   50,22
ἀρχηγός   70,29
ἀρχιεπίσκοπος   122,9
ἀρχιεράρχης   (of God) 52,5   (of clergy) 60,25; 76,23; 78,10
ἀρχιερατικός   102,13
ἀρχιερεύς   70,6; 82,14; 110,4; 112,10
ἀρχιμανδρίτης   44,12
ἀρχιποίμην   (of Christ) 46,15
ἀρχιτελετάρχης   58,22; 86,30; 143
ἄρχων   70,25
ἀσεβής   72,24; 80,3; 100,4
ἀσηκρῆτις   74,25; 78,18; 153
ἀσκέω   48,9; 52,15
ἄσκησις   50,6; 70,30
ἀσπάζομαι   60,11; 70,15; 84,18; 96,22; 112,11; 114,13; 122,21; 124,26,31; 126,25
ἀστρονομία   48,2
ἄσυλος   88,22; 114,3
ἄσχετος   72,22
αὐτάδελφος   52,27
αὐτοκράτωρ   76,21
ἀχώριστος   54,23
βαθμός   ('rank')   46,21
βασιλικός   78,20; 82,10   (of a monastery) 106,1; 116,22; 165
βαυκάλιον   52,13; 137-8
βέβηλος   72,24; 116,19
βίος   44,2
βλασφημέω   56,2; 80,2
βούνευρον   90,14
βρύχω   ('to gnash or grind the teeth')   62,3; 78,24
γνώριμος   128,11

GREEK INDEX

γράμματα (τῆς προπαιδείας) 46,26 (as engraved on faces of *Graptoi* brothers) 94,15,22
γραμματική 46,29,31; 52,25
δαίμων 64,12; 128,4,18
δήμιος (executioner) 94,9
δημιουργός 88,24
δημόσιος 82,3
διάβολος 64,11
διαγωγή 108,2
διαθήκη 66,22
διακονία 50,17
διϊππεύω 72,7
δίπτυχα 60,17; 145
δόγμα 72,24; 78,15,16,20; 80,21; 94,21; 98,3; 100,12,15; 102,2
δοξολογία 48,5; 52,23; 116,6; 120,3
δορυφορία 124,15
δράκων 68,2; 149
ἐγκολάπτω 84,21
ἐγκώμιον 112,1; 114,12
ἐθελοφρονέω 56,13
ἔθνος (τῶν φράγγων) 54,31
εἰδωλολατρεία 80,1
εἰδωλολατρέω 68,8
εἰδωλολάτρης 68,7; 76,27; 78,3; 98,1
εἴδωλον 68,26,27; 76,26; 80,5,9
εἰκονοκαύστης 58,11; 66,23; 72,17; 108,16; 110,28
εἰκονολάτρης 78,2
εἰκονομάχος 58,14; 74,31
εἰκών 64,8,13,19,21,25; 66,1,12,15,17,26; 68,11; 70,10,15; 72,3; 76,7,13,26; 80,4,7,15; 84,15; 86,27; 88,11; 92,17,22,23,24; 96,10,24,25; 100,12; 102,2,5,18; 122,24
ἐκκλησιαστικός 100,30
ἐκσφράγισμα 64,23
ἔμπνευσις 56,26
ἔμπνοος (στήλη) 100,23; 162
ἐμφράττω 110,28
ἐνανθρώπησις 80,11; 86,25
ἔνσαρκος 66,4
ἔνστασις 76,9; 80,24
ἐξεικονίζω 66,3
ἔπαρχος 82,19,21; 92,26; 94,13; 96,6

ἐπίγειος (of emperors) 122,22
ἐπιστομίζω 58,27; 144
ἐπιτάφιος 114,12
ἐπουράνιος 122,26
εὐαγής 116,20
εὐκτήριος (οἶκος) 44,21; 106,18, 20; 126,11
εὐπρόσδεκτος 46,2
εὐσεβέστατος 106,3
ἔφεσις 54,25
ἑωθινός 120,6; 126,12
ζόφος 74,13
ζωαρχικός 64,6
ἡσυχάζω 52,7,10; 137
θαυματουργέω 114,25
θαυματουργός 102,26
θεάρεστος 48,26; 116,12
θεοκυβέρνητος 62,24
θεομάχος 62,1
θεόσδοτος 46,22
θεόστεπτος (of emperors) 58,18; 82,14; 106,19; 116,18,21; 122,13,28
Θεοτόκος 64,19; 66,2; 80,4,10; 90,17; 114,7
θεοφιλής 44,20; 98;9; 116,11
θεοφόρος 96,8; 104,29; 106,15; 110,30; 114,11,22; 116,8; 118,3; 126,3; 147
θεσπέσιος 78,25; 108,15; 120,6
θήκη 112,2; 114,13; 124,21
θηριώνυμος 62,1; 108,8,14
θλῖψις 70,26; 78,5,7,28
θρυλλολέκτης 84,31; 157
θυμομαχέω 68,1; 90,19
θυσιαστήριον 44,27
ἴαμβος 84,21,24,30; 86,1,2; 88,28; 92,11; 94,11
ἱεράτευμα 80,14
ἱερατικός 56,12
ἱεροψάλτης 68,19
ἱλαστήριον 64,18
ἰουδαόφρονος 108,17
καθηγέομαι 96,7
καθηγητής 48,28
καθιδρύω 116,5
καθολικός 70,5; 78,3; 114,2; 116,28; 118,29; 122,30

καθομιλέω 74,2,4
καθυπογράφω 74,30
καθυπουργέω 74,3
καρπός (κοιλίας) 44,26; 134
καρτερέω 74,30
καρτερικός 108,27; 114,14; 126,7
καταβροντάω 94,25
κατακοσμέω 54,8; 118,2
καταμαλάσσω 48,7
καταμόνας 52,7
κατασκάπτω 114,28
κατασκιάζω 64,18
κατάστασις 122,20
κατατάσσω 48,29
καταφυγή 124,19
κατοικητήριον 48,8
κελλίον 52,7,12; 54,15; 124,3,10,12; 126,8,13
κεντέω 94,10
κέντρον 44,6
κηδεμών 98,15; 112,12
κλῆρος 46,17
κληρόω 46, 23
κοίμησις 112,2
κοινωνέω 60,14; 70,4; 92,27
κοινωνία ('Eucharist') 92,13,32
κορυφαῖος 54,28
κορυφή (of emperor) 106,19
κρούω 120,1
κυφότης 74,8; 78,29; 153
λαός (of God) 54,10; 86,18 (of the emperor) 94,26; 102,1,2
λαύρα 48,27
λειτουργία 50,16; 120,15
λειτουργός 44,26
λείψανον 54,27; 88,21; 108,24,27; 114,14; 124,20
λεοντιαῖος 78,24
λεοντώνυμος 68,2; 149
λογικὴ (ποίμνη) 112,5
λογικὸν (πρόβατον) 64,28; 147
λογοθέτης (τοῦ δρόμου) 90,32
λουτρόν (παλιγγενεσίας) 46,5 (baptism) 133
λύτρωσις 66,30

μαθητής 54,20; 78,12,25
μακροθυμέω 80,3
μαννούθιον 50,20; 136
μαρτυρέω 76,13
μάρτυς 88,9,27; 90,10; 92,19,28; 96,2,5; 100,22; 108,7; 110,6; 114,8,17; 116,3; 124,18,30,32; 128,16
μελῳδός 114,5
μετάστασις ('death') 118,5,11
μητροπολίτης 108,30
μισόχριστος 68,13,16; 72,16; 74,28; 76,8,17,20
μονάζω 48,16
μονήρης (βίος) 52,23
μονονουχί 44,24
μορφή 80,3; 86,20; 96,24,25
μυσαρός 58,28; 66,23
ναός 48,7; 124,16,31; 126,11
νεύω 84,20
νηστεία 50,18; 118,12; 124,7
νουθετικός 76,15
ξύλον ('stocks') 74,19; 78,31 ('sounding-board') 120,1,3
ξυνωρίς 52,16
ὀζώδης 74,13
οἰκονομέω 66,9; 116,7
οἰκονομία 66,4; 96,11
οἰκουμενικός 80,12; 122,20 (πατριάρχης)124,9 (διδάσκαλος)122,6 (σύνοδος) 104,24; 110,1
ὁμήγυρις 56,8; 68,6; 86,23
ὁμιλία ('conversation') 54,1
ὁμοθυμαδόν 56,20
ὁμοίωσις 64,8
ὁμολογέω 60,29; 76,6; 86,24; 92,21
ὁμολογητής 70,8; 74,6; 76,13; 80,18; 86,3; 96,2,8; 98,25; 100,22; 108,7,28; 110,23; 112,4; 114,15,16; 124,18; 126,1,3
ὁμολογία 76,16; 80,24; 86,27; 92,15; 128,14,17
ὁμόροφος 128,11
ὀπαδός 118,9
ὀρθόδοξος 70,8; 72,2,16,22; 74,9,29; 76,28,29; 78,4,14,15,19; 80,14,24; 88,5; 100,18; 102,2; 104,30; 106,1; 108,18; 112,28; 114,20; 122,11
ὀρθολεκτέω 56,24
ὀρθότης 54,12

GREEK INDEX

ὀρθρινός 120,2
ὁρμητήριον 128,19
ὁσιομάρτυς 102,5
ὅσιος 44,2; 112,2; 114,9; 120,10; 128,7
παιδίον 44,19
παιδοτρίβης 52,24; 138
παλάτιον 62,15; 116,27
παμβασιλεύς (of God) 52,4
παμβέβηλος 72,18; 76,20; 98,5; 102,8; 106,20
πάμμακαρ 106,30
παμμίαρος 80,5; 86,24
παμπόνηρος 70,17
πάναγνος 86,7,20; 88,23; 114,7
πανευδαίμων (of Constantinople) 72,27; 80,26; 104,14,22; 106,25; 112,9; 146
πανέχθιστος 108,7
πάνζοφος 74,17
πανήγυρις 114,6
πανόλβιος 98,13
πανόσιος 72,15; 74,10; 78,27; 104,16; 116,4
πάνσοφος 102,15,22; 110,18; 112,15; 114,14; 116,25,29
παραδίδωμι 66,21
παρακλητικός 76,1; 120,11
παρακούω 60,1
παραμονή (eve of a feast) 126,10
παράνομος 76,5; 80,27
πάροδος 76,24
παρρησία (in positive sense) 62,27; 68,12; 96,11,16; 114,19; 128,17
παρρησιάζομαι 76,6
πατριαρχεῖον 124,12
πατριάρχης 118,1; 122,1,2,13,16; 124,1,2; 143
πατροπαράδοτος 66,24
πέρας 52,28
περιγραπτός 70,10; 72,3; 76,7; 80,16
περιποιέω 74,1
περιφανέστατος 44,14
περσογενής 44,16
πλάσμα 80,6
πλαστουργέω 64,8
πλαστουργός 96,18
πνευματικὸν τέκνον 96,15; 110,18

ποιητής 84,13
ποιητική ('poetry') 48,2; 52,25
ποιμενάρχης 112,15
ποιμήν 50,3; 64,26 (of Peter); 114,20
πολιτεία 44,2; 50,18; 52,21; 116,27
πρεσβεία (intercession) 122,19; 124,24
πρεσβεύω 114,20
πρεσβύτερος 54,21; 104,11
πρόθεσις ('disposition') 52,9 ('counsel') 60,5; 144
πρόμαχος 98,10
πρόνοια (of God) 116,6
προόρασις 102,25
προσθήκη 56,13
προσκομίζω 112,6
προσκόπτω 76,28
προσκυνέω 64,26; 70,14; 76,7,26; 80,15; 92,17,21
προσκύνησις 54,27; 68,26; 98,7,10
προσομιλέω 52,8; 60,23; 78,32
πρόσταξις 46,28; 106,12
πρόσφατος 66,20
πρόσωπον 84,13,21; 86,3; 88,31; 94,11,13,21; 96,2,6,22; 110,11; 122,2
πρωτότοκος 88,24
πρωτότυπον 92,24
ῥητορική 46,30,31
σαρκίον 126,15
σαρκομοιόμορφος 66,12; 88,11
σεβάζω 70,15; 76,7; 92,21
σέβασμα 70,3
σεβάσμιος 86,9; 106,3,23,24; 108,1,25; 114,13; 122,18; 124,23; 126,18
σκάμνος 94,9
σκάνδαλον 118,28; 124,24
σκέμμα (ποιητικόν) 52,26; 84,27; 138
σκέπτομαι ('to compose') 84,24; 88,28; 92,11
σκηνόω 116,1
σκληραγωγία 52,1
σπαθάριος 76,14; 78,18; 102,28; 104,13; 153
σπαράσσω 128,8
σπηλοειδής 104,5
στάσις 50,18

GREEK INDEX

στενοχωρία   74,5; 116,3
στερροποιός   76,16
στήλη   100,23; 162
στηλογραφέω   66,11
στηλογραφία   66,8
στήριγμα   128,20
σύγκελλος   44,3; 54,14; 78,9; 102,15; 104,30; 131
σύγκλητος   62,16; 82,20; 102,1
σύγκοιτος (after death)   126,4
συγκροτέω   56,22 ('to assist') 74,1
συγχορευτής   126,5; 128,21
σύμβολον (meaning 'the Creed')   54,31; 56,8,14
συμβούλιον   56,17
συμμαχία   116,19
συμμύστης   128,12
συναγωνιστής   98,16; 102,26
συναυλία   108,2,23
συνοδία   50,1,8; 116,8,11,14,24; 120,2
σύνοδος   56,1; 68,6,25; 86,30; 88,1; 102,10,22,28,31; 104,15; 110,1
συνόμιλος   128,21
σύνταξις   84,26
συντάσσομαι   124,17,24,32; 126,6
συσσίτος   128,11
σύστημα   78,17
σχολάζω   44,21; 124,6
ταμιεῖον   62,13; 76,10; 106,11
ταχυδρόμος   78,26; 80,25; 104,16
τελεταρχέω   46,12; 56,6
τελετάρχης   60,24; 108,29
τεχνίτης   88,24
τιμωρία   72,17; 78,6
τοπάρχης   66,17
τύπος   64,21; 86,4
τύραννος   72,7; 76,4,9; 96,12
ὑμνῳδία   126,13
ὕπαρχος   84,20; 92,4,10,17,29; 94,7,14,24
ὑπασπιστής   76,20; 154
ὑπερένδοξος   88,17
ὑπερζέω   76,18
ὑπέρμαχος   116,7
ὑπερόριος   58,21; 98,17

GREEK INDEX

ὑπερούσιος   64,6
ὑπέρτιμος   88,19
ὑπόδειγμα   60,19; 88,4
ὑπολακίζω   70,11; 151
ὑπομονή   68,12; 98,2
φατριάρχης   58,27; 143
φιλόθεος   44,7
φιλοικτίρμων   54,4
φιλοσοφία   46,30; 48,1; 52,25
φιμόω   56,23
φοιτητής   54,17; 118,9; 120,4; 124,28; 126,14; 128,11
φωστήρ   54,5; 80,19; 88,18; 102,24; 116,27
χαίρω   60,11
χαρακτήρ   96,23; 160
χειροτονέω   54,21; 110,4
χειροτονία   50,28; 110,10,13
χιτώνιον   52,13
χρῆμα   76,10
ψηφίζω   56,20
ψῆφος   50,24; 102,3
ψιάθιον   52,13; 137
ᾠδή   68,10

Index to Biblical and other Quotations

Bible:

Genesis
3:24: 88,12-5
6:4: 54,30
41:40: 70,6

Exodus
1:7: 54,10

I Samuel (I Kings)
1:11: 44,24-7

I Kings (III Kings)
8:50: 70,28

Nehemiah
1:11: 70,28
9:27: 70,28

Job
5:16: 110,28

Psalms
26:14 (27:14): 96,27
30:24 (31:24): 96,27
32:18 (33:18): 70,27-8
34:16 (35:16): 62,3
36:12 (37:12): 62,3
45:10 (46:9): 52,28
62:12 (63:11): 110,28
90:12 (91:12): 76,28
106:42 (107:42): 110,28
111:10 (112:10): 62,3
113:13-5(115:5-7): 68,27-70,3
115:6: 126,30
124:3 (125:3): 98,27-9
131:11 (132:11): 44,22
140:5 (141:5): 68,19-20

Isaiah
1:6: 94,8
49:18: 100,25-8
54:11-2: 88,17-20
60:4: 100,25-8

I Maccabees
2:1: 54,30

Matthew
3:1: 54,30
4:6: 76,28
5:14: 106,7; 108, 3
8:11: 100, 25-8
10:16: 72,5-6
10:28: 82,24-6
11:18: 82,13
12:42: 52,28
16:18: 100,1-2
24:38: 54,30
25:40: 95,23
25:46: 88,9-10

Mark
1:26: 128, 8-9

Luke
1:28: 66,5-6
2:40: 116,25
2:52: 46,26-7; 116,25-6
4:11: 76,28
6:35: 80,6
7:33: 82,13
10:21: 54,3-4; 118,2
11:31: 52,28
12:4-5: 82,24-6
13:29: 100,25-8
16:9: 66,28
23:46: 112,23; 126,27

John
7:20: 82,13

8:48: 82,13
8:52: 82,13

Acts
2:18: 54,30
7:17: 54,10
7:54: 62,3
9:37: 54,30
20:28: 104,4

Romans
2:5: 88,9-10
9:32: 76,28
15:16: 46,1-2

II Corinthians
11:11: 128,3

Galatians
4:26-7: 88,24

Ephesians
2:21-2: 48,7-8

Philippians
1:23: 118,9

II Timothy
2:21: 48,7-8
4:7: 114,18
4:14: 126,24

Titus
3:5: 46,5

Hebrews
11:40: 128, 4-5
12:22: 88,24

I Peter
2:5: 46,1-2
2:9: 80,14
2:15: 56,23

5:4: 46,15

Revelation
9:6: 54,30
21:11-9: 88,17-20

Other:

Aristophanes, *Ranae*, 838: 56,23

Gregory Nazianzen, *Oratio* 31: 80,6; *Oratio* 38: 64,13-4

Homer, *Odyssey*, XVI, 206; XIX, 484; XXI, 208; XXIV, 322: 90, 4-5